Impact maths 3B

D1335940

About this book

Impact maths provides a complete course to help you achieve your best in your Key Stage 3 mathematics course. This book will help you understand and remember mathematical ideas, solve mathematical problems with and without the help of a calculator and develop your mental maths skills.

Exercises you should try without the help of a calculator are marked with this symbol:

Finding your way around

To help you find your way around when you are studying use the:

- **edge marks** shown on the front pages – these help you get to the right unit quickly

- **contents list** and **index** – these list all the key ideas covered in the book and help you turn straight to them.

- **links** in the margin – these show when an idea elsewhere in the book may be useful:

There is more about multiplying fractions on page 172.

Remembering key ideas

We have provided clear explanations of the key ideas you need throughout the book with **worked examples** showing you how to answer questions. **Key points** you need to remember look like this:

■ **The distance around the edge of a shape is its perimeter.**

and are listed in a **summary** at the end of each unit.

Investigations and information technology

Two units focus on particular skills you need for your course:
- **Using and applying mathematics** (unit 16) – shows you some ways of investigating mathematical problems.
- **Calculators and computers** (unit 17) – shows you some ways of using calculators and computers and will help with mental maths practice.

Heinemann Educational Publishers
Halley Court, Jordan Hill, Oxford, OX2 8EJ
a division of Reed Educational & Professional Publishing Ltd
Heinemann is a registered trademark of Reed Educational & Professional Publishing Ltd

OXFORD   MELBOURNE   AUCKLAND
JOHANNESBURG   BLANTYRE   GABORONE
IBADAN   PORTSMOUTH NH (USA)   CHICAGO

© Heinemann Educational Publishers

First published 2001

ISBN 0 435 01832 9

05 04 03 02 01
10 9 8 7 6 5 4 3 2 1

Designed and typeset by Tech-Set Ltd, Gateshead, Tyne and Wear
Illustrated by Barry Atkinson, Barking Dog and Tech-Set
Cover design by Miller, Craig and Cocking
Printed and bound by Edelvives, Spain

Acknowledgements

The authors and publishers would like to thank the following for permission to use photographs:

P1: Robert Harding/E. Simanor. P47: Empics/Mike Egerton. P102 (top): Collections/Brian Shuel. P102 (bottom): Eye Ubiquitous/Paul Thompson. P111: Empics/Aubrey. P121: Peter Sanders. P143: Robert Harding/ T Nakamura. P147: Action-Plus/Glyn Kirk. P149: Collections/Barry Payling. P165: Ancient Art and Architecture Collection Ltd.. P183: Empics/Mike Egerton. P186: Bruce Coleman Collection. P187: Robert Harding Picture Library. P229: Empics/Neal Simpson. P263: James Davis Worldwide. P295: Robert Harding/R Rainford.

Cover Photo by Tony Stone Images.

Publishing team

Editorial	Design	Author team	
Sue Bennett	Phil Richards	David Benjamin	Gina Marquess
Philip Ellaway	Colette Jacquelin	Sue Bright	Christine Medlow
Nigel Green	Mags Robertson	Tony Clough	Graham Newman
Shaheen Hassan		Gareth Cole	Sheila Nolan
Nick Sample	**Production**	Diana DeBrida	Keith Pledger
Harry Smith	David Lawrence	Ray Fraser	Ian Roper
Gwen Allingham	Jason Wyatt	Peter Jolly	Mike Smith
Des Brady		David Kent	John Sylvester
Ian Crane			
Sue Glover			
Katherine Pate			
Margaret Shepherd			

Tel:01865 888058 www.heinemann.co.uk

Contents

8 Handling data

9 Formulae and equations

10 Fractions and ratio

11 Probability

12 Number patterns

13 Decimals

14 Percentages

1 Positive and negative numbers

1.1 Ordering numbers

This castle is 41 m above sea level.

The middle of this lake is 98 m deep.

You can write this as −98 m.

■ **Positive numbers are greater than zero.**

■ **Negative numbers are less than zero. They are written with a minus sign in front. For example −4.**

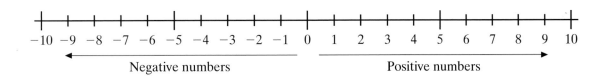

You can use a horizontal number line to answer questions about positive and negative numbers.

Example 1

Write down these numbers in order of size, starting with the smallest:

$$-3, \ 0, \ 3, \ -6, \ -1, \ 2, \ -8, \ -5$$

Mark the positions of the numbers on a number line.

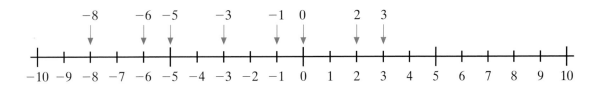

The order is −8, −6, −5, −3, −1, 0, 2, 3.

Example 2

Write down all the whole numbers that are greater than
−9, less than 4 and are odd.

The numbers are
greater than −9, so
−9 is not included.

The numbers are −7, −5, −3, −1, 1 and 3.

Exercise 1A

Use a number line to answer these questions.

1 Write these numbers in order of size, starting with the
smallest:
(a) 4, −8, −2, −5, 6, −3   **(b)** 7, −2, 2, −3, 1, −7
(c) 3, −6, −7, 2, −3, −5   **(d)** 1, −9, 2, −4, −6, −2

2 Write these numbers in order of size, starting with the
largest:
(a) −10, 3, −7, −9, −5, −2
(b) −6, 2, −13, −20, −8, −23
(c) 1, −9, 2, −4, −6, −2
(d) −10, 3, −7, −9, −5, −2

3 Write down all the whole numbers that are greater
than −5 and less than 4.

4 Write down all the whole numbers that are greater
than −7, less than 6 and are odd.

5 Write down all the whole numbers that are greater
than −9, less than 6 and are even.

6 Alice chose a whole number that is less than −4, greater
than −7 and is even. What number did Alice choose?

7 Write down all the whole numbers that are less than
14, greater than −7 and are multiples of 3.

1.2 Using the number line

You can answer questions by moving up or down the
number line.

Example 3

Use a number line to find the number that is:

(a) 4 more than −5   **(b)** 3 less than 1

(a) You have 4 more so the   **(b)** You have 3 less so the
number gets bigger.   number gets smaller.

Start at −5 and move   Start at 1 and move
4 spaces to the right.   3 spaces to the left.

   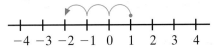

The number is −1.   The number is −2.

Example 4

Write down the next two numbers in this pattern:

$$10, 7, 4, 1, \ldots$$

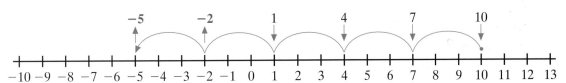

The next two numbers in the pattern are −2 and −5.

Exercise 1B

Use a number line to answer these questions.

1   Find the number that is:

     (a) 5 more than 4   **(b)** 6 more than −2
     (c) 2 less than −1   **(d)** 7 less than 4
     (e) 8 more than −3   **(f)** 5 less than 0
     (g) 8 more than −7   **(h)** 5 less than −4
     (i) 9 more than −9   **(j)** 7 less than 2
     (k) 4 more than −9   **(l)** 5 less than −3

2   Write down the next two numbers in each pattern:

(a) 7, 5, 3, 1, ...   (b) 8, 6, 4, 2, ...
(c) 11, 8, 5, 2, ...   (d) 3, 1, −1, −3, ...
(e) −7, −5, −3, −1, ...   (f) −13, −10, −7, −4, ...
(g) −9, −5, −1, 3, ...   (h) −11, −7, −3, 1, ...
(i) 1, −2, −5, −8, ...   (j) 9, 8, 6, 3, ...

3   Work out the two missing numbers in each number pattern:

(a) 9, 7, 5, 3, ☐, ☐, −3   (b) −15, −11, −7, −3, ☐, ☐, 9

(c) 13, 9, 5, 1, ☐, ☐, −11   (d) −11, −8, −5, −2, ☐, ☐, 7

(e) 10, 7, 4, 1, ☐, ☐, −8   (f) −11, −10, −8, −5, ☐, ☐, 10

4   What number is 8 more than the result of 2 less than −3?

5   What number is 5 less than the result of 3 more than −2?

6   Find the number that is 6 less than the result of 4 less than 3.

1.3 Adding and subtracting positive and negative numbers

You can use number tables to add and subtract positive
and negative numbers.

Example 5

Use number tables to find the answers:

(a) $2 + -3$ (b) $3 - -2$

(a)   First number

+	3	2	1	0	−1	−2	−3
3	6	5	4	3	2	1	0
2	5	4	3	2	1	0	−1
1	4	3	2	1	0	−1	−2
0	3	2	1	0	−1	−2	−3
−1	2	1	0	−1	−2	−3	−4
−2	1	0	−1	−2	−3	−4	−5
−3	0	−1	−2	−3	−4	−5	−6

Second number (rows labelled 3, 2, 1, 0, −1, −2, −3)

$2 + -3 = -1$

(b)   First number

−	3	2	1	0	−1	−2	−3
3	0	−1	−2	−3	−4	−5	−6
2	1	0	−1	−2	−3	−4	−5
1	2	1	0	−1	−2	−3	−4
0	3	2	1	0	−1	−2	−3
−1	4	3	2	1	0	−1	−2
−2	5	4	3	2	1	0	−1
−3	6	5	4	3	2	1	0

Second number (rows labelled 3, 2, 1, 0, −1, −2, −3)

$3 - -2 = 5$

■ **If you add a negative number the result is smaller.**

+	−	↓

Answer goes down

■ **If you subtract a negative number the result is bigger.**

−	−	↑

Answer goes up

Example 6

Use the rules shown to find the answers:

(a) $5 + -8$ b) $-4 - -7$

(a) $5 + -8$
Starting with 5, the answer goes down.
So $5 + -8 = 5 - 8 = -3$

(b) $-4 - -7$
Starting with -4, the answer goes up.
So $-4 - -7 = -4 + 7 = 3$

Exercise 1C

1   Use the number tables in Example 5 to find the answers:
      (a) $2 + -1$ (b) $-2 + -3$ (c) $-3 + 2$
      (d) $-2 - -3$ (e) $-2 - 1$ (f) $1 - -2$
      (g) $-2 - 2$ (h) $-2 + -2$ (i) $3 - 1$
      (j) $3 + -1$ (k) $1 - 3$ (l) $1 + -3$
      (m) $-1 - 2$ (n) $-1 + -2$ (o) $3 + -3$

2   Use the rules shown to find the answers:
      (a) $-6 - 1$ (b) $-5 + -2$ (c) $3 - 5$
      (d) $-8 - -2$ (e) $7 - -4$ (f) $-3 + 2$
      (g) $7 + -2$ (h) $-3 - -4$ (i) $-5 + -4$
      (j) $-7 - -3$ (k) $-2 - -6$ (l) $9 - -3$

answer

+	+	↑	goes up
+	−	↓	goes down

answer

−	+	↓	goes down
−	−	↑	goes up

3   Check your answers to questions **1** and **2** using a calculator.

4   Without using a calculator work out:
      (a) $2 + +5$ (b) $-3 + 6$ (c) $-5 + 2$
      (d) $3 + -5$ (e) $2 + -4$ (f) $1 + -6$
      (g) $-2 + -1$ (h) $-1 + -4$ (i) $-4 + -3$
      (j) $-7 + 3$ (k) $4 + -9$ (l) $-6 + -2$

1.4 Multiplying negative numbers

You already know how to multiply positive numbers.

■ **A positive number multiplied by a positive number is a positive number.**

First number	$\times$	Second number	=
$+$		$+$	$+$

This cablecar starts in the mountains.
There is one stopping point 200 m
down the mountainside.
This can be written as -200 m.

The second stopping point is a further
200 m down the mountainside.

The total distance the cablecar goes is
-200 m $+ -200$ m $= -400$ m.

You can write this as -200 m $\times 2 = -400$ m
and so $-200 \times 2 = -400$.

■ **A negative number multiplied by a positive number is a negative number.**

First number		Second number	=
$-$		$+$	$-$

-200 m $\times 2$ has the same value as 2×-200 m
so $-200 \times 2 = -400$ and $2 \times -200 = -400$.

Remember:
You can multiply in any order.
For example: $3 \times 5 = 5 \times 3 = 15$

■ **A positive number multiplied by a negative number is a negative number.**

First number		Second number	=
$+$		$-$	$-$

You can use a number line to help with multiplying
negative numbers.

Example 7

Use a number line to work out -3×5.

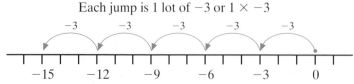

Each jump is 1 lot of -3 or 1×-3

You have moved back 15 places, so $-3 \times 5 = -15$.

You can multiply in any order, so $5 \times -3 = -15$.

If you only make 1 jump of -3, you move back 3 places.
If you make 0 jumps of -3, you do not move at all.

You can make -1 jump of -3 on the number line by reversing 1 jump.

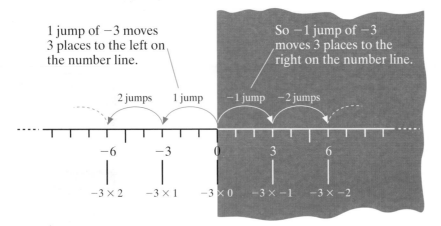

1 jump of -3 moves 3 places to the left on the number line.

So -1 jump of -3 moves 3 places to the right on the number line.

So $-3 \times -1 = 3$ and $-3 \times -2 = 6$.

■ **A negative number multiplied by a negative number is a positive number.**

First number	×	Second number	=
−		−	+

Example 8

Use the rules of multiplication to work out:
(a) -2×7 **(b)** 6×4
(c) 3×-4 **(d)** -5×-4

First number	×	Second number	=
−		+	−
+		−	−
−		−	+
+		+	+

(a) $-2 \times 7 = -14$ **(b)** $6 \times 4 = 24$
(c) $3 \times -4 = -12$ **(d)** $-5 \times -4 = 20$

Exercise 1D

1   The value of one Share in a company fell by 4p (a change of -4p) each day for 5 days. What is the change of value of one Share over this time?

2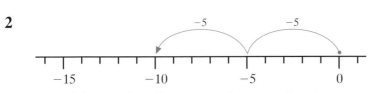

Use this number line to work out -5×2.

3 Use number lines to work out:

  (a) -4×4 **(b)** 6×-2

4

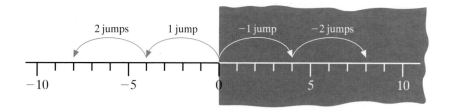

Use this number line to work out -4×-2.

5 Use the rules of multiplication to work out:

First number	×	Second number	=
−		+	−
+		−	−
−		−	+
+		+	+

  (a) 2×-7 **(b)** -4×5
  (c) 5×-5 **(d)** -2×-2
  (e) 1×1 **(f)** 1×-4
  (g) -7×3 **(h)** -6×-4
  (i) 7×-4 **(j)** 8×3
  (k) -8×-4 **(l)** -5×-6
  (m) -3×9 **(n)** -2×-3
  (o) -9×-4 **(p)** -3×6
  (q) 8×7 **(r)** 7×-6
  (s) -5×3 **(t)** -6×-8

6 Work out:

  (a) $3 \times -2 \times -4$ **(b)** $-2 \times 5 \times -3$
  (c) $2 \times -4 \times 5$ **(d)** $-3 \times -3 \times 2$
  (e) $1 \times -7 \times -4$ **(f)** $3 \times -5 \times -4$
  (g) $-2 \times 2 \times -6$ **(h)** $-3 \times -3 \times -4$
  (i) $2 \times -3 \times -5$

1.5 Dividing positive and negative numbers

You already know how to divide positive numbers.

■ **A positive number divided by a**
   positive number is a positive number.

First number	÷	Second number	=
+		+	+

You can use a number line to divide with negative numbers.

Example 9

Use a number line to work out $-8 \div 4$.

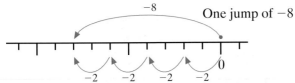

One jump of -8

You can split this into 4 equal jumps.
Each jump will be -2.

So $-8 \div 4 = -2$.

■ **A negative number divided by a
positive number is a negative number.**

First number	÷	Second number	=
−		+	−

You can also use a number line to divide
negative numbers by negative numbers.

Example 10

Use a number line to work out $-6 \div -3$.

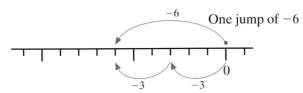

One jump of -6

How many jumps of -3 are there?
There are 2 jumps of -3 in one
jump of -6.

So $-6 \div -3 = 2$.

■ **A negative number divided by a
negative number is a positive number.**

First number	÷	Second number	=
−		−	+

You can find the result of dividing positive
numbers by negative numbers by starting
with a suitable multiplication.

Example 11

Work out $24 \div -4$ by finding a suitable multiplication.
What number fits into this equation?

$$\boxed{} \times -4 = 24$$
$$-6 \times -4 = 24$$

Divide both
sides by -4 $\div -4 \left(\right) \div -4$

$$-6 \;\; = 24 \div -4$$

So $24 \div -4 = -6$.

> Remember:
> dividing is the
> **inverse operation**
> to multiplying, so
> $-6 \times -4 \div -4 = -6$

■   **A positive number divided by a**
   negative number is a negative number.

First number	÷	Second number	=
+		−	−

Example 12

Use the rules of division to work out:

(a) $-32 \div 4$ **(b)** $45 \div -5$

(a) $-32 \;\; \div \;\; 4 \;\; = -8$ **(b)** $45 \;\; \div \;\; -5 \;\; = -9$

First number	÷	Second number	=
−		+	−

First number	÷	Second number	=
+		−	−

Exercise 1E

1   The depth of water in a swimming pool is 160 cm.
All the water is pumped out of the pool at a
steady rate (a change in water depth of -160 cm)
in 80 seconds. What is the change in water depth
each second?

2

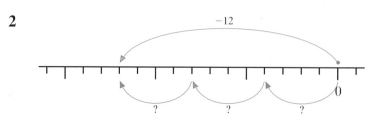

Copy this diagram and fill in the number you think
should go where the question marks are.
What is $-12 \div 3$?

3 Use the number line to work out:

(a) $-18 \div 2$ (b) $-15 \div 3$ (c) $-10 \div 2$
(d) $-12 \div 4$ (e) $-16 \div 4$ (f) $-22 \div 2$

4 Copy and complete these equations:

(a) $\boxed{} \times -7 = 14$ (b) $\boxed{} \times -3 = 24$

(c) $\boxed{} \times -4 = -24$ (d) $\boxed{} \times -3 = 27$

(e) $\boxed{} \times -5 = -35$ (f) $\boxed{} \times -7 = -42$

5 Use your answers to question **4** to find the answers:

(a) $14 \div -7$ (b) $24 \div -3$
(c) $-24 \div -4$ (d) $27 \div -3$
(e) $-35 \div -5$ (f) $-42 \div -7$

6 Use the rules of division to work out:

(a) $-48 \div 8$ (b) $-32 \div -4$
(c) $48 \div -8$ (d) $-26 \div -2$
(e) $-36 \div 9$ (f) $-18 \div -3$
(g) $30 \div -5$ (h) $-16 \div -8$
(i) $20 \div -4$

First number	$\div$	Second number	=
+		+	+
+		−	−
−		+	−
−		−	+

7 Use any of the methods in this chapter to work out:

(a) $5 - 2$ (b) $2 - 6$ (c) $4 - 7$
(d) $-2 - 1$ (e) $-1 - 4$ (f) $-3 - 5$
(g) $3 - 7$ (h) $-4 - 5$ (i) $1 - 5$
(j) $-3 - 6$ (k) $2 - 9$ (l) $-4 - 7$

8 Find the value of:

(a) $9 - 2$ (b) $2 - 7$ (c) $1 - 6$
(d) $2 - 9$ (e) $-6 + 4$ (f) $-5 + 8$
(g) $-2 + 4$ (h) $-4 - 3$ (i) $-5 - 3$
(j) $-9 + 4$ (k) $2 - 10$ (l) $-4 + 7$

9 Use any of the methods in this chapter to work out:

(a) $30 \div -6$ (b) $-64 \div -8$
(c) $-28 \div 4$ (d) $-63 \div -9$
(e) $28 \div -2$ (f) $-21 \div 7$
(g) $-3 \times (-2 + 5)$ (h) $(-5 - -3) \times 6$
(i) $(2 - 7) \times -3$ (j) $(-21 - 9) \div 5$
(k) $(-9 + -6) \div -5$ (l) $(33 + -9) \div -8$

Summary of key points

1   Positive numbers are greater than zero.

2   Negative numbers are less than zero. They are
written with a minus sign in front.
For example, −4.

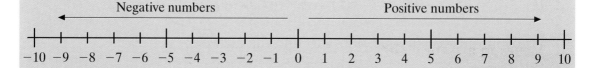

Negative numbers	Positive numbers

−10 −9 −8 −7 −6 −5 −4 −3 −2 −1 0 1 2 3 4 5 6 7 8 9 10

3   If you add a negative number
the result is smaller.

			answer
+	+	↑	goes up
+	−	↓	goes down

4   If you subtract a negative number
the result is bigger.

			answer
−	+	↓	goes down
−	−	↑	goes up

5   A positive number multiplied by a
positive number is a positive number

A negative number multiplied by a
positive number is a negative number

A positive number multiplied by a
negative number is a negative number

A negative number multiplied by a
negative number is a positive number

First number	×	Second number	=
+		+	+
−		+	−
+		−	−
−		−	+

6   A positive number divided by a
positive number is a positive number

A negative number divided by a
positive number is a negative number

A negative number divided by a
negative number is a positive number

A positive number divided by a
negative number is a negative number

First number	÷	Second number	=
+		+	+
−		+	−
−		−	+
+		−	−

2 Angles and bearings

2.1 Revision

Angle facts

You have met these angle facts before:

- **Angles in a corner add up to 90°.**

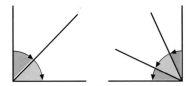

- **Angles on a straight line add up to 180°.**

- **Angles at a point add up to 360°.**

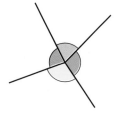

- **When two straight lines cross, the opposite angles are equal.**

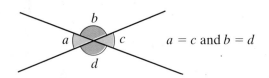

$a = c$ and $b = d$

Exercise 2A

Find the missing angles and write which angle fact you used to help you.

1

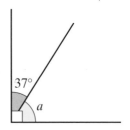

2

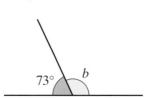

3

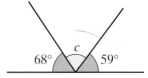

4

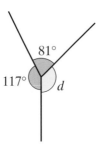

5

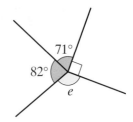

6

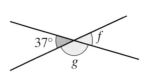

Angles in triangles, quadrilaterals and polygons

Angles in triangles, quadrilaterals and polygons have certain properties that you should know:

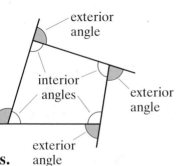

- The angles of a triangle add up to 180°.

- The angles of a quadrilateral add up to 360°.

- A *regular* polygon has equal sides and equal angles.

- The angles inside a shape are called interior angles. The angles outside a shape are called exterior angles. In any polygon:
  interior angle + exterior angle = 180°

- The sum of the exterior angles of a polygon is 360°.

Exercise 2B

Find the missing angles:

1
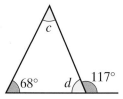

2
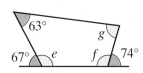

3
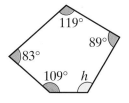

4
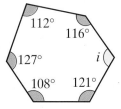

5
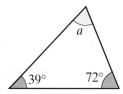

6
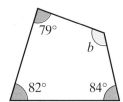

> **Hint:**
> The polygon in question 5 has got more than four sides. You need to work out the exterior angles first.

7 Find the sum of the interior angles of a polygon with 14 sides.

8 The size of each interior angle of a regular polygon is 140°.
   (a) Find the size of each exterior angle.
   (b) Find the number of sides the polygon has.

9 The size of each exterior angle of a regular polygon is 24°. Find the number of sides the polygon has.

10 A regular polygon has 20 sides. Find the size of each interior angle.

2.2 Angles between parallel lines

Lines are **parallel** if they are always the same distance apart. No matter how far you extend parallel lines, they never meet.

Arrows are used to show parallel lines on diagrams.

In the diagrams below, a straight line crosses two parallel lines. The pair of shaded angles are called **corresponding angles**. They are equal to each other.

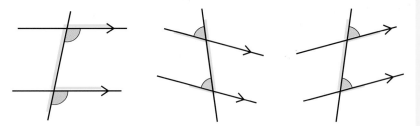

Corresponding angles are sometimes called **F angles**. Looking for an F shape can sometimes help you find corresponding angles.

■ **Corresponding angles between parallel lines are equal.**

These angles are called **alternate** angles. They are equal to each other.

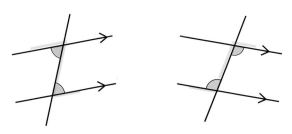

Alternate angles are sometimes called **Z angles**. Looking for a Z shape can sometimes help you find alternate angles.

■ **Alternate angles between parallel lines are equal.**

Example 1

Write down the angle which is
(a) corresponding to the shaded angle
(b) alternate to the shaded angle.

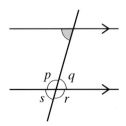

(a) s is the angle which is corresponding to the shaded angle.

(b) q is the angle which is alternate to the shaded angle.

Example 2

Find x. Give a reason for your answer.

$x = 105°$ (corresponding angles)

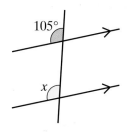

Example 3

Find x and y. Give reasons for your answers.

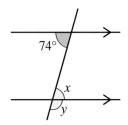

$x = 74°$ (alternate angles)

$x + y = 180°$ (angles on a straight line add to $180°$)

$74° + y = 180°$

$y = 180° - 74°$

$y = 106°$

Example 4

Find x, y and z. Give reasons for your answers.

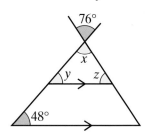

$x = 76°$ (opposite angles are equal)

$y = 48°$ (corresponding angles)

$x + y + z = 180°$ (angles of a triangle sum to $180°$)

$76° + 48° + z = 180°$

$124° + z = 180°$

$z = 180° - 124°$

$z = 56°$

Exercise 2C

1   Write down the angle which is:

(i)   corresponding to the shaded angle
(ii)   alternate to the shaded angle.

(a)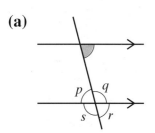

(b)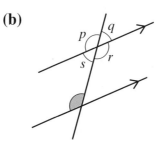

(c)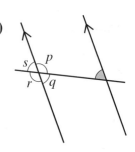

2   Find the missing angles and write which angle fact you used.

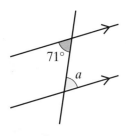

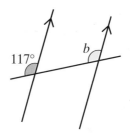

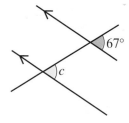

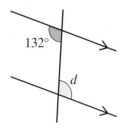

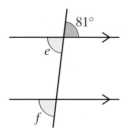

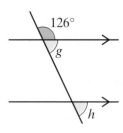

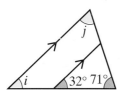

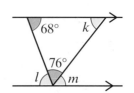

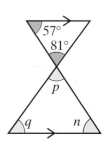

2.3 Three-figure bearings

You have probably used compass bearings to describe directions. This church is to the North-East.

You can describe directions more accurately using **three-figure bearings**.

A three-figure bearing describes a direction as an angle, measured clockwise from North:

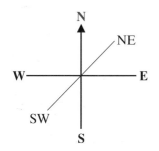

If the angle is less than 100°, you must put zeros in front of the angle so that the bearing has three figures.

You say 'the bearing of A from O is 140°'.

■ **A three-figure bearing is the angle measured clockwise from North.**

Example 5

Write these directions as three figure bearings:

(a) North East   **(b)** South West

(a) The angle measured clockwise from North to North East is 45°. The three-figure bearing is 045°.

(b) The angle measured clockwise from North to South West is 225° (180° + 45°). The bearing is 225°.

Example 6

Draw an accurate diagram to show a bearing of 137°.

Draw the obtuse angle using your protractor as shown here.

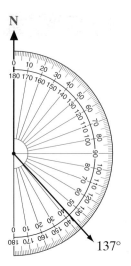

137°

You can use a semi-circular protractor to measure bearings up to 180°. For bearings greater than 180° you will either have to add 180° to the angle you measure or subtract it from 360°.

Example 7

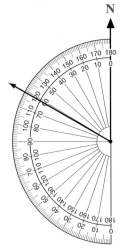

Express the direction shown in the diagram as a three-figure bearing.

Method 1
Measure the angle clockwise from South (119°) and add 180° to it.
Bearing = 119° + 180°
        = 299°

Method 2
Measure the angle anticlockwise from North (61°) and subtract it from 360°.
Bearing = 360° − 61°
        = 299°

You need to be able to calculate bearings using angle facts.

Example 8

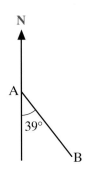

Work out the three-figure bearing of B from A.

Angles on a straight line add to 180°.
Bearing = 180° − 39°
        = 141°

Exercise 2D

1 Write these compass directions as three-figure bearings.

(a) West   (b) South-East   (c) North-West

2 Use a protractor to express the directions on the diagram as three-figure bearings.

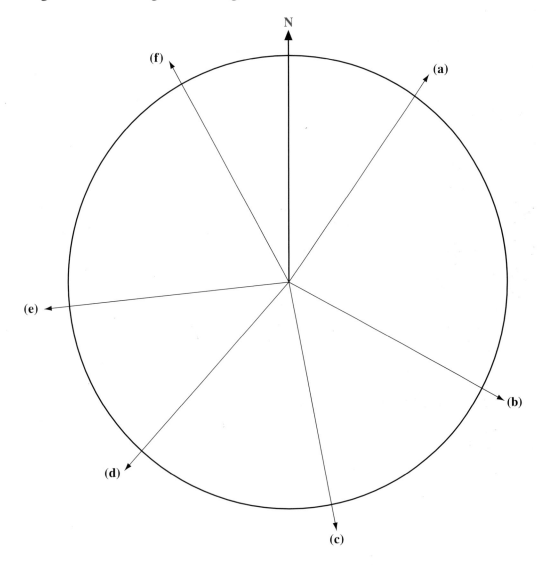

3 Using a protractor, draw a diagram similar to the one above to show these bearings.

(a) 042°   (b) 163°   (c) 209°   (d) 342°

4 Use angle facts to work out the three-figure bearing of B from A for each of the directions below.

(a)

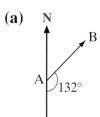

(b)

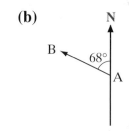

(c)

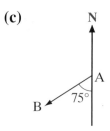

2.4 Scale drawings

Architects often make accurate drawings of houses. The drawing is much smaller than the actual house, but all the angles and proportions are the same. This is called a **scale drawing**.

The scale compares the size of the drawing with the size of the object. If 1 cm on the drawing represents 10 cm in real life, then the scale is 1 cm to 10 cm. You can also just say '1 to 10'.

■ **A drawing to a scale of 1 cm to 10 cm (or 1 to 10) is $\frac{1}{10}$ of the actual size.**

Example 9

This diagram is a scale drawing of the front of a microwave oven. The scale is 1 cm to 10 cm.

(a) Find the height of the oven.
(b) Find the width of the oven.

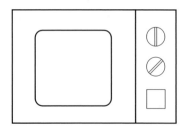

(a) On the drawing, the height of the oven is 3 cm. Its real height is 3 cm × 10 = 30 cm

(b) On the drawing, the width of the oven is 4.5 cm. Its real width is 4.5 cm × 10 = 45 cm

Example 10

Helen's bedroom is a rectangle 4 m by 3.2 m. Make a plan of her bedroom, using a scale of 1 cm to 1 metre.

1 cm on the plan represents 1 m in real life.
So 4 cm represents 4 m and 3.2 cm represents 3.2 m.

Helen's
bedroom

You can't write this scale as 1 to 1. This would mean it was full size. 1 cm represents 1 metre, which is 100 cm, so the scale could be written as 1 to 100.

Maps are examples of scale drawings.

Example 11

The map in the diagram shows three towns. The scale is 1 cm to 5 km. Find the distance in real life from:

(a) Wolverhampton to Bridgnorth
(b) Wolverhampton to Telford
(c) Bridgnorth to Telford.

Telford ●

● Wolverhampton

Bridgnorth ●

Hint:
Use a ruler to measure the distances in the diagram first.

1 cm on the map represents 5 km in real life. You need to multiply the distance on the map in centimetres by 5. This will give you the distance in real life in kilometres.

(a) On the map the distance is 4 cm. $4 \times 5 = 20$
The distance is 20 km.

(b) On the map the distance is 4.6 cm. $4.6 \times 5 = 23$
The distance is 23 km.

(c) On the map the distance is 2.9 cm. $2.9 \times 5 = 14.5$
The distance is 14.5 km.

Exercise 2E

1 This diagram is a scale drawing of the front of a speaker. The scale is 1 cm to 10 cm.
(a) Find the height of the speaker.
(b) Find the width of the speaker.

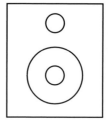

2 A rectangular dining room is 5 m by 3.8 m. Make a scale drawing of the room. Use a scale of 1 cm to 1 m.

> This scale could be expressed as 1 cm to 100 cm or 1 to 100.

3 A soccer pitch is 100 m long and 70 m wide. Make a scale drawing of the pitch. Use a scale of 1 cm to 20 m. How could you write this scale without using units?

4 This diagram is a scale drawing of the Eiffel Tower. The scale is 1 cm to 100 m. Find the actual height of the Eiffel Tower.

5 This map shows three towns. The scale is 1 cm to 5 km. Find the distance in real life from:
(a) Canterbury to Margate
(b) Canterbury to Sandwich.

● Margate

Canterbury ●   ● Sandwich

6 This diagram is a scale drawing of a man playing a trumpet. The scale is 1 cm to 50 cm. Find:
(a) the man's height
(b) the length of his trumpet.

7 A rectangular plot of land is 35 m by 27 m. Make a scale drawing of the plot. Use a scale of 1 cm to 5 m. Write this as a scale without units.

8 The map in the diagram shows four towns. The scale is 1 cm to 25 km. Find the actual distance from:

(a) Oxford to Milton Keynes
(b) Oxford to Birmingham
(c) Birmingham to Cambridge.

Birmingham ●

● Cambridge

● Milton
Keynes

Oxford ●

2.5 Locus

When a point moves according to a given rule, its path is called a **locus**. All the points on the locus obey the rule. You can draw a locus using a dotted line.

> The plural of locus is **loci**.

■ **A locus is the path of a point which moves according to a given rule.**

Example 12

A point moves so that it is always 2 cm from a fixed point A. Draw the locus.

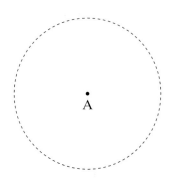

The locus is a circle, centre A, with a radius of 2 cm.

Example 13

A point moves so that it is always 1 cm from the line AB.
Draw the locus.

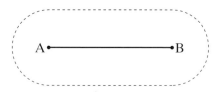

The locus is two lines
parallel to AB
and two semi-circles,
centres A and B,
each with a radius of 1 cm.

Example 14

A and B are two fixed points. A point moves so that it is
always the same distance from A as it is from B. Draw the
locus.

The locus is a straight line
halfway between A and B
at right angles to the line
AB. It is called the
perpendicular bisector of
the line AB.

You can find the perpendicular bisector by making a
tracing of the points A and B. If you fold B over so that it
is on top of A, the fold line is the perpendicular bisector.

Example 15

AB and AC are straight lines. A point moves to that it is
always the same distance from AB as it is from AC. Draw
the locus.

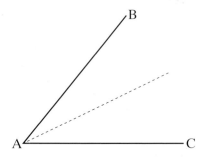

The locus is a straight line
halfway between AB and
AC. It cuts angle BAC in
half. It is called the
bisector of angle BAC.

You can find the bisector of angle BAC by making a
tracing of angle BAC. If you fold the line AB over so that it
is on top of the line AC, the fold line is the angle bisector.

Exercise 2F

1 A point moves so that it is always 3 cm from a fixed point A. Draw the locus.

2 Draw a line AB 4 cm long. A point moves so that it is always 2 cm from AB. Draw the locus.

3 Draw two points, A and B, 5 cm apart. A point moves so that it is always the same distance from A as it is from B. Draw the locus.

4 Draw angle BAC of 65°. A point moves so that it is the same distance from AB as it is from AC. Draw the locus.

5 Draw a circle with a radius of 2 cm. A point moves *outside* the circle so that it is always 1 cm from the circle. Draw the locus.

6 Draw a circle with a radius of 4 cm. A point moves *inside* the circle so that it is always 1 cm from the circle. Draw the locus.

7 Draw a rectangle 5 cm by 3 cm. A point moves *outside* the rectangle so that it is always 1 cm from the rectangle. Draw the locus.

8

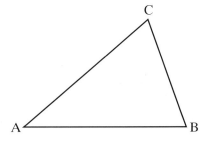

Hint:
Draw two loci, one for each rule. Where the loci cross, both the rules are obeyed.

Make a copy of triangle ABC. A point moves so that it is the same distance from A as it is from B *and* it is the same distance from AB as it is from AC. Find the point.

2.6 Compass and ruler constructions

Mathematicians in ancient Greece were particularly interested in geometrical constructions and they created many of the mathematical constructions we use today. These are sometimes called 'compass and straight edge' constructions, because the ruler is not used for measuring lengths.

Example 16

Construct an equilateral triangle with AB as one of its sides.

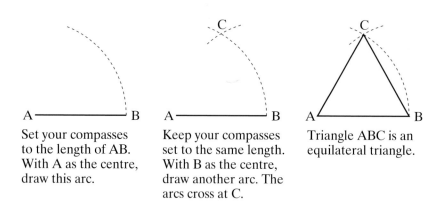

Set your compasses to the length of AB. With A as the centre, draw this arc.

Keep your compasses set to the same length. With B as the centre, draw another arc. The arcs cross at C.

Triangle ABC is an equilateral triangle.

You can use this method to construct an angle of 60°, since each angle of an equilateral triangle is 60°.

Example 17

Construct the perpendicular bisector of the line AB.

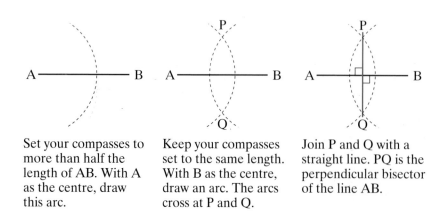

Set your compasses to more than half the length of AB. With A as the centre, draw this arc.

Keep your compasses set to the same length. With B as the centre, draw an arc. The arcs cross at P and Q.

Join P and Q with a straight line. PQ is the perpendicular bisector of the line AB.

Example 18

Construct the perpendicular from the point P to the line AB.

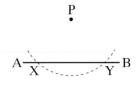

With P as centre draw an arc. Choose a radius so that the arc crosses AB twice, at X and Y.

Choose a radius more than half the length of XY. With X as centre, draw an arc below AB. Keep the radius the same and, with Y as centre, draw a second arc below AB. The two arcs cross at Q.

Join P and Q with a straight line. PQ is the perpendicular from P to the line AB.

Example 19

Construct the perpendicular from the point P on the line AB.

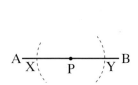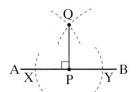

With P as centre draw two arcs of the same radius to cross AB at X and Y.

Choose a radius more than half the length of XY. With X as centre, draw an arc above AB. Keep the radius the same and, with Y as centre, draw a second arc above AB. The two arcs cross at Q.

Join P and Q with a straight line. PQ is perpendicular to the line AB.

Example 20

Construct the bisector of angle BAC.

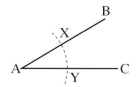 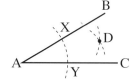 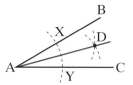

With centre A, draw an arc to cross AB and AC at X and Y respectively.

With centre X, draw an arc. Keep the radius the same and, with Y as centre, draw a second arc. The two arcs cross at D.

Join A and D with a straight line. AD bisects angle BAC.

Exercise 2G

1   Construct an equilateral triangle with sides 3.8 cm long.

2   Draw a line 4.7 cm long and construct the perpendicular bisector of the line.

3   Copy the diagram and construct the perpendicular from P to the line AB.

> Make your copies at least twice as big as the diagrams on the page, otherwise you won't have space to do your constructions.

P
•

A ——————————— B

4   Copy the diagram and construct the perpendicular from the point P on the line AB.

A ————•———— B
         P

5   Copy the angle below and construct its bisector.

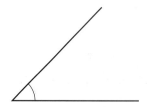

6   Copy the triangle below. Construct the perpendicular bisector of each its sides.

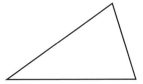

7   Copy the triangle below. Construct the bisectors of its angles.

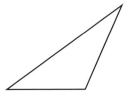

8   Copy triangle ABC. Construct:
   (a) the perpendicular bisector of AC
   (b) the bisector of angle BAC.

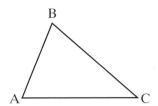

Summary of key points

1   Angles in a corner add up to 90°.

2   Angles on a straight line add up to 180°.

3   Angles at a point add up to 360°.

4   When two straight lines cross, the opposite angles are equal.

5   The angles of a triangle add up to 180°.

6   The angles of a quadrilateral add up to 360°.

7   A regular polygon has equal sides and equal angles.

8 The angles inside a shape are called interior angles. The angles outside a shape are called exterior angles.
In any polygon:
interior angle + exterior angle = 180°.

9 The sum of the exterior angles of a polygon is 360°.

10 Corresponding angles between parallel lines are equal.

11 Alternate angles between parallel lines are equal.

12 A three-figure bearing is the angle measured clockwise from North.

13 A drawing to a scale of 1 cm to 10 cm (or 1 to 10) is $\frac{1}{10}$ of the actual size.

14 A locus is the path of a point which moves according to a given rule.

3 Working with algebra

To solve problems in algebra you need to be able to work with letters or symbols with confidence.

Scientists use complicated algebra to work out the orbit of the satellite and the size of dish needed to pick up the television signal.

3.1 Collecting like terms

At Roger's Bakery the cost of each cake is:

Cake	Price
Doughnut	d
Jam tart	j
Swiss bun	s
Eccles cake	e
Cream slice	c

Example 1

A family orders these cakes from the bakery:

Susan   3 doughnuts + 3 jam tarts + 1 swiss bun
Becky   1 jam tart + 3 eccles cakes
Oliver   2 doughnuts + 1 eccles cake + 2 cream slices

(a) Work out the cost of each order.
(b) What is the total cost?

(a) Susan $d + d + d + j + j + j + s$
      Becky $j + e + e + e$
      Oliver $d + d + e + c + c$

(b) Total cost $= d + d + d + j + j + j + s + j + e + e$
               $+ e + d + d + e + c + c$

> Remember:
> terms that have the same letter are called *like* terms.

You can collect like terms:

$$\underbrace{d + d + d + d + d}_{5d} + \underbrace{j + j + j + j}_{4j} + \underbrace{s}_{s} + \underbrace{e + e + e + e}_{4e} + \underbrace{c + c}_{2c}$$

> Remember:
> s means $1s$

■ **Bringing terms together is called 'collecting like terms'.**

Example 2

Simplify:

(a) $5x + 4x$ (b) $3a - 2b + 6a + 5b$

(c) $6x + 7y + 9$ (d) $8t + 6 - 7t - 4$

> Remember:
> **Simplify** means collect like terms.

(a) $5x + 4x = 9x$

(b) $3a - 2b + 6a + 5b$

      $= 3a + 6a - 2b + 5b$

      $= \quad 9a \qquad -3b$

(c) There are no like terms so $6x + 7y + 9$ cannot be simplified.

(d) $8t + 6 - 7t - 4$

      $= 8t - 7t + 6 - 4$

      $= t + 2$

Exercise 3A

1   Simplify:

(a) $3x + 3y + 3x + 3y$ (b) $5r + 3t + 4r + 2t$

(c) $6c + 5d - 3c - 2d$ (d) $7r + 3w + r - w$

(e) $12x - 6y - 5x + 9y$ (f) $6c + 7d - 6c + 3d$

(g) $5 + 3a + 2 - a$ (h) $9p + 3n + 5n - 3p$

(i) $6v + 2s - s + 8v$ (j) $3r + 6s - 2r - s + 5$

(k) $4d - 3d - 2d + 6d$ (l) $3 + 4r + 5 + 3r - 1$

(m) $15p - 2q + 3p + 8q$ (n) $6m + 2n - 3n - 2n + m$

(o) $6x - 2y + 3w - t$ (p) $6e + 7f - 10f + 6e$

(q) $5g + 3e + 2f + 3e - 5g$ (r) $15a - 10a - 6a + 3a$

(s) $17y - 11x + 3y + 12y$ (t) $8x - 6 + 8x - 6 + 4x$

3.2 Multiplying terms together

At Roger's bakery they need to work out how much icing to make for slab cakes

Each slab cake is divided into slices x wide and y long.

Then the whole slab cake is:

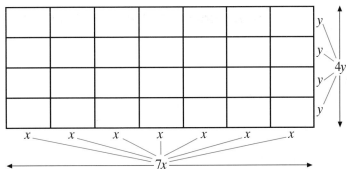

Area of icing $= 7x \times 4y$

$\qquad = 7 \times x \times 4 \times y$

$\qquad = 7 \times 4 \times x \times y$

$\qquad = 28xy$

You can use this method to simplify more complicated expressions.

Example 3

Simplify $5ab \times 3c$

$5ab \times 3c = 5 \times a \times b \times 3 \times c$

$\qquad\quad = 5 \times 3 \times a \times b \times c$

$\qquad\quad = 15abc$

> The letters should be written in alphabetical order.

Example 4

Simplify:

(a) $3r \times 4st$ **(b)** $15mn \times 8pq$

(a) $= 3 \times r \times 4 \times s \times t$

$\qquad = 3 \times 4 \times r \times s \times t$

$\qquad = 12rst$

(b) $= 15 \times m \times n \times 8 \times p \times q$

$\qquad = 15 \times 8 \times m \times n \times p \times q$

$\qquad = 120mnpq$

Exercise 3B

1 Simplify:

(a) $2a \times 3b$ **(b)** $4c \times 5d$ **(c)** $5x \times 6y$

(d) $x \times y \times z$ **(e)** $5d \times e$ **(f)** $5e \times 5g$

(g) $4ab \times 2c$ **(h)** $3x \times 4yz$ **(i)** $7cd \times 3x$

(j) $5ab \times 5cd$ **(k)** $3a \times 4bc$ **(l)** $10x \times 9yz$

(m) $8rs \times wy$ **(n)** $7pq \times 3rs$ **(o)** $3abc \times 4ef$

(p) $5mn \times 2pqr$

3.3 Brackets in algebra

In algebra you need to be able to expand and simplify expressions like $2(3x + 4y)$ and $3(2x + y) + 4(x + 2y)$.

■ **Removing brackets in an expression is called expanding the bracket,**

e.g. $3(a + 3b) = 3a + 9b$

Example 5

Expand and simplify:
(a) $3(2x + 5y)$
(b) $3(4x + 3y) + 2(2x - 3y)$

(a) $3(2x + 5y)$ Expand the brackets
$= 3 \times 2x + 3 \times 5y$
$= 6x + 15y$

> Remember:
> Multiply each term inside the bracket by the term outside the brackets.

(b) $3(4x + 3y) + 2(2x - 3y)$ Expand the brackets
$= 3 \times 4x + 3 \times 3y + 2 \times 2x + 2 \times -3y$
$= 12x + 9y + 4x - 6y$
$= 12x + 4x + 9y - 6y$ Simplify by collecting like terms.
$= 16x + 3y$

> Remember:
> $+2 \times -3 = -6$

■ **Simplify means collect like terms together.**

Exercise 3C

1 Expand the expressions and then simplify:
(a) $2(x + y)$
(b) $3(2a + 3b)$
(c) $5(3s - 2r)$
(d) $6(3a - 2b + 3c)$
(e) $4(a - b + 2c)$
(f) $2(x + y) + 3(2x + y)$
(g) $5(m + n) + 2(m - 2n)$
(h) $3(d + 3e) + 4(2d + 3e)$
(i) $6(7a - 3b) + 3(a + 2b)$
(j) $11(2x + 3y) + 4(x - 5y)$
(k) $5(3p - 2q) + 4(p + 5q)$
(l) $4(x + y) + 3(x - y)$
(m) $8(3f - 2g) + 3(4f - g)$
(n) $2(5s + 2r) + 7(2s + 3r)$
(o) $9(3a - 2b) + 9(2a + 3b)$
(p) $4(a - b) + 4(a + b)$
(q) $5(2x + b) + 2(a - 2b)$
(r) $3(3d - 2e) + 3(2d + 3e)$

3.4 Subtracting expressions with brackets

You will need to be able to subtract expressions like:

$$4(3x + 4y) - 2(2x - 3y)$$

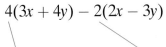

This means multiply each term in the bracket by 4.

This means multiply each term in the bracket by -2 (minus 2).

So $\quad 4(3x + 4y) - 2(2x - 3y)$

$= 4 \times 3x + 4 \times 4y - 2 \times 2x - 2 \times -3y$ — Expand the brackets.

$= 12x + 16y - 4x + 6y$

$= 12x - 4x + 16y + 6y$ ———— Simplify by collecting like terms.

$= 8x + 22y$

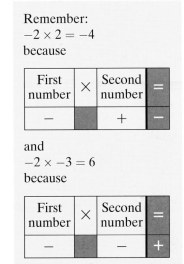

Remember:
$-2 \times 2 = -4$
because

First number	$\times$	Second number	=
$-$		$+$	$-$

and
$-2 \times -3 = 6$
because

First number	$\times$	Second number	=
$-$		$-$	$+$

For a reminder about multiplying with negative numbers see page 6.

Example 6

Simplify $4(3x - 2y) - (x + 4y)$

Remove the brackets:

$\quad 4(3x - 2y) - (x + 4y)$

$= 4 \times 3x + 4 \times -2y - 1 \times x - 1 \times 4y$

$= 12x - 8y - x - 4y$

$= 12x - x - 8y - 4y$ ———— Collect like terms.

$= 11x - 12y$

$-(x + 4y)$ means
$-1(x + 4y)$

Example 7

Simplify $2(a - 6b) + 3(a + 3b)$

Remove the brackets:

$\quad 2(a - 6b) + 3(a + 3b)$

$= 2 \times a + 2 \times -6b + 3 \times a + 3 \times 3b$

$= 2a - 12b + 3a + 9b$

$= 2a + 3a - 12b + 9b$ ———————— Collect like terms.

$= 5a - 3b$

Example 8

Simplify $3(2x + 3y) - 2(2x + 5y)$

Remove the brackets:

$$3(2x + 3y) - 2(2x + 5y)$$
$$= 3 \times 2x + 3 \times 3y - 2 \times 2x - 2 \times 5y$$
$$= 6x + 9y - 4x - 10y$$
$$= 6x - 4x + 9y - 10y \text{ ————— Collect like terms.}$$
$$= 2x - y$$

You write $-1y$ as $-y$

Exercise 3D

Expand the brackets and then simplify:

1 $2(2a + b) - 3(a + b)$ 2 $6(2x + 3y) - 2(x + 3y)$
3 $4(4a - 3b) - (2a + b)$ 4 $2(p + q) - 3(p - q)$
5 $5(4a + 3b) - 3(a - b)$ 6 $3(2p + q) - 2(p + q)$
7 $4(3x - 2y) - 2(5x - 3y)$ 8 $11(x - 2y) - 11(x + 2y)$
9 $7(4r - 3s) - 2(5r - 6s)$ 10 $6(3m - 2n) - 3(2m + 7n)$
11 $3(2a + 5b) - (7a + b)$ 12 $(x + y) - (x - y)$
13 $2(a + 3b) - 2(a - 3b)$ 14 $4(5a + 7b) - 9(3a - 4b)$
15 $7(x + 3t) - 6(x + 4t)$ 16 $5(2x - 7y) + 8(3x - 4y)$
17 $5(3w + 4z) - 3(2w + 7z)$ 18 $2(2s + 3t) - 2(s + 4t)$
19 $5(x + 2y) - 6(x + y)$ 20 $4(3a + 2b) - 3(2a + 3b)$
21 $2(x - y) + 3(2x - 3y) - (x + 2y)$

3.5 Factorising simple expressions

■ **Factorising is the reverse process to removing brackets.**

Factorising lets you write algebraic expressions in a
different form using brackets.

Example 9

Factorise $5x + 10$

Look for common factors of the terms $5x$ and 10.
5 goes exactly into $5x$ and 10, so 5 is a common factor.
You can write the common factor outside a bracket:

$$5x + 10 = 5(x + 2)$$

Hint: You can check
your answer by
expanding the
expression again:

$$5(x + 2) = 5x + 10$$

Example 10

Factorise $6a + 3$

$6a + 3$ Look for common factors of the terms $6a$ and 3.
$= 3(2a + 1)$ Because 3 goes exactly into $6a$ and 3, 3 is a
       common factor. It can be taken outside a bracket.

Example 11

Factorise $10y - 15x$

$10y - 15x$ Look for common factors of the terms $10y$ and $15x$.
$= 5(2y - 3x)$ 5 is a common factor so it can be taken outside
       a bracket.

Exercise 3E

Factorise these expressions:

1	$2a + 4$	**2**	$9c + 6d$
3	$10x + 5$	**4**	$18p - 6q$
5	$10 + 5x$	**6**	$12 - 4b$
7	$6x + 9y$	**8**	$12r - 8s$
9	$15a + 30b$	**10**	$11w - 33x$
11	$14d + 21e$	**12**	$18x - 24y$
13	$14a + 7b$	**14**	$6x - 9y$
15	$18c + 6$	**16**	$24a - 18b$
17	$9r - 15s$	**18**	$4x - 14y$
19	$15x - 6y$	**20**	$18r - 27s$

3.6 Powers in algebra

You can use powers to multiply letters that are the same:

	You write:	You say:
$y \times y$	y^2	y to the power of 2, or y squared
$y \times y \times y$	y^3	y to the power of 3, or y cubed
$y \times y \times y \times y$	y^4	y to the power of 4, or y to the fourth
$y \times y \times y \times y \times y$	y^5	y to the power of 5, or y to the fifth

y on its own is a special case. It can be written as y^1. You
say 'y to the power of one'.

You can use powers for numbers too:

	You write:	You say:
4×4	4^2	4 to the power of 2, or 4 squared
$4 \times 4 \times 4$	4^3	4 to the power of 3, or 4 cubed
$4 \times 4 \times 4 \times 4$	4^4	4 to the power of 4, or 4 to the fourth

Example 12

Write using powers:

(a) $a \times a$ **(b)** $b \times b \times b \times b$

(a) $a \times a = a^2$ —————————— 2 lots of a multiplied together.
(b) $b \times b \times b \times b = b^4$ ————— 4 lots of b multiplied together.

Example 13

Write in a simpler form:

(a) x to the power of 4   **(b)** a cubed
(c) y squared   **(d)** b to the power of eight.

(a) x^4 **(b)** a^3
(c) y^2 **(d)** b^8

Example 14

Write these terms in full (without powers):

(a) a^3 **(b)** x^5

(a) $a \times a \times a$ **(b)** $x \times x \times x \times x \times x$

Exercise 3F

1 Write using powers:

     (a) $b \times b$ **(b)** $c \times c \times c$
     (c) $r \times r \times r \times r \times r$ **(d)** $f \times f \times f \times f$
     (e) $w \times w \times w$ **(f)** $t \times t \times t \times t \times t \times t$
     (g) $d \times d \times d \times d \times d \times d$ **(h)** $a \times a \times a \times a$

2 Write these terms in full:

     (a) 3^2 **(b)** 5^3 **(c)** 5^4 **(d)** a^3
     (e) x^2 **(f)** y^4 **(g)** b^5 **(h)** c^3
     (i) d^6 **(j)** r^7 **(k)** w^3 **(l)** t^9

3   Write in a simpler form:
   (a) *a* squared   **(b)** *b* cubed
   (c) *x* to the power of 4 **(d)** *y* to the power of 1
   (e) *w* to the power of 6 **(f)** *r* to the fifth

3.7 Multiplying powers of the same number or letter

You need to be able to multiply powers of the same number together.

$$2^3 \times 2^2 = (2 \times 2 \times 2) \times (2 \times 2) = 2^5$$
$$3^2 \times 3^4 = (3 \times 3) \times (3 \times 3 \times 3 \times 3) = 3^6$$

You can multiply powers of the same letter together in the same way:

$$y^3 \times y^2 = (y \times y \times y) \times (y \times y) = y^5$$
$$t^2 \times t^4 = (t \times t) \times (t \times t \times t \times t) = t^6$$

> Notice that:
> $2^3 \times 2^2 = 2^{3+2} = 2^5$
> $3^2 \times 3^4 = 3^{2+4} = 3^6$
> The power tells you how many times a number is multiplied together.

■ **To multiply powers of the same number or letter add the powers: $y^a \times y^b = y^{a+b}$**

Example 15

Simplify by writing as a single power:
(a) $4^2 \times 4^3$ **(b)** $3^4 \times 3^5$ **(c)** $p^2 \times p^3$ **(d)** $y^3 \times y^6$

(a) $4^2 \times 4^3 = 4^{2+3} = 4^5$ **(b)** $3^4 \times 3^5 = 3^{4+5} = 3^9$
(c) $p^2 \times p^3 = p^{2+3} = p^5$ **(d)** $y^3 \times y^6 = y^{3+6} = y^9$

Example 16

Simplify:
(a) $2a^2 \times 3a^3$ **(b)** $4a \times a^3$

(a) $2a^2 \times 3a^3$
        means $2 \times a^2 \times 3 \times a^3$
Multiply the numbers together and multiply the letters together:
$$2a^2 \times 3a^3 = 2 \times 3 \times a^2 \times a^3$$
$$= \quad 6 \quad \times \quad a^{2+3}$$
$$= 6a^5$$

(b) $4a \times a^3$
$= 4 \times 1 \times a \times a^3$
$= 4 \times a^{1+3}$
$= 4a^4$

> Remember:
> *a* means a^1
> a^3 means $1a^3$

Exercise 3G

Simplify:

1	$3^2 \times 3^4$	**2**	$4^3 \times 4^2$
3	$2^4 \times 2^5$	**4**	6×6^3
5	$4^5 \times 4^5$	**6**	$7^2 \times 7^4$
7	$5^6 \times 5^{17}$	**8**	9×9
9	$y^2 \times y^3$	**10**	$x^5 \times x^2$
11	$w \times w^3$	**12**	$p^2 \times p^2$
13	$t^3 \times t^6$	**14**	$r^4 \times r^5$
15	$x^2 \times x^3 \times x^4$	**16**	$y^5 \times y \times y^2$
17	$2x^2 \times 3x^3$	**18**	$4y^2 \times 2y^3$
19	$4t^2 \times 3t$	**20**	$5w^5 \times 4w^4$
21	$2y^3 \times 3y^7$	**22**	$4x^3 \times 3x^2 \times x^2$
23	$4 \times 5t^2 \times 6t^3$	**24**	$5a^3 \times 4a \times 3$

3.8 Multiplying expressions in brackets

Sometimes you will need to multiply together two expressions in brackets, like $(x + 3)(x + 2)$.

You need to multiply each term in the 2nd bracket by each term in the 1st bracket:

$$
\begin{array}{c}
x \times 2 \\
\boxed{x \times x} \\
(x + 3)(x + 2) \\
\boxed{3 \times x} \\
3 \times 2
\end{array}
$$

$$= x \times x + x \times 2 + 3 \times x + 3 \times 2$$

$$= x^2 + 2x + 3x + 6 \qquad \text{Collect like terms.}$$

$$= x^2 + 5x + 6$$

> $x \times 2$ is the same as $2 \times x = 2x$

■ **To multiply together two expressions in brackets, multiply each term in the 2nd bracket by each term in the 1st bracket,**

$$
\begin{array}{c}
x \times 2 \\
\boxed{x \times x} \\
\text{e.g. } (x + 3)(x + 2) \\
\boxed{3 \times x} \\
3 \times 2
\end{array}
$$

Example 17

Expand and simplify $(x + 4)(x + 1)$

Expand means multiply the brackets together.

$$x \times 1$$
$$x \times x$$
$$(x + 4)(x + 1)$$
$$4 \times x$$
$$4 \times 1$$

$$= x \times x + x \times 1 + 4 \times x + 4 \times 1$$
$$= x^2 + x + 4x + 4 \quad\text{————————Collect like terms.}$$
$$= x^2 + 5x + 4$$

$$x \times 1 = 1 \times x = x$$

Example 18

Expand and simplify $(x + 2)(x - 3)$

$$x \times -3$$
$$x \times x$$
$$(x + 2)(x - 3)$$
$$2 \times x$$
$$2 \times -3$$

$$= x \times x + x \times -3 + 2 \times x + 2 \times -3$$
$$= x^2 - 3x + 2x - 6$$
$$= x^2 - x - 6$$

$$x \times -2 = -2x$$
$$2 \times -3 = -6$$

$$-3x + 2x = -1x = -x$$

Example 19

Expand and simplify $(x - 3)(x + 3)$

$$(x - 3)(x + 3)$$

$$= x \times x + x \times 3 - 3 \times x - 3 \times 3$$
$$= x^2 + 3x - 3x - 9$$
$$= x^2 - 9$$

Exercise 3H

Expand and simplify:

1 $(x + 4)(x + 2)$ 2 $(x + 6)(x + 3)$

3 2 $(x + 5)(x + 1)$ 4 $(x + 2)(x + 5)$

5 $(x + 4)(x - 1)$ 6 $(x - 2)(x + 1)$

7 $(x + 7)(x - 6)$ 8 $(x - 4)(x + 3)$

9 $(x - 1)(x + 3)$ 10 $(x - 2)(x + 2)$

11 $(x + 5)(x - 2)$ 12 $(x + 8)(x - 3)$

13 $(x + 7)(x - 7)$ 14 $(x - 4)(x + 4)$

Summary of key points

1 Bringing terms together is called 'collecting like terms'.

2 Removing the brackets in an expression is called expanding the bracket,

for example $3(a + 3b) = 3a + 9b$

3 'Simplify' means collect like terms together.

4 Factorising is the reverse process to removing brackets,

for example $4a + 8 = 4(a + 2)$

5 To multiply powers of the same number or letter add the powers:

$$y^a \times y^b = y^{a+b}$$

6 To multiply together two expressions in brackets, multiply each term in the 2nd bracket by each term in the 1st bracket.

$x \times 2$

$x \times x$

$(x + 3)(x + 2)$

$3 \times x$

3×2

4 Averages

The average British household has two mobile phones.

This chapter will show you how to work out different types of averages.

4.1 Some revision

You should already know these facts:

- **The mode of a set of data is the value which occurs most often.**

- **In a frequency table, the mode is the value with the highest frequency.**

- **The median is the middle value when the data is arranged in order of size.**

- $$\text{mean} = \frac{\text{sum of values}}{\text{number of values}}$$

- **range = highest value − lowest value**

The mode is sometimes called the **modal value**.

Example 1

Akbar writes down the number of letters in the forenames of ten of his friends. The results are shown below.

5 letters, 6 letters, 4 letters, 7 letters, 4 letters,
8 letters, 6 letters, 4 letters, 3 letters and 9 letters.

Work out the mean, mode, median and range.

To find the **mean** find the sum of the values and divide by the number of values:

$$\text{mean} = \frac{5 + 6 + 4 + 7 + 4 + 8 + 6 + 4 + 3 + 9}{10} = \frac{56}{10} = 5.6$$

The mean is 5.6 letters.

To find the **mode** find which value occurs most often.

4 occurs three times. 4 letters is the mode.

To find the **median** arrange the values in order of size and find the middle value.

There are two middle values

3, 4, 4, 4, 5, 6, 6, 7, 8, 9.

There are two middle values. The median is:

$$\frac{5+6}{2} = 5.5 \text{ or } 5\frac{1}{2}$$

The **range** is the largest value minus the smallest value

The range is $9 - 3 = 6$ letters.

Example 2

This frequency table shows the number of attempts needed to get through to the internet.

Number of attempts	Frequency
1	15
2	10
3	5
4	3
5	2

largest frequency

Work out the mean, mode and range.

The mode is the value with the largest frequency.
The mode is 1 attempt.

To find the mean you need to know the total number of attempts made. Add an extra column to the table:

Number of attempts	Frequency	Number of attempts × frequency
1	15	$1 \times 15 = 15$
2	10	$2 \times 10 = 20$
3	5	$3 \times 5 = 15$
4	3	$4 \times 3 = 12$
5	2	$5 \times 2 = 10$
Total	35	72

$$\text{mean} = \frac{72}{35} = 2.06 \quad (3 \text{ s.f.})$$

The range is $5 - 1 = 4$ attempts.

Exercise 4A

1   For the following sets of data work out the mean, mode, median and range.
   (a) 12, 17, 15, 12, 16, 18, 21
   (b) 5, 6, 12, 6, 15, 3, 2
   (c) 16, 30, 15, 20, 31, 30, 15, 12, 16
   (d) 25, 12, 31, 26, 31, 19, 16, 30

2   The heights of eight rugby forwards are:

   2.1 m, 1.98 m, 1.88 m, 2.02 m,
   2.02 m, 2.07 m, 1.87 m, 1.84 m

   Work out:
   (a) the mean height of the players
   (b) the median height of the players
   (c) the modal height of the players
   (d) the range of the heights of the players.

3   This frequency table shows the number of packets of crisps eaten by each pupil in a school in one week:

Number of packets of crisps	Frequency
0	30
1	50
2	60
3	120
4	100
5	70
6	30
7	30
8	10

Without using a calculator, work out:
   (a) the mode
   (b) the mean
   (c) the range.

Hint:
The total frequency equals 500.

4 This chart shows the number of weeks holiday abroad taken in a year by a group of families:

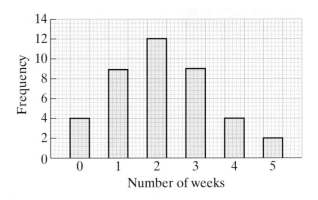

(a) Draw a frequency table for this data.

(b) Work out the mean of the data.

(c) Work out the mode for the data.

(d) Work out the range for the data.

5 Neil is comparing the reliability of two machines. He records the weekly number of breakdowns for 3 weeks.

Machine A has a mean of 6 breakdowns per week and a range of 3 breakdowns per week.

Machine B has a mode of 10 breakdowns per week and a mean of 12 breakdowns per week.

(a) Write down three numbers that could give the results for machine A.

(b) What is the maximum number of weekly breakdowns Neil could have recorded for machine A?

(c) What was the range for machine B?

4.2 Finding the median from a frequency table

When a frequency table is used the median can be found by adding an extra column called the cumulative frequency. This is the running total of all the frequencies so far.

■ **The cumulative frequency is the running total of all the frequencies so far.**

Example 3

Tony keeps a record of the number of phone calls he answers an hour. His results for a week are shown in the frequency table opposite.

Number of calls	Frequency
0	1
1	3
2	6
3	7
4	5
5	8
6	3
7	0
8	2

To find the median add a cumulative frequency column to the table:

Number of calls	Frequency	Cumulative frequency
0	1	$1 = 1$
1	3	$1 + 3 = 4$
2	6	$4 + 6 = 10$
3	7	$10 + 7 = 17$
4	5	$17 + 5 = 22$
5	8	$22 + 8 = 30$
6	3	$30 + 3 = 33$
7	0	$33 + 0 = 33$
8	2	$33 + 2 = 35$

The 17th value is 3 calls

The 18th value is 4 calls as 18 is larger than 17 but less than 22

There are 35 values altogether. The median is the middle value:

$$\frac{35 + 1}{2} = \frac{36}{2} = 18$$

So the median is the 18th value.
The median is 4 calls an hour.

Example 4

The number of shots Sue takes per hole for two rounds of golf are shown in this frequency table.

Find the median number of shots she takes.

Number of shots	Frequency
2	2
3	7
4	9
5	10
6	8

Add a cumulative frequency column to the table:

Number of shots	Frequency	Cumulative frequency	
2	2	$2 = 2$	
3	7	$2 + 7 = 9$	
4	9	$9 + 9 = 18$	——— 18th value $= 4$
5	10	$18 + 10 = 28$	——— 19th value $= 5$
6	8	$28 + 8 = 36$	

There are 36 values altogether.

$$\frac{36 + 1}{2} = 18\tfrac{1}{2}$$

There are two middle values. The median is half way between them:

$$\text{median} = \frac{18\text{th value} + 19\text{th value}}{2} = \frac{4 + 5}{2} = 4\tfrac{1}{2}$$

Exercise 4B

1   The number of callouts a week an inshore lifeboat makes during the season is shown in this table:

Number of callouts	Frequency
0	4
1	3
2	5
3	2
4	4
5	2
6	1
7	3
8	1

Calculate the median number of callouts during the season.

2   The number of pupils late to school per day is shown in this table.

Number of pupils late	Frequency
0	12
1	25
2	36
3	25
4	30
5	21
6	18
7	13
8	10

Calculate the median for this data.

3 Copy and complete this cumulative frequency table
showing the number of penalties conceded by
60 football teams in a cup tournament. The median
number of penalties is $3\frac{1}{2}$.

Number of penalties conceded	Frequency	Cumulative frequency
0	2	
1	6	8
2		
3	10	
4		48
5	8	56
6	3	
7	1	60

4.3 Using stem and leaf diagrams to calculate the median

Frequency tables are very useful when your data values are
in separate groups. If you have a lot of different data values
it is usually more useful to draw a **stem and leaf diagram**.

Ruth collected data on the number of cars parked on a
street each hour for a whole day:

1, 2, 5, 7, 12, 12, 16, 18, 19, 20, 23, 24,
29, 31, 31, 31, 33, 35, 37, 39, 41, 43, 48, 49.

Ruth decided to record this data in groups called **stems**.
The values from 10–19 all have stem 1, since all these
values start with the digit 1.

The stems for this data are:

0
1
2
3
4

Ruth adds the leaves one at a time.
She records 39 like this:

```
0 |
1 |
2 |
3 | 9
4 |
```

This is the complete stem and leaf diagram:

```
0 | 1 2 5 7
1 | 2 2 6 8 9
2 | 0 3 4 9
3 | 1 1 1 3 5 7 9
4 | 1 3 8 9
```

For the value 7, the stem is 0 and the leaf is 7.

stem = 10 cars —— This shows that to read values off the diagram you have to multiply the stem by 10 and add on the leaf.

Stem and leaf diagrams are useful for calculating the median of a set of values.

There are 24 values in the above data set. The median will be half way between the 12th and 13th values:

```
0 | 1 2 5 7
1 | 2 2 6 8 9
2 | 0 3 4 9
3 | 1 1 1 3 5 7 9
4 | 1 3 8 9
```

$$\text{median} = \frac{24 + 29}{2} = 26\frac{1}{2}$$

Stem and leaf diagrams are not very useful for finding the mean.

By looking at the stem and leaf diagram, it is easy to see that the modal value is 31.

Exercise 4C

1 This stem and leaf diagram shows the scores for a rugby team in one season:

```
0 | 3 3 5 5 7 7 8 8 9
1 | 1 2 2 3 3 4 4
2 | 0 0 3 4 5 6 6 6 9
3 | 2 2 3 5 6 8 9
4 | 0 2 4 4 6
```

stem = 10 points

Remember:
3 | 6 means 36

(a) How many games did the rugby team play?
(b) Work out the median.
(c) Write down the mode.

2 Sibtain delivers pizzas. The length of time he drives
— each day for a month (21 working days) is shown
below.

1 h 25 min,	2 h 35 min,	1 h 40 min,
3 h 50 min,	3 h 10 min,	4 h 20 min,
1 h 15 min,	30 min,	3 h 20 min,
2 h 15 min,	1 h 35 min,	2 h 10 min,
55 min,	2 h 20 min,	1 h 50 min,
2 h 15 min,	4 h 0 min,	2 h 10 min,
1 h 40 min,	2 h 0 min,	1 h 20 min.

(a) Draw a stem and leaf diagram to represent this
data. Use hours for the stems and minutes for
the leaves.
(b) Work out the median and the mode for the data.

3 This graph shows the mathematics test results for a
class:

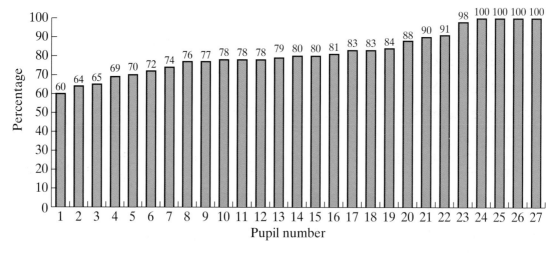

(a) Draw a stem and leaf diagram to show this data.
(b) Work out the median and mode.
(c) Say which of the two averages is not representative
of the data and explain your answer.

4 Write down examples of work covered in other subjects
where you could use a stem and leaf diagram.

4.4 Different types of average

By choosing to use either the mean, median or mode it is possible to show different things. You need to be able to choose the most appropriate type of average.

Example 5

Richard earns £4.10 an hour at his local supermarket. He finds out the average hourly rate for other part-time jobs:

mean = £4.87   median = £4.15   mode = £3.90

Which average should Richard use to convince the supermarket manager he should get a pay rise?

Richard should use the mean because it has the highest value.

Example 6

The number of hours a group of children watch television in a week is shown below.

12   10   38   11   7   10   13   11   9   10

Work out the mean, mode and median. Comment on your results.

$$\text{mean} = \frac{12 + 10 + 38 + 11 + 7 + 10 + 13 + 11 + 9 + 10}{10} = \frac{131}{10} = 13.1 \text{ hours}$$

mode = 10 hours

The median is found by arranging the values in order and finding the middle value.

7   9   10   10   10   11   11   12   13   38

median = 10.5 hours.

All three of the averages are different.

The very large single value of 38 hours makes the mean bigger than the median and mode.

■   **The mean is affected by very large or very small values.**

■   **The mean doesn't have to be one of the values in the data.**

Exercise 4D

1   Jane works in a supermarket. She encourages people to taste a certain brand of cracker and then keep a tally of how many packets they buy.

Number of packets	Frequency
0	12
1	9
2	6
3	5
20 (complete box)	8

(a) Calculate the mean, mode and median of this data.
(b) Jane is asked for the average number of packets. For each of the averages you worked out say why she should or should not quote that average.

2   At a job interview 20 candidates were asked how many miles they had travelled. Here are their replies:

   10, 15, 12, 10, 9, 36, 42, 10, 15, 21,
   1380, 23, 29, 41, 52, 21, 33, 17, 10, 3

(a) Work out the mean, mode and median for the data.
(b) The firm wants to make it seem that it is popular and candidates will travel a long way for an interview. Which average would it quote?

3   Three newspapers surveyed the weekly wages of the same 10 people:

Write down ten possible weekly wages which could give all of the averages quoted.

Investigation

Find some newspaper articles that quote averages.

Say whether you think they have used the mean, the median or the mode.

Does the average they have used illustrate a point they are trying to make?

Do you think the average used is an accurate representation of the data?

Exercise 4E

Do not use your calculator in this exercise. Show your working carefully.

1 The number of shots Laura takes per hole for a round of golf is shown below.

3, 5, 4, 4, 5, 4, 3, 5, 4, 4, 3, 9, 4, 5, 4, 4, 6, 5

Work out:
(a) the mean
(b) the median
(c) the mode
(d) the range.

2 The stem and leaf diagram below shows the runs scored by Asif in 25 innings.

```
0 | 0 0 0 5 7 9
1 | 1 2 5 8 9
2 | 2 5 5 6 6 9
3 | 0 3 7 9
4 | 0 1 5 7
```
   stem = 10 runs

(a) Work out the median, mode and range.
(b) Write down a list of the scores and calculate the mean.

3 The number of spelling mistakes per page in a draft of a 100 page book is shown below.

Number of mistakes	Frequency
0	27
1	22
2	17
3	13
4	10
5	11

(a) Calculate the mean, median and mode for the data.
(b) An extra page is added to the book. Because of a computer fault it contains 113 errors. Say which of the averages would change and which would not.
(c) Calculate the mean for the 101 pages.

Exercise 4F

You may use your calculator for these questions.

1 The number of callouts per day for a local fire brigade last year is shown in the table below.

Number of callouts	0	1	2	3	4	5
Frequency	115	118	79	36	12	5

(a) Calculate the median.
(b) Calculate the mean.
(c) State the mode.
(d) State the range.

2 John throws three coins 120 times and records the number of heads. His results are shown below:

Number of heads	0	1	2	3
Frequency	22	53	35	10

(a) Calculate the mean, median and mode for this data.
(b) When the coins are fair the mean and the median should be $1\frac{1}{2}$. Do you think that the coins are fair? Give a reason for your answer.

Summary of key points

1   The mode of a set of data is the value which occurs most often.

2   In a frequency table, the mode is the value with the highest frequency.

3   The median is the middle value when the data is arranged in order of size.

4   $$\text{mean} = \frac{\text{sum of values}}{\text{number of values}}$$

5   range = highest value − lowest value

6   The cumulative frequency in the running total of all the frequencies so far.

7   The mean is affected by very large or very small values.

8   The mean doesn't have to be one of the values in the data.

5 Graphs

5.1 Coordinates

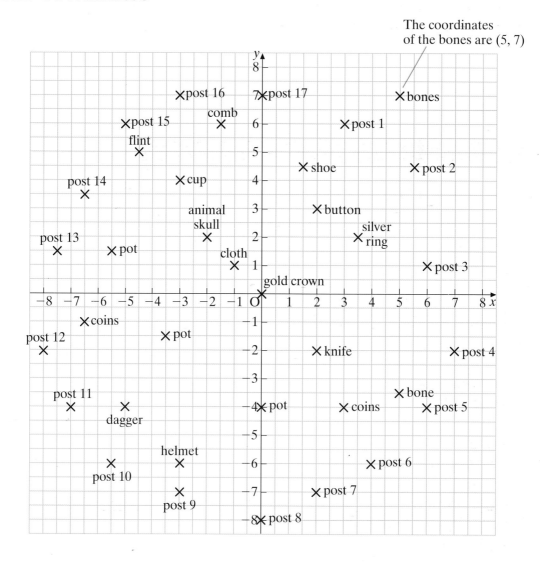

The coordinates of the bones are (5, 7)

This grid shows the plan of an archaeological dig.

The gold crown was found at the centre of the grid.

It has coordinates (0, 0).

The point (0, 0) is called the **origin**.

Sometimes positions do not have whole number coordinates. The silver ring has coordinate $(3\frac{1}{2}, 2)$.

- The horizontal coordinate is called the *x*-coordinate.
  The vertical coordinate is called the *y*-coordinate.
  You always write the *x*-coordinate first.

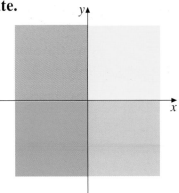

- Each quarter of the coordinate
  grid is called a quadrant.

Exercise 5A

Look at the plan of the archaeological dig.

1 What is at:
- **(a)** $(2, 3)$
- **(b)** $(1\frac{1}{2}, 4\frac{1}{2})$
- **(c)** $(2, -2)$
- **(d)** $(0, -4)$
- **(e)** $(5, -3\frac{1}{2})$
- **(f)** $(-6\frac{1}{2}, -1)$
- **(g)** $(-5, -4)$
- **(h)** $(-2, 2)$
- **(i)** $(-5\frac{1}{2}, 1\frac{1}{2})$
- **(j)** $(-3, 4)$

2 The archaeologists uncovered 17 roof posts in a
circular pattern. Give the coordinates of each post.

3 Write down the name and coordinates of all the objects
on the grid that are not listed in questions **1** and **2**.

4 Draw a coordinate grid from -8 to 8 in both directions.
Plot each set of points and join them in order.
- **(a)** $(3, 5)$ $(5, 8)$ $(7, 5)$ $(5, -2)$ $(3, 5)$
- **(b)** $(-8, 6)$ $(-6\frac{1}{2}, 7\frac{1}{2})$ $(\frac{1}{2}, 7\frac{1}{2})$ $(-1, 6)$ $(-8, 6)$
- **(c)** $(4, -2\frac{1}{2})$ $(6, -2\frac{1}{2})$ $(6, -4\frac{1}{2})$ $(-1, -4\frac{1}{2})$ $(-1, -2\frac{1}{2})$
  $(1, -2\frac{1}{2})$ $(1, -3\frac{1}{2})$ $(4, -3\frac{1}{2})$ $(4, -2\frac{1}{2})$
- **(d)** $(-6, 4)$ $(-6, 3)$ $(-7, 3)$ $(-7, 2)$ $(-6, 2)$
  $(-6, -2\frac{1}{2})$ $(-7, -2\frac{1}{2})$ $(-7, -3\frac{1}{2})$ $(-6, -3\frac{1}{2})$
  $(-6, -4\frac{1}{2})$ $(-5, -4\frac{1}{2})$ $(-5, -3\frac{1}{2})$ $(-4, -3\frac{1}{2})$
  $(-4, -2\frac{1}{2})$ $(-5, -2\frac{1}{2})$ $(-5, 2)$ $(-4, 2)$ $(-4, 3)$
  $(-5, 3)$ $(-5, 4)$ $(-6, 4)$

5.2 Straight line graphs

This grid shows the starting positions of musicians in a marching band.

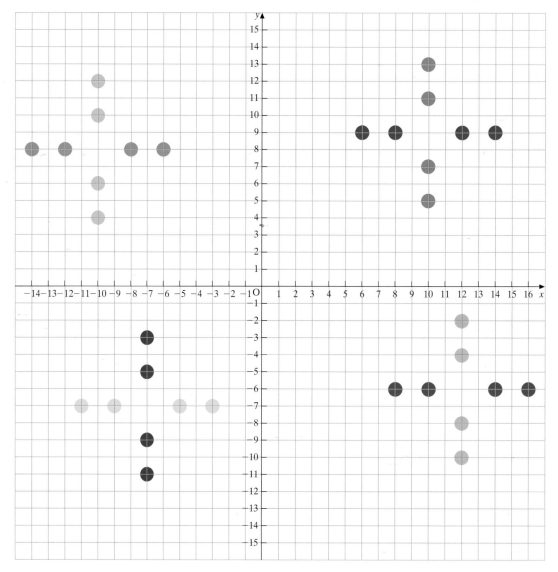

The four 'red' musicians are in a straight line.

You can give the line a name by investigating the coordinates of the 4 people.

These are (10, 5), (10, 7), (10, 11) and (10, 13)

The *x*-coordinates are all 10

The name of this line is $x = 10$.

The four 'yellow' musicians on page 62 have coordinates

$(-11, -7), \ (-9, -7), \ (-5, -7) \ \text{and} \ (-3, -7)$

The y-coordinates are all -7.

The line is $y = -7$.

At the end of their routine the musicians are in these positions:

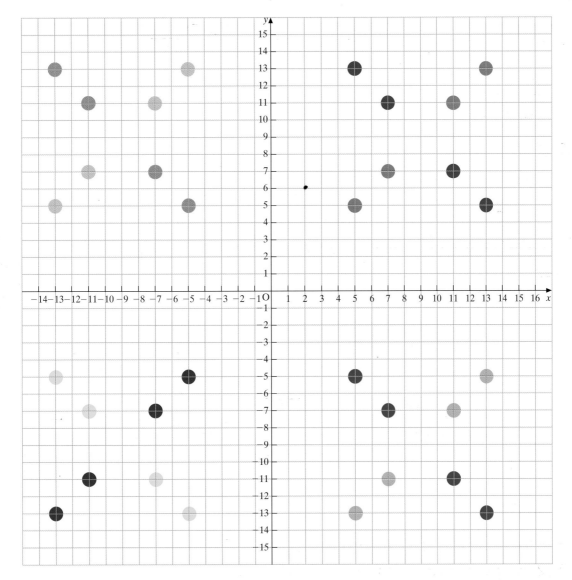

The four 'red' musicians are again in a straight line.

Their coordinates are

$(5, 5), \ (7, 7), \ (11, 11), \ (13, 13)$

When lines slope $\diagup$ or $\diagdown$ you need to find a link between the x- and y-coordinates.

Here the *x*- and *y*-coordinates are the same for each musician.

They are on the line $y = x$.

The 'orange' musicians are at points

$(13, -5),\ (11, -7),\ (7, -11),\ (5, -13)$

The line this time is $y = x - 18$.

x	y
$13 - 18 = -5$
$11 - 18 = -7$
$7 - 18 = -11$
$5 - 18 = -13$

■ **In general, if a line looks like this:**

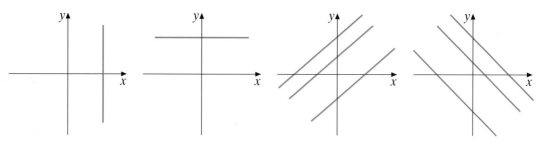

The equation looks like this:

$x = \square$ $\qquad$ $y = \square$ $\qquad$ $y = x + \square$ $\qquad$ $y + x = \square$

$\qquad\qquad\qquad\qquad\qquad\qquad\qquad$ **or** $y = x - \square$

Exercise 5B

1 Find the equations of the lines on page 62 for these musicians:

 (a) blue   **(b)** green
 (c) orange   **(d)** purple
 (e) brown   **(f)** pink

2 Find the equations of the lines on page 63 for these musicians:

 (a) blue   **(b)** green
 (c) yellow   **(d)** purple
 (e) pink   **(f)** brown

3 Work out the equations of these lines from their coordinates:

 (a) $(-3, 4)\ (1, 4)\ (4, 4)$ **(b)** $(-5, 0)\ (-2, 0)\ (4, 0)$
 (c) $(3, -2)\ (3, 1)\ (3, 6)$ **(d)** $(0, -5)\ (0, -3)\ (0, -1)$
 (e) $(4, -1)\ (5, -1)\ (9, -1)$ **(f)** $(7, 6)\ (8, 6)\ (9, 6)$

(g) $(-2, -4)$ $(-2, -2)$ $(-2, 7)$ **(h)** $(6, 0)$ $(6, 2)$ $(6, 4)$
(i) $(1, 3)$ $(5, 7)$ $(7, 9)$ **(j)** $(-1, -2)$ $(2, 4)$ $(5, 10)$
(k) $(7, 6)$ $(8, 7)$ $(9, 8)$ **(l)** $(2, 6)$ $(3, 9)$ $(4, 12)$
(m) $(-5, -5)$ $(0, 0)$ $(4, 4)$ **(n)** $(-1, 2)$ $(2, 5)$ $(4, 7)$
(o) $(-1, 1)$ $(2, -2)$ $(4, -4)$ **(p)** $(-4, -7)$ $(-4, 9)$ $(-4, 19)$
(q) $(3, 9)$ $(5, 13)$ $(6, 15)$ **(r)** $(1, 2)$ $(3, 8)$ $(5, 14)$

4 From each set of graphs, choose the one which most closely matches the equation:

(a) $x = 6$

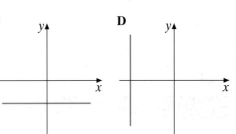

(b) $y = -4$

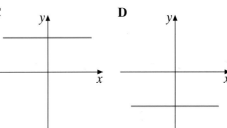

(c) $y = x + 1$

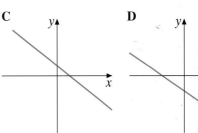

(d) $y = x - 2$

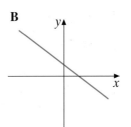
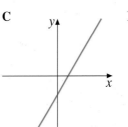
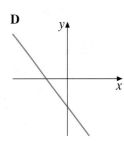

5 Find the equations of the lines on the grid.
(Hint: use the points marked to help you.)

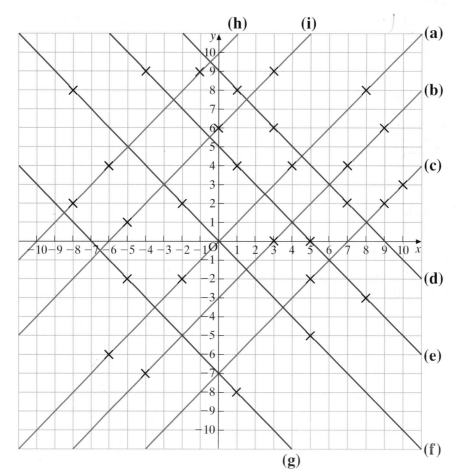

5.3 Drawing sloping lines

You can draw sloping lines from a table of values.

Example 1

Draw the line with equation $y = 3x - 2$.

Choose a set of values for x:

$$-4, \ -3, \ -2, \ -1, \ 0, \ 1, \ 2, \ 3, \ 4$$

Show them in a table:

x	-4	-3	-2	-1	0	1	2	3	4
y									

Work out $y = 3x - 2$ for each value of x

For example, for $x = -4$

$$y = 3 \times -4 - 2$$
$$= -12 - 2$$
$$= -14$$

Complete the table:

x	-4	-3	-2	-1	0	1	2	3	4
y	-14	-11	-8	-5	-2	1	4	7	10

The coordinate of the points on the line are:

$(-4, -14)$, $(-3, -11)$, $(-2, -8)$, $(-1, -5)$,
$(0, -2)$, $(1, 1)$, $(2, 4)$, $(3, 7)$, $(4, 10)$

You must draw and label your axes so
that they can contain all the
coordinates from the table.

For this line you need:

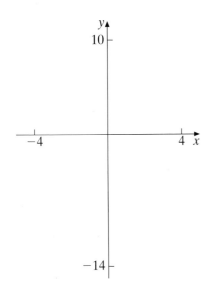

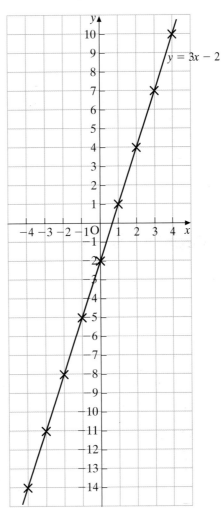

Plot the points.
Draw and label the line.

Exercise 5C

1   For each equation:
  - copy and complete the table of values
  - plot the points on a coordinate grid
  - draw and label the line.

(a) $y = x + 5$

x	−4	−3	−2	−1	0	1	2	3	4
y		2						8	

(b) $y = x - 4$

x	−4	−3	−2	−1	0	1	2	3	4
y		−7							0

(c) $y = 2x + 5$

x	−4	−3	−2	−1	0	1	2	3	4
y			1				9		

(d) $y = 3x - 4$

x	−4	−3	−2	−1	0	1	2	3	4
y									

(e) $y = 5x + 2$

x	−4	−3	−2	−1	0	1	2	3	4
y									

(f) $y = 2x - 5$

x	−4	−3	−2	−1	0	1	2	3	4
y									

(g) $y = 4 - x$

x	−4	−3	−2	−1	0	1	2	3	4
y									

(h) $y = 3 - 2x$

x	−4	−3	−2	−1	0	1	2	3	4
y									

5.4 Intercept and gradient

The grid shows the line $y = 2x + 1$

The line crosses the y-axis at $(0, 1)$.

This point is called the **intercept**.

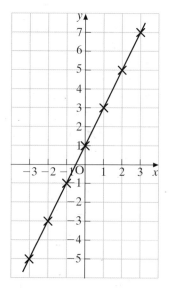

■   The intercept of a line is the point $(0, \boxed{})$
  where the line crosses the y-axis.
  The number $\boxed{}$ is the value of y when $x = 0$.

Example 2

Find the intercept of the line $y = 8x - 27$

The intercept is the point $(0, \boxed{})$.

Put $x = 0$ in the equation:

$$y = 8 \times 0 - 27$$
$$y = 0 - 27$$
$$y = -27$$

The intercept is $(0, -27)$.

This tobogganist is on a steep hill.

The steepness of the hill is called the gradient.

Steep hills have large gradients.

Shallow hills have small gradients.

■   **Gradient is the maths word for steepness.**

The bigger the gradient, the steeper the slope.

■   ● **A line that slopes up has a *positive* gradient.**

   ● **A line that slopes down has a *negative* gradient.**

   ● **Flat lines have *zero* gradient.**

Example 3

Put these lines in order according to their gradients, greatest first.

Write down whether each gradient is positive, negative, or zero.

The order is:

(c)	**(b)**	**(a)**	**(d)**
+	+	0	−

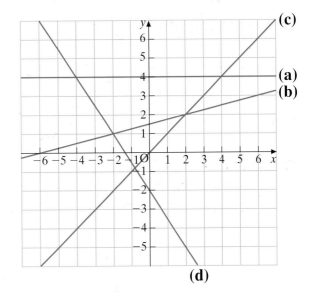

Exercise 5D

1 Find the intercept of each line:
  (a) $y = x + 5$ **(b)** $y = x - \frac{1}{2}$
  (c) $y = 4 - x$ **(d)** $y = 3x + 8$
  (e) $y = 2x - 6$ **(f)** $y = 2x + 1$
  (g) $y = 5 - 2x$ **(h)** $y = -3x + 1$
  (i) $y = 3x + 7$ **(j)** $y = 7x - 6$
  (k) $y = 3 - 3x$ **(l)** $y = -x$

2 Draw a coordinate grid from -4 to 4 on both axes.
  (a) Using tables of values, draw and label these lines:
    • $y = x + 3$ • $y = 2x + 3$
    • $y = 3x + 3$ • $y = 4x + 3$
  (b) Write the lines in order according to their gradients, greatest first.
    What do you notice?
  (c) What can you say about the intercepts?

3 Draw a coordinate grid from -4 to 4 on both axes.
  (a) Using tables of values, draw and label these lines:
    • $y = x$ • $y = 2x$ • $y = 3x$
  (b) What do you notice about the gradients?

4 Arrange these graphs in order of gradient, smallest first.

Hint: some of the gradients are negative.

(a) (i) 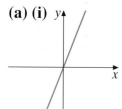   **(ii)** 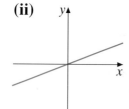   **(iii)** 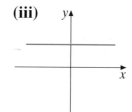   **(iv)**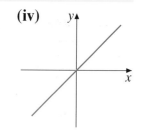

(b) (i) 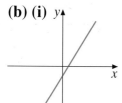   **(ii)** 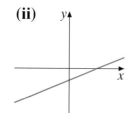   **(iii)** 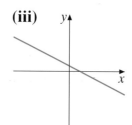   **(iv)**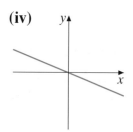

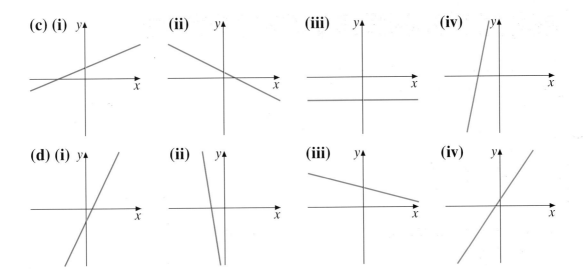

(c) (i)   **(ii)**   **(iii)**   **(iv)**

(d) (i)   **(ii)**   **(iii)**   **(iv)**

5.5 Equations of curves

You need to be able to draw the lines of more complicated equations.

Example 4

Draw the line with equation $y = x^2$.

Choose some values for x:

$$-4, \ -3, \ -2, \ -1, \ 0, \ 1, \ 2, \ 3, \ 4$$

Work out y for each value of x.

For example, when

$$x = -3, \ y = (-3)^2 = -3 \times -3 = 9.$$

Draw a table of values:

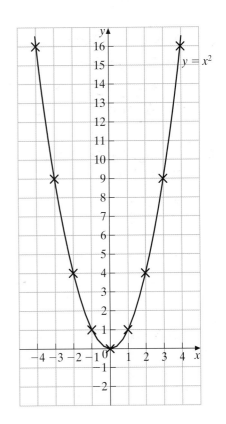

x	-4	-3	-2	-1	0	1	2	3	4
y	16	9	4	1	0	1	4	9	16

The coordinates of the points on the line are:

$$(-4, 16), \ (-3, 9), \ (-2, 4), \ (-1, 1),$$
$$(0, 0), \ (1, 1), \ (2, 4), \ (3, 9), \ (4, 16)$$

The points are not in a straight line.

Join the points together with a **smooth curve** and label the line.

Exercise 5E

For each equation:
- copy and complete the table of values
- plot the points on a coordinate grid
- draw and label the line.

For the first questions help is given
with choosing your scale, e.g.

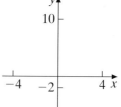

1 $y = x^2 + 1$

x	−4	−3	−2	−1	0	1	2	3	4
y	17					2			

Hint: when drawing
curves you might
find it easier to turn
the paper and draw
a curve like this:

instead of like this:

2 $y = x^2 + 2$

x	−4	−3	−2	−1	0	1	2	3	4
y		11					6		

3 $y = x^2 − 1$

x	−4	−3	−2	−1	0	1	2	3	4
y	15								

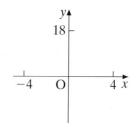

4 $y = 1 − x^2$

x	−4	−3	−2	−1	0	1	2	3	4
y		−8				−3			

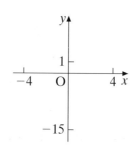

5 $y = 2x^2$

x	−4	−3	−2	−1	0	1	2	3	4
y								18	

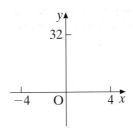

6 $y = 2x^2 + 4$

x	−4	−3	−2	−1	0	1	2	3	4
y		22							

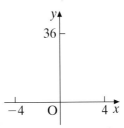

7 $y = 3x^2 - 1$

x	−4	−3	−2	−1	0	1	2	3	4
y			11						

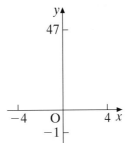

8 $y = 2x^2 - 3$

x	−4	−3	−2	−1	0	1	2	3	4
y									

9 $y = x^2 + x$

x	−4	−3	−2	−1	0	1	2	3	4
y									

10 $y = x^2 - x$

x	−4	−3	−2	−1	0	1	2	3	4
y									

Simplifying the procedure

Equations that give straight lines look like this:

$y = x$ $y = 2x$ $y = x + 1$ $y = 3x - 1$ $y + x = 7$ $y + 3x = 8$

Equations you have seen that give curves look like this:

$y = x^2$ $y = 2x^2$ $y = x^2 + 1$ $y = 1 - x^2$ $y = 3x^2 - 2$

The two sets of equations look different.

■ **If the equation looks like:**

$y = mx + c$

**where m and c are numbers (positive, negative or 0),
then the line will be straight.**

Check: $y = 2x$ $\overset{c = 0}{y = mx + c}$
                              $m = 2$

              $y = 3x - 1$ $\overset{c = -1}{y = mx + c}$
                              $m = 3$

If an equation gives a straight line graph you can draw it by
plotting only 3 points.

Example 5

Draw the graph of

    $y = 3x + 7$

Choose 3 values for x.

    $x = 0$ and $x = 1$

are always sensible choices.

$x = 4$ (or 3 or 5) would do for the third value.

Use these values of x to work out the values of y.

If $x = 0$

    $y = 3 \times 0 + 7 = 7$

Plot (0, 7).

If $x = 1$

    $y = 3 \times 1 + 7 = 10$

Plot (0, 10).

If $x = 4$

    $y = 3 \times 4 + 7 = 19$

Plot (4, 19).

Join the points using a ruler and pencil.

Extend the line to the edge of the
grid in both directions.

Label your line.

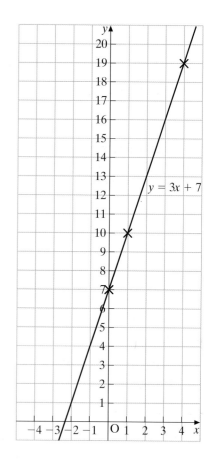

Exercise 5F

1 Which of these equations give straight lines?
- **(a)** $y = x^2$
- **(b)** $y = x - 4$
- **(c)** $y = 2x + 5$
- **(d)** $y = x^2 - 1$
- **(e)** $y = 3x^2 - 4$
- **(f)** $y = x^2 + x$
- **(g)** $y + x = 6$
- **(h)** $y - x = 4$
- **(i)** $y = 7x - 3$
- **(j)** $y = 3 - 2x$
- **(k)** $y = 1 - x$
- **(l)** $y = 2 - 4x$
- **(m)** $y = 3x^2 + 4$
- **(n)** $y = 8x^2 - 6$
- **(o)** $y = x^2 + 2x$
- **(p)** $y = 11 - 4x$

2 For each equation in question **1** that gives a straight line, draw the graph by plotting 3 points only.
(Use $x = 0$, $x = 1$ and $x = 4$.)

5.6 Information graphs

This graph shows a car journey.

The graph is made up of 6 straight lines.

Each line describes part of the journey.

The vertical axis ↑ gives information on distance travelled. Each square represents 10 km.

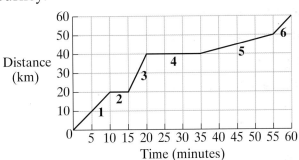

On information graphs, always look to see what information each axis gives and what one square represents.

The horizontal axis → gives information on time. Each square represents 5 minutes.

■ **On information graphs, always look to see what information each axis gives and what one square represents.**

On the graph:

Section 1   20 km are covered in 10 minutes
The line is straight so the speed is constant.

Section 2   A horizontal line means 0 distance travelled.
The car has stopped, maybe for petrol.

Section **3** 20 km travelled in 5 minutes.
Notice that the gradient is steeper than in Section 1. The car is travelling faster.

Section **4** The car is stationary for 15 minutes.

Section **5** The car travels 10 km in 20 minutes.
A small gradient so a slow speed.

Section **6** The journey finishes with the car travelling 10 km in 5 minutes.

Being able to tell the story of a graph is an important skill.

Example 6

Look at the graph of the car journey.

Use it to answer these questions:

(a) How long did the journey take?
(b) How far did the car travel?
(c) When was the car travelling fastest?
(d) How long did they have for breaks, in total?
(e) What was the average speed for the journey?
(f) What was the car's fastest speed?
(g) What was the car's slowest speed?

(a) The journey took 60 minutes in total.
(b) The car travelled 60 km.
(c) The car travelled fastest between 15 and 20 minutes (steepest slope).
(d) The breaks were 5 minutes and then 15 minutes.
Total: 20 minutes.
(e) Speed = distance ÷ time
Average speed = 60 km ÷ 60 min

$$= \frac{60 \text{ km}}{60 \text{ min}} = 1 \text{ km per minute}$$

or 60 km in 1 hr (= 60 min) = 60 km per hour.
(f) Fastest speed was 20 km in 5 min.

$$\text{Speed} = \frac{20 \text{ km}}{5 \text{ min}} = 4 \text{ km/min}$$

(g) Slowest speed was 10 km in 20 min

$$\frac{10 \text{ km}}{20 \text{ min}} = \frac{1}{2} \text{ km/min}$$

$$= 0.5 \text{ km/min}$$

Exercise 5G

1   Look at this graph of a car journey.
    Use the graph to help you answer the questions.

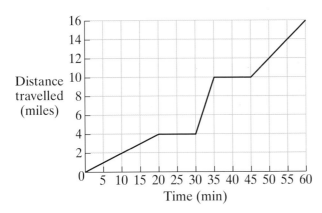

(a) What does each square represent:
    • horizontally
    • vertically?
(b) How far did the car travel?
(c) How long did the journey take?
(d) How long did the car stop for, in total?
(e) When did the car travel fastest?
(f) Work out the average speed for the whole journey.

2   This graph shows the depth of water in Peter's bath.

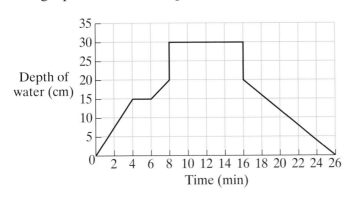

(a) What happened at 8 minutes?
(b) How deep was the water just before Peter got in?
(c) How long did Peter stay in the bath?
(d) How long did it take for the bath to empty?
(e) Make up a bath graph of your own and describe
    each stage.

3 The graph shows the flight of a hot air balloon.

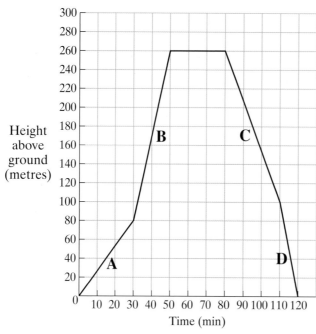

(a) What does each square represent:
  • horizontally
  • vertically?
(b) How high does the balloon rise above the ground?
(c) How long does it stay at its maximum height?
(d) What is its average speed as it rises?
(e) What is its average speed as it descends?
(f) Find the speed in sections **A**, **B**, **C** and **D**.

4 The graph shows the distance of a train from a station.

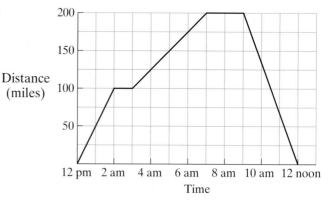

(a) How far was the train from the station at 3 am?
(b) How far was the train from the station at 11 am?
(c) At what two times is the train 150 miles from the station?
(d) For how long is the train stationary in total?
(e) What is the average speed for the outward journey?
(f) What is the average speed for the return journey?

5 This graph shows a rocket in flight.

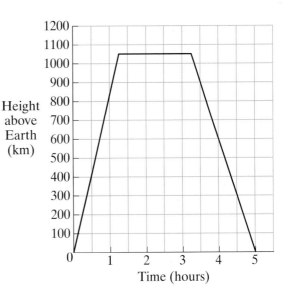

(a) What does each square represent:
  • horizontally
  • vertically?

(b) What height above the Earth does the rocket reach?

(c) At its maximum height the rocket is in orbit. How long does the rocket stay in orbit?

(d) How long was the total flight?

(e) When was the rocket travelling fastest?

(f) What was the rocket's speed as it went up?

(g) What was the rocket's speed as it came down?

6 The graph shows Bina's journey to the shops and back.

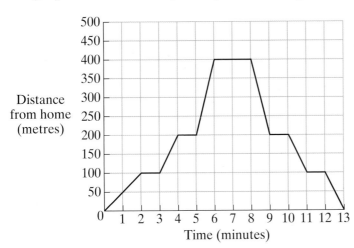

(a) How far does Bina live from the shops?

(b) How long does it take her to get to the shops?

(c) How long does she spend at the shops?

(d) How long does it take Bina to get home?

(e) How many roads do you think Bina crosses on her way to the shops?

(f) What is her average speed on her way to the shops?

(g) What is her average speed on her way home?

7   Draw a grid.

Horizontally each square represents 10 minutes, up to 120 minutes.
Label the horizontal axis 'Time (minutes)'.
Vertically each square represents 5 miles, up to 50 miles.
Label the vertical axis 'Distance from home (miles)'.

Draw the car journey described below on your grid.
The car is always travelling away from home.

Section 1   The car travels 15 miles in 20 minutes at a constant speed.
Section 2   The car stops for 10 minutes.
Section 3   The car travels 10 miles in 10 minutes.
Section 4   The car stops for 20 minutes.
Section 5   The car travels 25 miles in 40 minutes.

Use your graph to answer these questions:
(a) How far does the car travel in total?
(b) How long does the journey take?
(c) How long does the car stop for?
(d) In which section did the car travel fastest?
(e) What was the car's speed in
      (i) section 1   (ii) section 2   (iii) section 3?
(f) What was the average speed for the whole journey?

8   Draw a grid.

Horizontally each square represents 10 minutes, up to 120 minutes.
Label the horizontal axis 'Time (minutes)'.
Vertically each square represents 100 metres, up to 1000 metres.
Label this axis 'Height above ground (metres)'.

Plot the balloon flight described below on your grid.

Section 1   The balloon rose 500 m in 30 minutes.
Section 2   It stayed at this height for 10 minutes.
Section 3   It rose 300 metres in 10 minutes.
Section 4   It fell 400 metres in 20 minutes.
Section 5   It rose 500 metres in 20 minutes.
Section 6   It descended to the ground in 10 minutes.

Use your graph to answer these questions:
(a) How long was the flight?
(b) How high did the balloon get?
(c) How long did the balloon take to reach its maximum height?

(d) What was the balloon's speed as it descended to the ground?

(e) Work out the speed for each section during which the balloon was rising.

Summary of key points

1   The horizontal coordinate is called the **x-coordinate**.
The vertical coordinate is called the **y-coordinate**.
You always write the *x*-coordinate first.

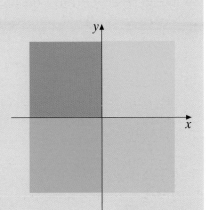

2   Each quarter of the coordinate grid is called a **quadrant**.

3   In general, if a line looks like this:

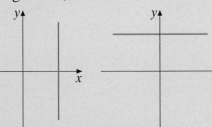 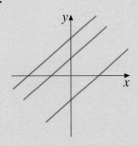 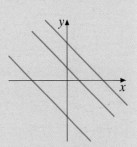

The equation looks like this:

$x = \boxed{}$ $y = \boxed{}$ $y = x + \boxed{}$ $y + x = \boxed{}$

or $y = x - \boxed{}$

4   The **intercept** of a line is the point $(0, \boxed{})$ where the line crosses the *x*-axis.
The number $\boxed{}$ is the value of *y* when $x = 0$.

5   **Gradient** is the maths word for steepness.
The bigger the gradient, the steeper the slope.

• A line that slopes up has a *positive* gradient.

• A line that slopes down has a *negative* gradient.

• Flat lines have *zero* gradient. ———

6 If the equation looks like:

$$y = mx + c$$

where m and c are numbers (positive, negative or 0),
then the line will be straight.

7 On information graphs, always look to see what information each axis gives and what one square represents.

6 Number

6.1 Numbers up to a billion

The decimal number system uses only these ten digits and the idea of place value to write any whole number:

0, 1, 2, 3, 4, 5, 6, 7, 8 and 9

■ **To read a large number it is useful to think of a place value diagram:**

The next three columns after billions are called trillions but you're unlikely to use these in everyday situations.

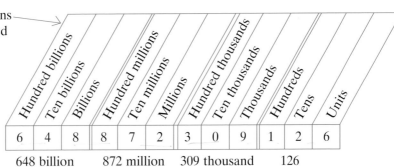

648 billion 872 million 309 thousand 126

You say 'six hundred and forty-eight billion, eight hundred and seventy-two million, three hundred and nine thousand, one hundred and twenty-six'.

Example 1

For each number say:
(i) how many billions there are
(ii) how many millions there are
(iii) how many thousands there are.

(a) 54 366 823 729

(b) 465 223 870 547

(a) **(i)** 54 billions
    (ii) 54 366 millions
    (iii) 54 366 823 thousands

(b) **(i)** 465 billions
    (ii) 465 223 millions
    (iii) 465 223 870 thousands

Example 2

Put these numbers in order of size, largest first:

507 296 403 205   48 329 047 643
48 677 987   269 293
875 293 582 849   898 701 732
     754 894

You could order them first into numbers starting with ...

billions:	507 296 403 205
	48 329 047 643
	875 293 582 849

| millions: | 48 677 987 |
| | 898 701 732 |

| thousands: | 269 293 |
| | 754 894 |

Next order the billions, millions and thousands ...

billions:	875 293 582 849
	507 296 403 205
	48 329 047 643

| millions: | 898 701 732 |
| | 48 677 987 |

| thousands: | 754 894 |
| | 269 293 |

Exercise 6A

For each number say:

1 **(i)** how many billions there are
(ii) how many millions there are
(iii) how many thousands there are.
(a) 635 778 290 132   **(b)** 48 576 220 943
(c) 456 837 241 987   **(d)** 6 458 043 256

2 Put these numbers in order of size, largest first:

(a)

45 763
476 345 899 023
76 388 645
576 435 823 564
421 576
7 345 734 987
445 760 000

(b)

86 476 923
345 765 829 072
67 987
79 654 286 678
432 609
675 098 706
354 678 834 998

(c)

6 487 436
278 663 409 875
377 543 357
287 465 998 300
456 867
563 557 444
564 576

6.2 Multiples and factors

You already know about multiples, factors and primes.

The multiples of 5 are the answers in the 5 times table. The multiples of 5 go on forever: 5, 10, 15, 20, 25 ... 165, 170 ...

The factors of a number are those numbers that divide into it exactly. For example 1, 2, 5 and 10 are the factors of 10. Factors are always whole numbers.

Numbers that have exactly two factors are called prime numbers. These factors are 1 and the number itself. 1 is not a prime number as it only has one factor. 2, 3, 5, 7, 11 13, 17, 19, 23 ... are prime numbers.

Exercise 6B

1 True or false:
   (a) There is always a multiple of 3 between any two multiples of 4.
   (b) There is always a multiple of 4 between any two multiples of 3.
   (c) If you add a multiple of 2 to a multiple of 4 you always get an even number.
   (d) If you add a multiple of 3 to a multiple of 5 you always get an odd number.

2 Write down numbers that make these statements true:
   (a) There is always a multiple of ☐ between any two multiples of 5.
   (b) If you add a multiple of 4 to a multiple of 6 you always get a multiple of ☐.

3 The number 9 can be placed in this table as shown because:
   ● it is a multiple of 3
   ● it is an odd number
   Place the rest of the numbers 1 to 16 in the table.

	Not a multiple of 3	Multiple of 3	Less than 10	Greater than 10
Even				
Odd		9		
Prime				
Not prime				

4 Which number less than 50 has the most factors?

5 The factors of 6 are 1, 2, 3 and 6.
Their sum is $1 + 2 + 3 + 6 = 12$ and $12 = 2 \times 6$.
Find the other number less than 30 with factors which add up to twice itself.

6 Choose any two digits from the cloud. Use them to make a 2-digit number and find all its factors.

   (a) Which 2-digit number has the greatest number of factors?

   (b) Which 2-digit number has the least number of factors?

For example, you could choose 4 and 5.
45 has 6 factors:
1, 3, 5, 9, 15 and 45.

7 13 is a prime number.
If you reverse its digits you get another prime number, 31. Find another prime number for which this works.

8 True or false:

   (a) Every number has a factor which is a prime number.

   (b) If you add 2 to any odd prime number you always get another prime number.

   (c) The difference between any two prime numbers is always an even number.

9 Christian Goldbach was a mathematician who lived from 1690 to 1764. He thought that every even number bigger than 2 could be written as the sum of two prime numbers.

   (a) Write every even number from 4 to 50 as the sum of two prime numbers.

   (b) He also thought every odd number bigger than 5 could be written as the sum of three prime numbers. Write every odd number from 7 to 49 as the sum of three prime numbers.

Common multiples

To add together fractions such as $\frac{1}{2}$ and $\frac{1}{3}$ you need to know about common multiples.

There is more about adding fractions on page 168.

The multiples of 2 are 2, 4, **6**, 8, 10, **12**, 14, 16, **18**, 20 ...
The multiples of 3 are 3, **6**, 9, **12**, 15, **18**, 21, **24**, 27, **30**, 33, **36**, 39, ...

■ The numbers 6, 12, 18, 24 ... are multiples of both 2 and 3. They are called the common multiples of 2 and 3.
6 is called the Lowest Common Multiple of 2 and 3.
The Lowest Common Multiple is sometimes called the LCM.

Example 3

(a) What are the first three common multiples of 3 and 4?
(b) What is the LCM of 3 and 4?

Write out the multiples of 3: 3, 6, 9, **12**, 15, 18, 21, **24**, 27, 30, 33, **36**, 39 ...
Write out the multiples of 4: 4, 8, **12**, 16, 20, **24**, 28, 32, **36**, 40 ...

(a) The first three common multiples of 3 and 4 are **12**, **24**, **36**.
(b) The Lowest Common Multiple of 3 and 4 is **12**.

Exercise 6C

1 What are the first three common multiples of:
(a) 3 and 5 (b) 4 and 6 (c) 2 and 5 (d) 3 and 7
(e) 5 and 6 (f) 3 and 9 (g) 4 and 9 (h) 6 and 9
(i) 5 and 4 (j) 8 and 6 (k) 6 and 7 (l) 15 and 20

2 What is the Lowest Common Multiple of:
(a) 4 and 10   (b) 6 and 2
(c) 9 and 3   (d) 8 and 5
(e) 8 and 12   (f) 4 and 7
(g) 20 and 30   (h) 10 and 15
(i) 50 and 40   (j) 2, 3 and 4
(k) 3, 6 and 9   (l) 4, 5, 6

3 Find two pairs of numbers that have an LCM of:
(a) 12   (b) 20
(c) 16   (d) 24

4 Find a pair of numbers that have the following common multiples.
(a) 4, 8, 12, ...   (b) 6, 12, 18, ...
(c) 5, 10, 15, ...   (d) 10, 20, 30, ...
(e) ... 16, 20, 24, ...   (f) ... 24, 32, 40, ...
(g) ... 20, 25, 30, ...   (h) ... 40, 60, 80, ...

5   Write down numbers that make these statements true:

(a) the LCM of 4 and ☐ is 12

(b) the LCM of 9 and ☐ is 18

(c) the LCM of ☐ and 8 is 24

(d) the LCM of ☐ and 10 is 40

(e) the LCM of ☐ and 14 is 28

(f) the LCM of 15 and ☐ is 30

(g) the LCM of ☐, 5 and ☐ is 20

(h) the LCM of ☐, ☐ and 6 is 18

Common factors

To simplify ratios and fractions you need to know about common factors.

The factors of 12 are   **1, 2,** 3, **4,** 6, 12
The factors of 16 are   **1, 2, 4,** 8, 16

■   **The numbers 1, 2, and 4 are called the common factors of 12 and 16.**
    4 is called the Highest Common Factor of 12 and 16.
    The Highest Common Factor is sometimes called the HCF.

Example 4

(a) Find the common factors of 60 and 45.
(b) What is the Highest Common Factor of 60 and 45?

The factors of 60 are **1,** 2, **3,** 4, **5,** 6, 10, **15,** 20, 30, 60.
The factors of 45 are **1, 3, 5,** 9, **15,** 45.

(a) The common factors are 1, 3, 5, 15.
(b) The HCF is 15.

Exercise 6D

1   What are the common factors of:

(a) 4 and 10   (b) 12 and 18   (c) 14 and 21   (d) 12 and 6
(e) 8 and 20   (f) 18 and 24   (g) 18 and 27   (h) 24 and 16

2 What is the Highest Common Factor of:

(a) 5 and 7   **(b)** 6 and 9   **(c)** 8 and 12   **(d)** 9 and 15

(e) 20 and 30   **(f)** 28 and 16   **(g)** 9, 12, and 15   **(h)** 12, 18 and 24

3 Each of these pupils have chosen a pair of numbers from the blackboard. Which pair of numbers has each pupil chosen?

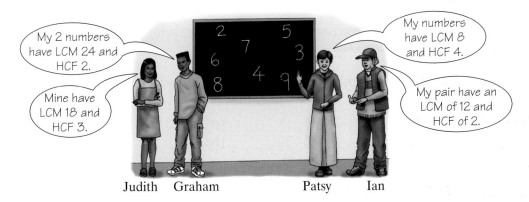

Judith   Graham   Patsy   Ian

4 Can the LCM and the HCF of two numbers ever be the same? Explain your answer.

5 **(a)** Choose two numbers and find their LCM and their HCF. Multiply the two numbers together. Multiply their LCM and their HCF together.
What do you notice?

     (b) Try this for other pairs of numbers. Can you explain what is happening?

Prime factors

The factors of 18 are 1, 2, 3, 6, 9, 18.
The numbers 2 and 3 are prime numbers.
18 can be written as $2 \times 3 \times 3$.
This is called writing 18 as a product of its prime factors.

> $18 = 2 \times 3 \times 3$
> $48 = 2 \times 2 \times 2 \times 2 \times 3$
> $450 = 2 \times 3 \times 3 \times 5 \times 5$
> $385 = 5 \times 7 \times 11$
> $80 = 2 \times 2 \times 2 \times 2 \times 5$

■ **Any number can be written as a product of its prime factors.**
For example 2 and 3 are the prime factors of 18, and $18 = 2 \times 3 \times 3$.

Example 5

Write 40 as a product of its prime factors.

The factors of 40 are 1, 2, 4, 5, 8, 10, 20, 40.
The prime factors of 40 are 2 and 5.
Multiply 2s and 5s to make 40: $2 \times 2 \times 2 \times 5 = 40$

40 written as a product of its prime factors is $2 \times 2 \times 2 \times 5$.

Exercise 6E

1   Write each of these numbers as a product of its prime factors:

  (a) 14   **(b)** 12   **(c)** 16   **(d)** 24
  (e) 25   **(f)** 28   **(g)** 30   **(h)** 35

2   Write each of these numbers as a product of its prime factors:

  (a) 32   **(b)** 36   **(c)** 42   **(d)** 48
  (e) 27   **(f)** 81   **(g)** 100   **(h)** 75

3   Which numbers less than 100 have prime factors 2 and 3 only?

4   Write the numbers 4, 9, 16, 25, 36, 49, 64, 81, 100 as a product of their prime factors. What do you notice?

6.3 Powers

You will already have seen powers of numbers.

10^2 means $10 \times 10 = 100$. You say 10 to the power of 2 or 10 squared.

10^3 means $10 \times 10 \times 10 = 1000$. You say 10 to the power of 3 or 10 cubed.

10^4 means $10 \times 10 \times 10 \times 10 = 10\,000$. You say 10 to the power of 4.

Example 6

Write 216 as a power of 6

$216 = 6 \times 6 \times 6 = 6^3$

Example 7

Work out 2^5

$2^5 = 2 \times 2 \times 2 \times 2 \times 2 = 32$

Exercise 6F

You may need a calculator for some of these questions.

1 Write:
- **(a)** 9 as a power of 3
- **(b)** 125 as a power of 5
- **(c)** 256 as a power of 4
- **(d)** 343 as a power of 7
- **(e)** 81 as a power of 3
- **(f)** 10 000 as a power of 10
- **(g)** 625 as a power of 5
- **(h)** 729 as a power of 9
- **(i)** 7776 as a power of 6
- **(k)** 4096 as a power of 8

2 Work out:
- **(a)** 2^3
- **(b)** 4^5
- **(c)** 6^4
- **(d)** 3^5
- **(e)** 7^4
- **(f)** 5^5
- **(g)** 8^3
- **(h)** 10^5

3 Find the missing numbers:
- **(a)** $\boxed{}^2 = 16$
- **(b)** $\boxed{}^3 = 27$
- **(c)** $5^{\boxed{}} = 25$
- **(d)** $6^{\boxed{}} = 216$
- **(e)** $\boxed{}^4 = 16$
- **(f)** $\boxed{}^3 = 1000$
- **(g)** $3^{\boxed{}} = 729$
- **(h)** $\boxed{}^3 = 64$

Multiplying and dividing powers

There is a quick way to multiply and divide powers of the same number.

Example 8

Write $10^3 \times 10^4$ as a power of 10

$10^3 = 1000$

$10^4 = 10\,000$

so $10^3 \times 10^4 = 1000 \times 10\,000 = 10\,000\,000$

but $10\,000\,000 = 10^7$

so $10^3 \times 10^4 = 10^7$

notice that $3 + 4 = 7$

Example 9

Write $2^5 \div 2^2$ as a power of 2

$2^5 = 32$

$2^2 = 4$

so $2^5 \div 2^2 = 32 \div 4 = 8$

but $8 = 2^3$

so $2^5 \div 2^2 = 2^3$

notice that $5 - 2 = 3$

■ **To multiply powers of the same number you add the powers**
To divide powers of the same number you subtract the powers.

$$3 + 4 = 7$$
$$10^3 \times 10^4 = 10^7$$

$$5 - 2 = 3$$
$$2^5 \div 2^2 = 2^3$$

Example 10

Work out $5^2 \times 5^4 \div 5^3$, leaving your answer as a power.

$$2 + 4 - 3 = 3$$
so $\quad 5^2 \times 5^4 \div 5^3 = 5^3$

Example 11

Write down $7^5 \times 7^3 \div 7^6$
(a) as a power of 7
(b) as a whole number.

(a) $\qquad 5 + 3 - 6 = 2$
$\quad$ so $\quad 7^5 \times 7^3 \div 7^6 = 7^2$

(b) $7^2 = 49$

Exercise 6G

1 Work out, leaving your answer as a power:
(a) $3^2 \times 3^4$ $\qquad$ **(b)** $4^3 \times 4^2$
(c) $10^5 \div 10^3$ $\qquad$ **(d)** $6^3 \times 6^4$
(e) $7^6 \div 7^4$ $\qquad$ **(f)** $8^7 \times 8^3$

2 Work out, leaving your answer as a power:
(a) $5^3 \times 5^2 \times 5^4$ $\qquad$ **(b)** $4^5 \times 4^2 \times 4^3$
(c) $9^5 \times 9^3 \div 9^4$ $\qquad$ **(d)** $6^5 \times 6^2 \div 6^4$
(e) $7^3 \times 7^6 \div 7^4$ $\qquad$ **(f)** $8^7 \div 8^3 \times 8^5$

3 Write each answer as a power and as a whole number:
(a) $5^3 \times 5^3 \div 5^4$ $\qquad$ **(b)** $6^3 \times 6^4 \div 6^5$
(c) $4^5 \times 4^3 \div 4^6$ $\qquad$ **(d)** $7^4 \times 7^6 \div 7^8$
(e) $10^4 \times 10^5 \div 10^6$ $\qquad$ **(f)** $3^2 \times 3^5 \div 3^4$

4 Match each question to a value in the cloud:
(a) $10^6 \div 10^3$ $\qquad$ **(b)** $5^6 \times 5^2 \div 5^5$
(c) $3^2 \times 3^4 \div 3^3$ $\qquad$ **(d)** $2^3 \times 2^2$
(e) $4^6 \div 4^5 \times 4^2$ $\qquad$ **(f)** $6^3 \times 6^3 \div 6^4$

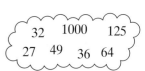

32 $\quad$ 1000 $\quad$ 125
27 $\quad$ 49 $\quad$ 36 $\quad$ 64

(g) Make up a question using powers to give the remaining value in the cloud.

6.4 Roots

You have used square roots and cube roots before.

The square root of 16 can be written as $\sqrt[2]{16}$ or $\sqrt{16}$.
$\sqrt{16} = 4$ because $4 \times 4 = 16$.
The cube root of 216 can be written as $\sqrt[3]{216}$
$\sqrt[3]{216} = 6$ because $6 \times 6 \times 6 = 216$.

You can use this method to write other roots.

The fourth root of 625 is written as $\sqrt[4]{625}$.
$\sqrt[4]{625} = 5$ because $5^4 = 625$.

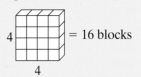

Squares and cubes

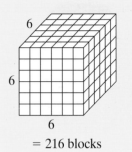

4 $= 16$ blocks

$= 216$ blocks

Example 12

Find the value of
(a) $\sqrt[4]{1296}$ **(b)** $\sqrt[5]{32}$

(a) $\quad 6^4 = 1296$ **(b)** $\quad 2^5 = 32$
$\quad$ so $\sqrt[4]{1296} = 6$ $\quad$ so $\sqrt[5]{32} = 2$

Example 13

Show that the following statement is true:
$\sqrt{4} \times \sqrt{100} = \sqrt{400}$

$\sqrt{4} \times \sqrt{100} = 2 \times 10 = 20$
$\sqrt{400} = 20$
so $\sqrt{4} \times \sqrt{100} = \sqrt{400}$

Exercise 6H

1 Find the value of:
   (a) $\sqrt[4]{16}$ **(b)** $\sqrt[4]{10\,000}$ **(c)** $\sqrt[4]{81}$
   (d) $\sqrt[6]{64}$ **(e)** $\sqrt[6]{1\,000\,000}$

2 Show that the following statements are true:
   (a) $\sqrt{4} \times \sqrt{9} = \sqrt{36}$ **(b)** $\sqrt{16} \times \sqrt{4} = \sqrt{64}$
   (c) $\sqrt[2]{1} = \sqrt[3]{1}$ **(d)** $\sqrt[3]{8} = \sqrt{4}$
   (e) $\sqrt[2]{100} = \sqrt[3]{1000}$
   (f) $\sqrt{4} \times \sqrt{9} \times \sqrt{100} = \sqrt{3600}$

6.5 Rounding to 1 significant figure to check answers

Kath, Ted and Ray have been collecting signatures for a petition.

Kath actually collected 76 signatures.
The units digit was greater than 5 so she rounded up to 80.
Ted actually collected 652 signatures.
The tens digit was 5 so he rounded up to 700.
Ray actually collected 3497 signatures.
The hundreds digit was less than 5 so he rounded down to 3000.

Kath, Ted and Ray each rounded their number to **1 significant figure**.

■ **The first significant figure in a whole number
   is the digit (or figure) on the left of the
   number.**

   For example:

   **The first significant figure in 7486 is 7
   The first significant figure in 25 314 is 2
   The first significant figure in 362 is 3**

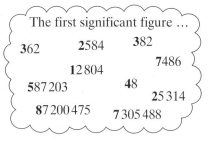

■ **To round to one significant figure look at
   the next figure after it.**
   ● **If it is less than 5 round down.**
   ● **If it is 5 or more round up.**

   For example:

   **7486 rounded to 1 significant figure is 7000
   25 314 rounded to 1 significant figure is 30 000
   362 rounded to 1 significant figure is 400**

Example 14

Round each number to 1 significant figure to find an approximate answer:

(a) 3476×467 **(b)** $86\,241 \div 252$

(a) 3000×500
    $= 15\,000 \times 100$
    $= 1\,500\,000$

To multiply by 500 multiply by 5 then multiply by 100

(b) $90\,000 \div 300$
    $= 900 \div 3$
    $= 300$

To divide by 300, divide by 100 then divide by 3. This is the opposite of multiplying by 300

Exercise 6I

1 Round each number to 1 significant figure to find an approximate answer:

    (a) 42×728 **(b)** 47×234 **(c)** 752×2487
    (d) 461×3742 **(e)** 752×3842 **(f)** 6362×2548
    (g) 3685×5723 **(h)** $87\,035 \times 3598$ **(i)** $751 \times 47\,442$

2 Round each number to 1 s.f. to find an approximate answer:

1 s.f. means 1 significant figure.

    (a) $752 \div 21$ **(b)** $891 \div 34$ **(c)** $7823 \div 416$
    (d) $1837 \div 494$ **(e)** $5743 \div 25$ **(f)** $8123 \div 37$
    (g) $8076 \div 235$ **(h)** $5843 \div 1598$ **(i)** $6585 \div 723$

3 By rounding to 1 s.f. find the correct answer in the cloud for each calculation:

    (a) $79\,422 \times 84$ **(b)** $13\,278 \times 2643$
    (c) $19\,336 \div 4834$ **(d)** $355\,386 \div 183$
    (e) $78\,714 \times 158$ **(f)** $730\,881 \div 2601$

4   1942
     281
         35 093 754
6 671 448   12 436 812

4 Four pupils each did 767×345 on their calculators. Only one of them got the correct answer. Find an approximate answer to help you decide who had the correct answer.

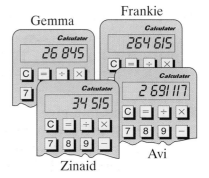

Gemma   Frankie

Zinaid   Avi

5   Who had the correct answer to this calculation:

$$17\,578 \div 374$$

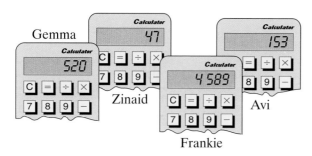

6   **(a)** Copy this table rounding each number to 1 significant figure.

(b) Decide which of the following statements are true and which are false:

   (i)   The area of Sweden is about ten times the area of Switzerland.

   (ii)   Denmark is about half the size of the Czech Republic.

   (iii) Hungary is roughly a quarter the size of Germany.

(c) Make up a statement like this of your own.

Country	Area in km²
England	130 357
Sweden	411 479
Switzerland	41 228
Hungary	93 033
Czech Republic	78 864
Denmark	43 076
Germany	357 868

6.6 Rounding to more than 1 significant figure

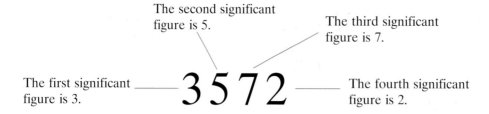

The first significant figure is 3.

The second significant figure is 5.

The third significant figure is 7.

The fourth significant figure is 2.

■   **To round to a given number of significant figures look at the next figure after it.**
   • **If it is less than 5 round down.**
   • **If it is 5 or more round up.**

Example 15

Round 3572 to

(a) 1 s.f.   (b) 2 s.f.   (c) 3 s.f.

(a) 4000   (b) 3600   (c) 3570

Example 16

Round 6997 to

(a) 1 s.f.   (b) 2 s.f.   (c) 3 s.f.

(a) 7000   (b) 7000   (c) 7000 ———————————

> When you round 6997 up to the nearest 10 you get 7000.

Example 17

The length of the River Nile is 6690 km to 3 s.f.
What is:

(a) the shortest it could be?
(b) the longest it could be?

(a) The shortest it could be is 6685 km.
(b) The longest it could be is 6694 km.

Exercise 6J

1   Round to 2 significant figures:
    (a) 4634   (b) 7356
    (c) 849   (d) 2452
    (e) 10 643   (f) 41 289
    (g) 35 478   (h) 146 089
    (i) 5496   (j) 4972

> Hint:
> Look at the third significant figure.

2   Round to 3 significant figures:
    (a) 5481   (b) 23 492
    (c) 78 452   (d) 365 423
    (e) 4697   (f) 68 072
    (g) 346 712   (h) 695 498
    (i) 59 962   (j) 9996

3   The length of each of these rivers has been given correct to 3 s.f. Copy and complete the table to show the shortest each river could be and the longest each river could be.

River	Length in km to 3 s.f.	Shortest length in km	Longest length in km
Amazon	6570		
Mississippi	6020		
Yangtze	5980		
Congo	4630		
Mekong	4180		
Niger	4100		

4   This table shows the depth of some of the world's deepest caves rounded to 3 s.f.
The cloud contains the actual depth of each cave.
Copy and complete the table to show the actual depth of each cave.

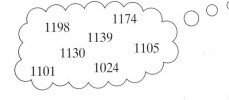

Cave	Depth in metres to 3 s.f.	Actual depth in metres
Badalona	1130	
Batmanhöle	1110	
Schneeloch	1100	
Berger	1200	
Lamprechtshofen	1020	
Zitu	1140	
Dachstein-Mammuthöle	1170	

6.7 Using inverse operations to check solutions when using a calculator

You will need a calculator for this section. In section 5 you used rounding to check calculations. You can also check calculations using inverse operations.

You can think of the calculation as a number machine:

Think of the inverse number machine:

■ **You can check an answer by performing the inverse operation on it. If you end up with your original number you know your answer was correct.**

operation	inverse
×	÷
÷	×
+	−
−	+

For example, to check 973 × 78 you would divide your answer by 78 (÷ is the inverse operation to ×). If you get 973 you know your answer is correct.

Example 18

Supraj worked out 43 216 ÷ 72 using a calculator.

He got the answer 592.

Check his answer by the method of inverse operations.

592 × 72 = 42 624 so his answer is wrong.

Example 19

Ann worked out 7904 − 1328 using a calculator.

She got the answer 6576.

Check her answer by the method of inverse operations.

6576 + 1328 = 7904 so her answer is correct.

Exercise 6K

1 Use the method of inverse operations to decide which of these calculations is correct:

   (a) $463 \times 58 = 26\,854$

   (b) $748 \times 87 = 58\,344$

   (c) $76\,463 - 8652 = 67\,711$

   (d) $45\,893 + 8364 = 54\,257$

   (e) $14\,352 \div 624 = 24$

   (f) $14\,400 \div 450 = 34$

2 Use the method of inverse operations to work out the missing numbers in the following calculations.

   (a) $\boxed{} \times 45 = 1620$ **(b)** $\boxed{} \div 27 = 341$

   (c) $\boxed{} + 4578 = 345\,932$ **(d)** $\boxed{} - 473 = 88\,493$

   (e) $\boxed{} \times 456 = 56\,088$ **(f)** $\boxed{} \div 365 = 1847$

Summary of key points

1 To read a large number it is useful to think of a place value diagram:

The next three columns after billions are called trillions but you're unlikely to use these in everyday situations.

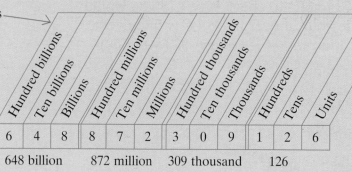

648 billion   872 million   309 thousand   126

2 The numbers 6, 12, 18, 24 … are multiples of both 2 and 3. They are called the common multiples of 2 and 3.
6 is called the Lowest Common Multiple of 2 and 3.
The Lowest Common Multiple is sometimes called the LCM.

3 The numbers 1, 2 and 4 are called the common factors of 12 and 16.
4 is called the Highest Common Factor of 12 and 16.
The Highest Common Factor is sometimes called the HCF.

4 Any number can be written as a product of its prime factors. For example 2 and 3 are the prime factors of 18, and $18 = 2 \times 3 \times 3$.

5 To multiply powers of the same number you add the powers:
To divide powers of the same number you subtract the powers:

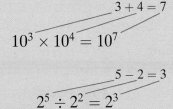

$$3 + 4 = 7$$
$$10^3 \times 10^4 = 10^7$$

$$5 - 2 = 3$$
$$2^5 \div 2^2 = 2^3$$

6 The first significant figure in a whole number is the digit on the left of the number. For example:
The first significant figure in 7486 is 7
The first significant figure in 25 314 is 2
The first significant figure in 362 is 3

7 To round to 1 significant figure look at the next figure after it.
- If it is less than 5 round down.
- If it is 5 or more round up.

For example:
7486 rounded to 1 significant figure is 7000
25 314 rounded to 1 significant figure is 30 000
362 rounded to 1 significant figure is 400

8 To round to a given number of significant figures look at the next figure after it.
- If it is less than 5 round down.
- If it is 5 or more round up.

9 You can check an answer by performing the inverse operation on it. If you end up with your original number you know your answer was correct.

For example, to check 973×78 you would divide your answer by 78 ($\div$ is the inverse operation to $\times$). If you get 973 you know your answer is correct.

operation	inverse
$\times$	$\div$
$\div$	$\times$
$+$	$-$
$-$	$+$

7 Transformations

This chapter covers four types of transformation:

translation

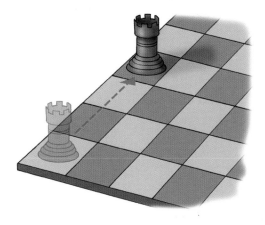

A sliding movement is called a **translation**.

rotation

A circular movement around a point is called a **rotation**.

reflection

The image of an object in a mirror is called a **reflection**.

enlargement

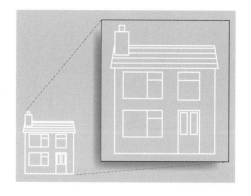

An **enlargement** changes the size of an object.

■ **In any transformation the original shape is called the object and the transformed shape is called the image.**

7.1 Reflection

This shape is reflected in the mirror line:

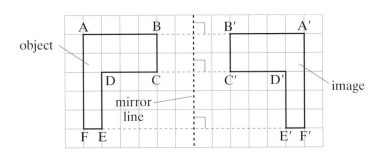

To mark the reflection of pointer A you write A′. You say 'A prime'.

Measure the distance of the object and image from the mirror line at right angles.

They are both the same distance away.

■   **In a reflection the image is the same distance behind the mirror line as the object is in front.**

Example 1

Draw the image of this shape in the mirror line.

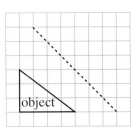

Imagine these lines being drawn:

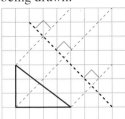

Mark the corners …

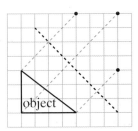

… and complete the shape.

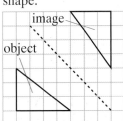

Example 2

Using the *x*-axis as the mirror line, reflect the triangle ABC.

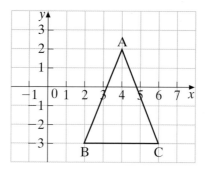

The part of the shape above the mirror line is reflected below the mirror line and the part of the shape below the mirror line is reflected above the mirror line.

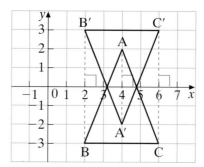

<hr>

Exercise 7A

1 Copy these diagrams onto squared paper and draw the image in the mirror line.

(a)
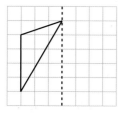

(b)
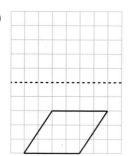

(c)
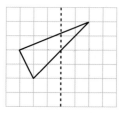

(d)
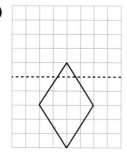

(e)
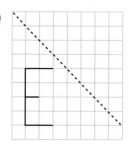

(f)
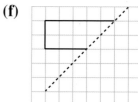

2 For each diagram:
- copy the diagram
- draw the image using the given mirror line.

(a)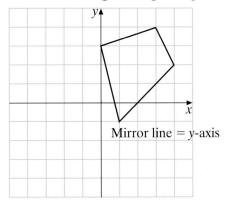

Mirror line = y-axis

(b)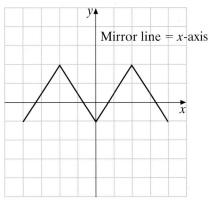

Mirror line = x-axis

3 **(a)** On squared paper, draw x-axis from −6 to 6 and y-axis from −6 to 6. Plot the following points A(−1, 0), B(2, 3), C(3, −1) and reflect the shape using the x-axis as the mirror line. Label the image A′B′C′.

(b) Reflect the shape A′B′C′ in the y-axis and label this image A″B″C″.

Finding the line of reflection

In the diagram, triangle ABC has been reflected and A′B′C′ is the image.

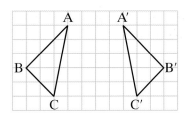

To find the mirror line:

Imagine these lines:

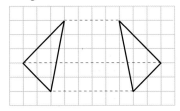

Mark the mid-points …

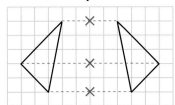

… and join them up:

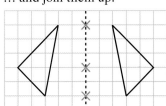

The mirror line **bisects** the distance from ABC to A′B′C′.

Hint:
Bisect means 'cut in half'.

Example 3

Find the line of reflection.

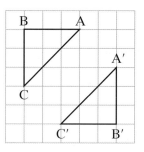

Find the mid points of A to A′, B to B′ and C to C′.

Join the mid points to form the mirror line.

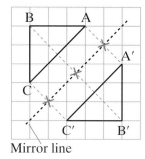

Mirror line

Exercise 7B

1   Copy each diagram onto squared paper and find the line of reflection.

(a)

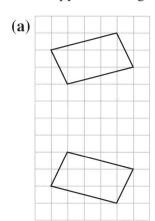

(b)

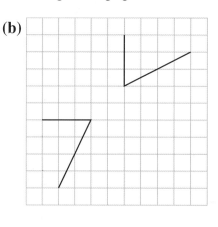

(c)

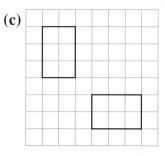

2   Trace each diagram and find the mirror line.

    (a)

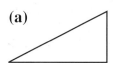
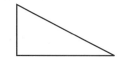

                                   (b)

7.2 Translation

Samina and Chi are playing a board game.

Chi's counter has moved 3 squares to the right. Samina's counter has moved 4 squares up the ladder.

Both these movements are **translations**.

- **A translation is a sliding movement with no twisting or turning.**

Example 4

Describe the translation that moves A to A'.

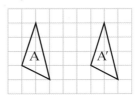

Each point on shape A has moved 5 squares to the right, so the translation is **5 units to the right**.

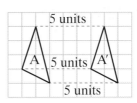

Example 5

Describe the translation that moves B to B'.

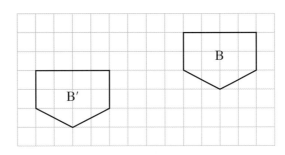

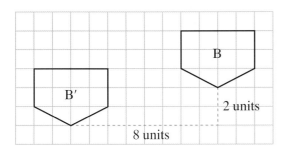

Each point on B has moved 8 squares to the left and 2 squares down. The translation is **8 units to the left and 2 units down**.

Hint: Always give the movement across first, then the movement up or down.

Exercise 7C

1 For each diagram, describe the translation from A to A′.

(a)

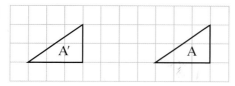

(b)

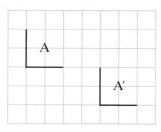

(c)

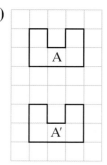

(d)

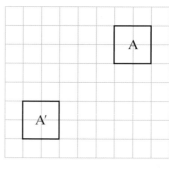

(e)

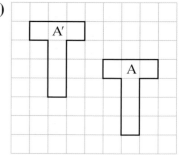

2 Copy this diagram onto squared paper and draw and label the images of the rectangle using these translations:

(a) 2 units to the left and 4 units down. Label this rectangle M.

(b) 3 units to the right and 1 unit up. Label this rectangle N.

(c) 7 units down. Label this rectangle P.

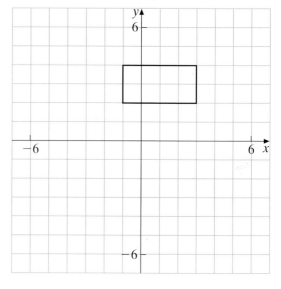

3 Draw x- and y-axes from −8 to 8 and plot the points A(2, 5), B(4, 3), C(6, 5), D(4, 7).

(a) Reflect the shape ABCD using the x-axis as a mirror line. Label the image A′B′C′D′.

(b) Translate the shape A′B′C′D′ seven units to the left and one unit down. Label the image A″B″C″D″.

(c) Reflect the shape A″B″C″D″ using the x-axis as a mirror line. Label the image A‴B‴C‴D‴.

4 Copy the diagram.

(a) Translate triangle ABC two units to the right and five units down, label the image A'B'C' and write the coordinates of this triangle.

(b) Reflect the triangle A'B'C' using the y-axis as a line of reflection, label the image A″B″C″ and write down the coordinates of this triangle.

(c) Can you translate triangle ABC to triangle A″B″C″? Give a reason for your answer.

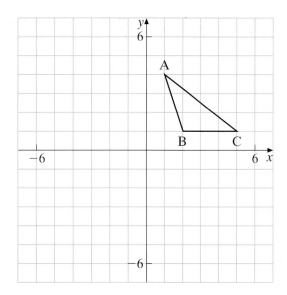

7.3 Translations using distance and direction

The boat needs to reach the lighthouse before dark.

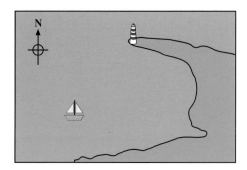

The captain could:

set her course east and then north:

set her course north-east:

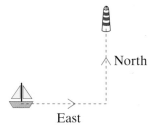

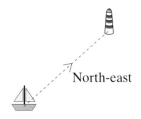

> Hint:
> The direction is always given as a bearing.
> There is more on bearings on p. 19.

North-east would be much quicker!

■ **You can describe a translation by giving a distance and a direction.**

Example 6

Describe this translation using
a distance and a direction:

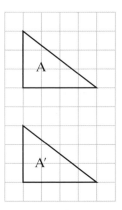

Each point on shape A has moved
5 units south (or 180°).

The translation is written as (5, 180°).

Exercise 7D

1 For each diagram, describe the translation using
   distance and direction.

(a)
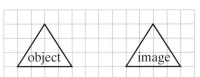

(b)
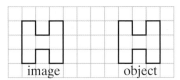

(c)
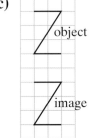

2 Copy this diagram for each of (a)–(f):
   • Plot and label the point.
   • Describe the point as a translation
     of P, using a distance and direction.

   (a) Q (5, 6)
   (b) R (1, 4)
   (c) S (3, 0)
   (d) T (3, 8)
   (e) U (7, 4)
   (f) V (1, 2)

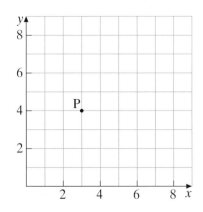

7.4 Rotation

As part of their routine this group of
synchronised swimmers rotate in a circle.

■ **A circular movement around a
point is called a rotation.
The point is called the centre
of rotation.**

The triangle has been rotated 90°
anticlockwise, about point B.
You can check this using tracing
paper. Trace triangle ABC, put
the tip of your pencil on point B
and turn the tracing paper 90°
(a quarter of a turn) anticlockwise.

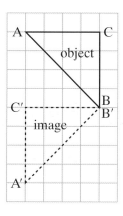

About point B
means that the
centre of rotation is
point B.

■ **You describe a rotation by
giving the centre of rotation
and the amount of turn.
The direction is always
anticlockwise.**

Example 7

Rotate ABCD 180° about point A.

To help you do this:

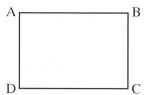

- Trace the shape.
- Put your pencil on shape A and rotate the paper 180°.
- Mark the corners with a sharp point.
- Remove the paper and join up the corners.

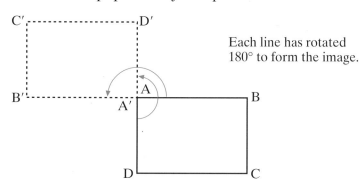

Each line has rotated
180° to form the image.

Example 8

Rotate this shape 90° about the origin.

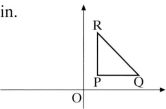

Imagine these lines: Rotate each one 90° ...   ... and join up the points.

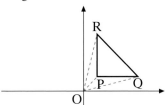 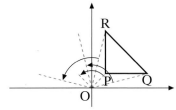 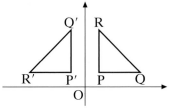

Notice that the distance from the origin is the same for the object and the image.

Example 9

The diagram shows an object and its image after it has been rotated *anticlockwise* about the point P.

(a) What angle has been formed by rotating SP to S′P′?
(b) What angle is formed by rotating QP to its new position Q′P′?
(c) What is the angle of rotation for this transformation?

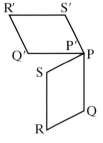

(a) SP has been rotated anticlockwise 270°.
(b) The angle formed by rotating QP to Q′P′ is 270°.
(c) Every point on the shape has rotated 270° so the angle of rotation for the transformation is 270°.

Exercise 7E

1   For each of the following diagrams, state the angle of rotation.

   The centre of rotation is P and the image is in red.

   (a)   (b)   (c)

          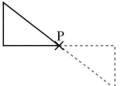

(d)   **(e)** 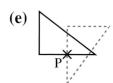 **(f)**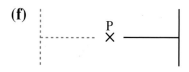

2   Copy each diagram onto squared paper and draw the image
    following the rotation. The centre of rotation is marked P.

(a)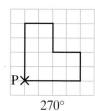
    Angle of turn 90°

(b)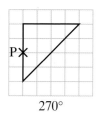
    180°

(c)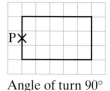
    270°

(d)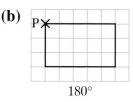
    270°

(e)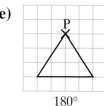
    180°

(f)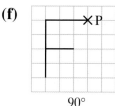
    90°

(g)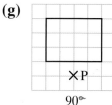
    90°

(h)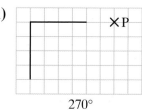
    270°

3   Draw x- and y-axes from -6 to 6 in both directions. Plot the
    points A$(-6, 5)$, B$(-6, 2)$, C$(-2, 2)$ and join to form a triangle.
    (a) Reflect triangle ABC in the x-axis and label the image A′B′C′.
    (b) Rotate triangle A′B′C′ 180° about the point $(0, -2)$.
        Label the image A″B″C″.

4   Draw x- and y-axes from -8 to 8 in both directions. Plot the
    points L$(1, -3)$, M$(3, -1)$, N$(5, -3)$ and join the points to
    form a triangle.
    (a) Rotate triangle LMN 90° about $(3, 0)$ and label the image L$_1$M$_1$N$_1$.
    (b) Reflect triangle L$_1$M$_1$N$_1$ in the y-axis and label the image L$_2$M$_2$N$_2$.

7.5 Enlargement

Yvonne has a print of a painting. The print is twice as big as the painting. All the lengths of the print are twice the lengths of the painting.

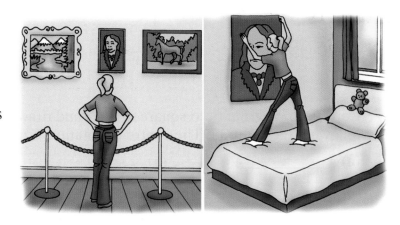

You say the scale factor is 2.

■ **An enlargement changes the size of the original shape.**

Example 10

Enlarge rectangle ABCD by a scale factor of 3.

Every length of rectangle ABCD is multiplied by 3.

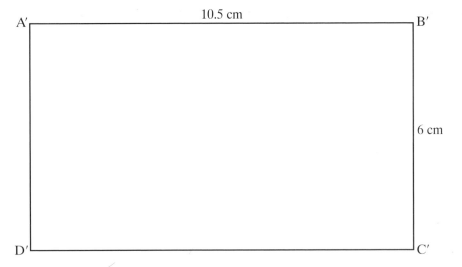

Yvonne's brother sends her a postcard of the painting. The postcard is ten times smaller than the painting. This means the scale factor of painting to postcard is $\frac{1}{10}$ because all lengths of the postcard are $\frac{1}{10}$ of the painting.

■ **The image may be larger or smaller than the object.**

Example 11

Enlarge triangle EFG by a scale factor of $\frac{1}{2}$.

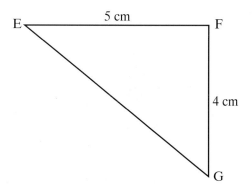

Every length of triangle EFG is multiplied by $\frac{1}{2}$ so E′F′G′ is:

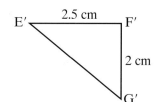

Notice that it is still called an enlargement when the image is smaller than the object.

Example 12

Find the scale factor that has enlarged triangle PQR to triangle P′Q′R′.

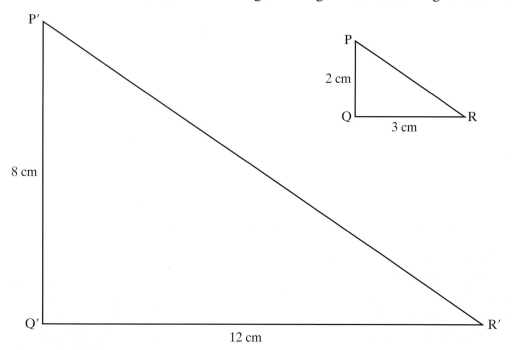

The length QR = 3 cm has been enlarged to Q′R′ = 12 cm.

You know that 3 cm × scale factor = 12 cm

So, $\quad\quad\quad\quad$ scale factor $= \dfrac{12\,\text{cm}}{3\,\text{cm}}$

and the scale factor is 4.

■ **Scale factor** $= \dfrac{\textbf{length of image}}{\textbf{corresponding length of original}}$

Scale factor is sometimes written as S.F.

Exercise 7F

1 Copy each diagram onto squared paper and enlarge it by the given scale factor.

(a)

Scale factor 3

(b)
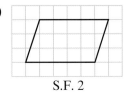
S.F. 2

(c)
S.F. 3

(d)

S.F. $\frac{1}{2}$

(e)

S.F. 4

(f)
S.F. $2\frac{1}{2}$

2 Find the scale factor for each object and image.

(a)
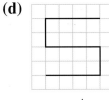
object

image

(b)
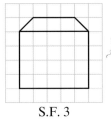
object $\quad$ image

(c)
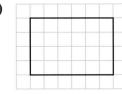
object

image

(d)
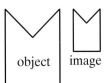
object $\quad$ image

(e)

object

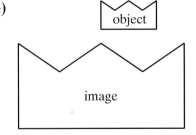
image

3 Triangle ABC has been enlarged to make A′B′C′.

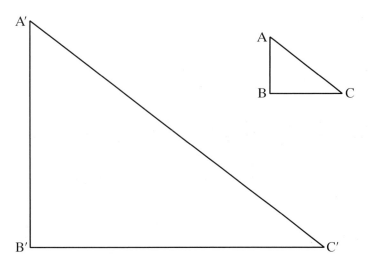

(a) Measure the length B′C′.
(b) Measure the length BC.
(c) Copy and complete this sentence:

$$\text{Scale factor} = \frac{\text{length of image}}{\text{length of object}} = \frac{\text{length B}'\text{C}'}{\text{length BC}} = \frac{\boxed{}\text{cm}}{\boxed{}\text{cm}}$$

$$\text{Scale factor} = \boxed{}$$

7.6 Centre of enlargement

Each of these shapes has been enlarged by a scale factor of 2.

The **centre of enlargement** positions the image.

$\times$ = centre of enlargement

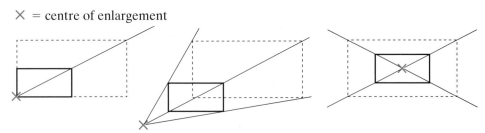

Example 13

Enlarge the shape ABC by a scale factor of 2.
The centre of enlargement is O.

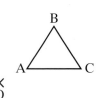

The scale factor is 2 so:

A′ is twice as far from the centre of enlargement as A
B′ is twice as far as B is from O
C′ is twice as far as C is from O

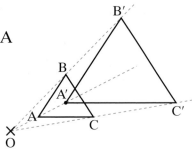

Example 14

Copy this diagram and draw the enlarged image of ABCD with scale factor $\frac{1}{2}$ and centre of enlargement O.

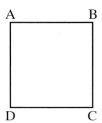

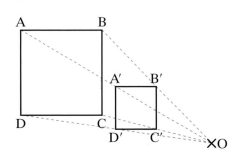

Draw the lines and mark:

A′ halfway along the line OA
B′ halfway along the line OB
... and repeat for points C and D

Notice that each side of the image is half the length of the object.

Exercise 7G

1

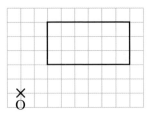

(a) Copy this diagram onto squared paper. Draw the image when the scale factor is 2 and the centre of enlargement is O.
(b) Repeat part (a) with the same centre of enlargement, but with a scale factor of $\frac{1}{2}$.

2 (a) Copy the diagram onto squared
        paper. Draw the image when
        the scale factor is 3 and the
        centre of enlargement is O.
    (b) Repeat part (a) with the same
        centre of enlargement, but with
        a scale factor of $1\frac{1}{2}$.

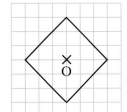

3 Copy the diagram. Using O as the
    centre of enlargement and a scale
    factor of $2\frac{1}{2}$, draw the enlargement.

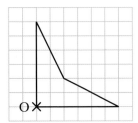

4 Draw x- and y-axes from 0 to 12. Plot and join the
    points A(2, 2), B(5, 2) and C(5, 4).
    Draw the image of triangle ABC, with a scale factor of
    2 and the origin as centre of enlargement.

5 For each object and image, copy the diagrams onto
    squared paper. Find the centre of enlargement by
    following these instructions:
    (a) Using dotted lines, join the points A to A', B to B',
        etc.
    (b) Extend the dotted lines so that they meet at a
        point, O.
        This is the centre of enlargement.

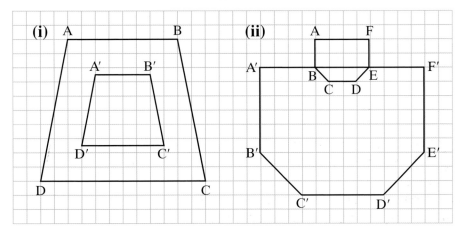

7.7 Congruence

This diagram shows triangle A after:

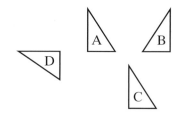

- a reflection (B)
- a translation (C)
- a rotation (D)

All the triangles are exactly the same size and shape. They are all **congruent**.

- ■ **If two figures are the same shape and size they are congruent.**

- ■ **The image of an object after a reflection, translation or rotation (or a combination of these) is always congruent to the object.**

Example 15

State whether the following figures are congruent to **(a)**.

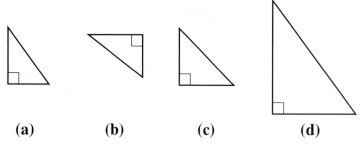

| (a) | (b) | (c) | (d) |

Trace triangle **(a)** and use the tracing to help.

(b) is congruent to **(a)**, it is the same shape and size.
(c) is not congruent to **(a)** as the sides are not the same length.
(d) is not congruent to **(a)** as it is larger.

Exercise 7H

1   Group the congruent shapes together. There may be more than two congruent shapes.

(a)   **(b)**   **(c)**   **(d)**

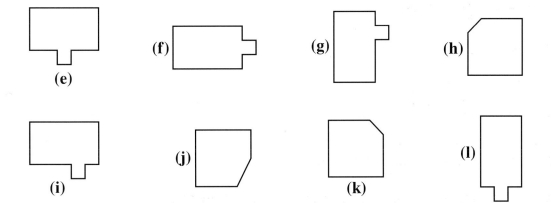

2 In each case, name the two congruent shapes.

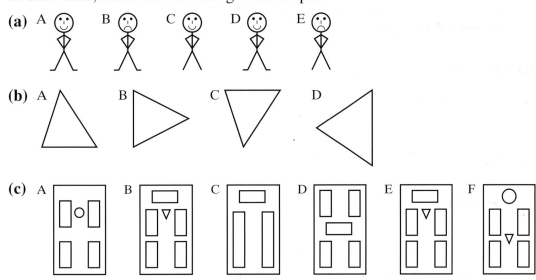

7.8 Tessellations

Wallpaper, carpet and print designs are often repeated patterns of a fairly simple shape.

■ **If a repeating pattern has no gaps or overlaps it is called a tessellation.**

Example 16

Use a regular hexagon to design a tessellating pattern.

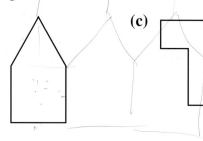

This is a tessellation because there are no gaps and no overlapping.

Exercise 7I

1 Create a tessellation using an equilateral triangle.

2 Create a tessellation using two different sized squares.

3 Use these shapes to create a design that tessellates.

(a) **(b)** **(c)**

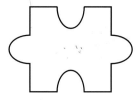

7.9 Plan and elevation

This architect has drawn the view of the building from above (the plan) and the view from the front and sides (the elevations).

■ **The plan of a solid is the two-dimensional view when seen from above.**

■ **The front elevation is the view from the front.**

■ **The side elevation is the view from the right-hand side.**

Example 17

Sketch the plan and elevations of this model house.

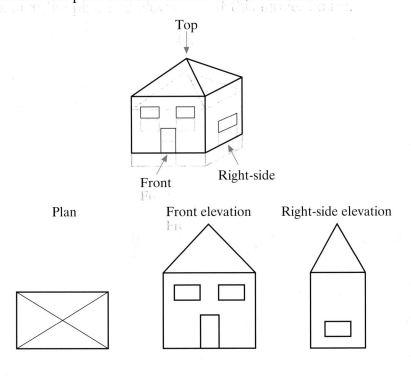

Top

Front   Right-side

Plan   Front elevation   Right-side elevation

Exercise 7J

1 Sketch the plan and front elevation of each solid.

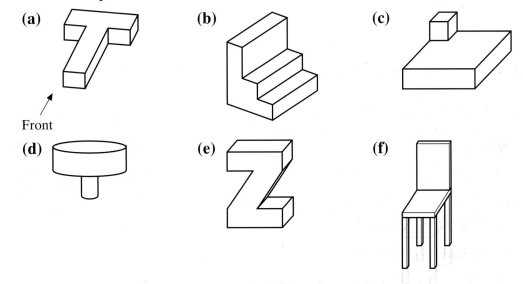

(a)   **(b)**   **(c)**

Front

(d)   **(e)**   **(f)**

2 Sketch the plan and front and side elevations of your desk.

3 In each case, sketch the shape with the given plan and elevations.

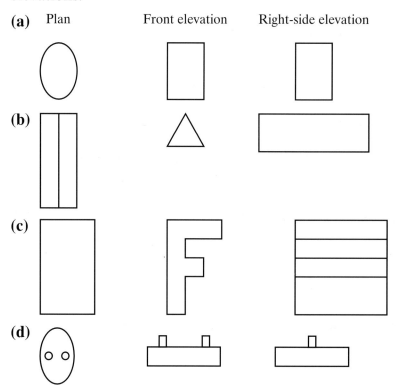

7 An enlargement changes the size of the original shape.

8 The image may be larger or smaller than the object.

9 Scale factor $= \dfrac{\text{length of image}}{\text{corresponding length of object}}$

10 If two figures are the same shape and size they are congruent.

11 The image of an object after a reflection, translation or rotation (or a combination of these) is always congruent to the object.

12 If a repeating pattern has no gaps or overlaps it is called a tessellation.

13 The plan of a solid is the two-dimensional view when seen from above.

14 The front elevation is the view from the front.

15 The side elevation is the view from the right-hand side.

8 Handling data

8.1 Questionnaires

A good way of collecting information is to use a questionnaire.

You need to be clear about what you want to know and what sort of questions to ask to get the information you want.

It is a good idea to keep the questions as simple as possible, giving choices or tick boxes for the answers:

Are you male? ☐   female? ☐

How much homework did you do last night?	none	
	< 1 hour	
	1 < 2 hours	
	2 < 3 hours	
	3 hours or more	

Avoid answers like 'a lot' or 'a little' because these can mean different things to different people.

Try to avoid questions like:

You don't like milk do you? | Y | N |

This is a **biased** question because it expects the answer to be 'no'.

Have you ever stolen a library book? | Y | N |

You may not get a truthful answer if you ask this question!

Exercise 8A

1   Write down what you think is wrong with these questions and rewrite them to make them more suitable.

   (a) How many hours TV did you watch last night? Please tick.

0–1 hour	
1–2 hours	
2–3 hours	
more than 3 hours	

(b) You will go to the dance won't you? Yes/No

(c) How much money do you get for baby sitting?

not much	
not enough	
under a fiver	
over £5	

2   Write suitable questions to find out each of the following:

(a) How pupils get to school.

(b) Where people do their shopping.

(c) Which newspaper is the most popular.

(d) Approximately how much someone earns.

(e) The amount of time people spend playing sport.

(f) How much money people spend on entertainment.

3   **(a)** Write a series of questions to find out the type of holiday people had. (Hint: You could ask about where they went, how they travelled, where they stayed, cost, what facilities were there).

(b) A leisure centre is to be built nearby. Design a questionnaire to find out if people agree with the idea and what facilities it should have in it.

(c) Design a questionnaire to find out what pets people keep, the time and cost of keeping them.

4   Use one of the above and conduct a survey. (Ask at least ten people). Write down a summary of what you found out.

5   Write a questionnaire to find out about computer games played by pupils in your school. (Format, time spent, cost, favourite...)

8.2 Sorting and presenting data

To be able to order data, spot patterns or features, and compare results for different sets of data you will need to know a variety of ways of presenting data.

A dictionary uses alphabetical order to help find information quickly:

stylish or spirited.
Word Family: **dashingly**, adverb
dastardly (*say* **dasst'd-lee**) *adjective, adverb*
mean and cowardly.
data (*say* **dayta** *or* **dahta**) *plural moun*
singular is **datum**
the facts or information on a particular
subject.
[Latin, the given things]
data base
Computers: a store of computerized i̶
mation which can be retrie̶
of ways.
̶) *noun*

This experiment uses a graph to show how solid A took longer to cool down than solid B.

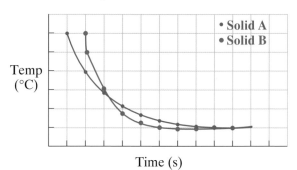

Here is some data which can be presented in a number of different ways. This list shows the number of correct answers achieved by 30 teams in a general knowledge quiz:

27	31	7	20	42	37	22	48	16	28
11	43	25	46	36	5	43	34	45	37
29	19	38	14	22	33	27	11	8	23

Because there is a spread of values, it is useful to order this data in a frequency table using sensible class intervals:

Number of correct answers	Tally	Frequency
0–9	|||	3
10–19	⊬⊬⊦	5
20–29	⊬⊬⊦ ||||	9
30–39	⊬⊬⊦ ||	7
40–49	⊬⊬⊦		6

Remember:
Class intervals must **not** overlap
e.g.   0–10
       10–20
       20–30 etc.

You could also use a stem and leaf diagram. Here you can actually see the scores for each class interval.

```
0 | 5 7 8
1 | 1 1 4 6 9
2 | 0 2 2 3 5 7 7 8 9
3 | 1 3 4 6 7 7 8
4 | 2 3 3 5 6 8
```

Stem = 10 correct answers

This data could then be presented in different diagrams depending on how you want the data to be used:

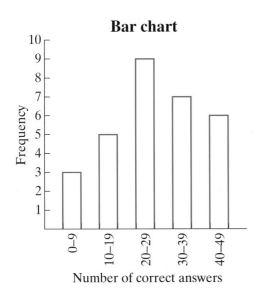

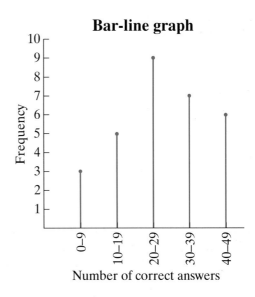

Pictogram

Number of correct answers	
0–9	✓ ✓ ✓
10–19	✓ ✓ ✓ ✓ ✓
20–29	✓ ✓ ✓ ✓ ✓ ✓ ✓ ✓ ✓
30–39	✓ ✓ ✓ ✓ ✓ ✓ ✓
40–49	✓ ✓ ✓ ✓ ✓ ✓

✓ represents 1 team

Exercise 8B

1 The number of passes achieved by pupils in the summer examination were:

```
4   9   5    7   6   8   4   6   9    5   8   7   3   8   5
6   3   8   10   2   9   8   9   7    4   7   5   9   6   7
9   7   6    5   4   6   7   5   9   10   6   9   4   8   3
5   3   4    7   8   5   8   7   6    9   7   2   6   7   4
```

   (a) Draw up a frequency chart to represent this data.
   (b) Write down the mode.
   (c) How many pupils achieved 7 passes or more?
   (d) Draw a bar-line graph to represent this data.

2 The number of empty seats on flights to Paris one day were:

23 58 4 33 9 41 10 26 52 12 25 8 56 37 40
31 11 22 45 18 25 5 52 28 5 38 47 20 8 28
 8 42 7 21 56 37 42 36 16 34 20 6 37 37 18
26 15 36 58 39 8 23 50 2 27 55 18 25 3 58

(a) Draw a frequency chart to represent this data.

(b) Copy and complete the stem and leaf diagram. The 40–49 group has been done for you.

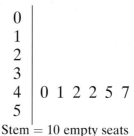

```
0 |
1 |
2 |
3 |
4 | 0 1 2 2 5 7
5 |
```
Stem = 10 empty seats

(c) Draw a bar chart to represent this data.

3 This table gives the marks out of sixty in a French oral.

16   30   44   35   41   19   50   43   37   35
31   14   21   7   24   33   38   25   28   17
42   35   47   36   15   48   52   46   55   36
17   54   28   36   23   11   32   8   16   57
58   45   9   51   49   50   42   20   54   41

(a) Draw a frequency chart to represent this data.

(b) Draw a stem and leaf diagram to represent this data.

(c) List the marks in the 40–49 group.

(d) Draw a horizontal bar chart to represent this data.

(e) In which group would you find the median?

> For a reminder about averages see Chapter 4.

4 This pictogram shows the number of letters delivered to a shop last week:

Monday	✉ ✉ ✉
Tuesday	✉ ✉ ✉ ✉
Wednesday	✉ ✉ ◺
Thursday	✉ ✉ ✉ ◺
Friday	✉ ✉ ✉ ✉ ✉
Saturday	✉ ◺

✉ represents 4 letters

(a) On which day were most letters delivered?

(b) How many letters were delivered altogether?

5 The table shows the number of years employees have worked with a firm:

No. of years	0–2	3–4	5–6	7–8	9–10	11–12	13–14	15–16	over 16
No. of employees	12	16	11	15	8	10	6	9	13

(a) Using ⚲ to represent 2 employees draw a pictogram to show this data.

(b) How many employees have worked six years or less?

6 The dual bar chart shows the number of parcels delivered to two firms:

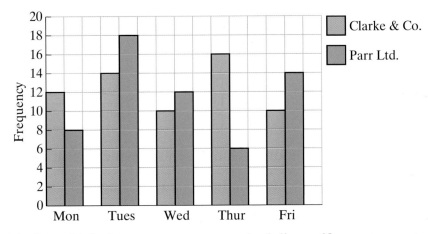

Clarke & Co.

Parr Ltd.

(a) On which day were most parcels delivered?

(b) Which firm had the least parcels delivered?

(c) How many parcels were delivered to Clarke & Co. on Thursday?

(d) How many parcels were delivered altogether?

7 A doctor holds morning and afternoon surgeries. The table shows the number of patients attending each surgery one week:

	Mon	Tues	Wed	Thur	Fri	Sat
Morning	24	20	25	31	27	17
Evening	32	26	19	24	30	Closed

(a) Draw a dual bar chart to represent this data.

(b) What is the average number of patients attending a surgery when it is open?

(c) How many more patients visited on Thursday than Tuesday?

When the surgery was closed no patients attended!

8 State whether each of the following is discrete or continuous data:
   (a) The length of a pea pod.   **(b)** The number of peas in a pod.
   (c) The age of a pupil.   **(d)** The height of a pupil.
   (e) The speed of a motorcycle.
   (f) The weight of a tube of sweets.
   (g) The number of red sweets in each tube.
   (h) The number of size six and a half shoes sold.

> Remember: Discrete data is data you can count. Continuous data is data you have to measure.

9 Draw line graphs to represent each of the following:
   (a) The maximum temperature, in degrees Celsius, over a seven month period.

Month	March	April	May	June	July	August	September
Temp.	18	20	21	23	28	30	24

   (b) The number of motorcycles sold over a seven month period.

Month	March	April	May	June	July	August	September
M/c sold	14	12	18	22	19	15	21

10 This table gives the monthly hours of sunshine in Bournemouth:

Month	March	April	May	June	July	August	September
Sunshine	130	155	185	210	240	230	195

   (a) Draw a line graph to represent this data.
   (b) Calculate: **(i)** the mean monthly sunshine **(ii)** the range.

8.3 Pie charts

■ **A pie chart uses a circle to represent data.**

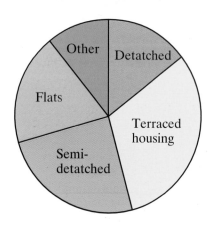

This pie chart shows the different types of housing in the St Mary's area.

The sections clearly show the proportion of people living in different types of housing.

Most people in St Mary's live in terraced housing.

Drawing a pie chart involves using angles to make the sections the correct sizes.

There are 360°
in a full circle.

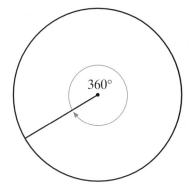

When dividing the pie chart into sections, you have to divide this 360° in the correct proportions.

Example 1

A warden made 30 sightings of wild animals during one of her visits to the wildlife preservation area. Use her table of results to draw a pie chart for this data.

Animal	Frequency
giraffe	4
wildebeest	15
lion	2
zebra	6
elephant	3

There were 30 sightings altogether. These will be represented by 360° in the pie chart.

Each sighting will be represented by

$$360° \div 30 = 12°$$

so   4 giraffes will be $4 \times 12° = 48°$
   15 wildebeest will be $15 \times 12° = 180°$
   2 lions will be $2 \times 12° = 24°$
   6 zebras will be $6 \times 12° = 72°$
   3 elephants will be $3 \times 12° = 36°$

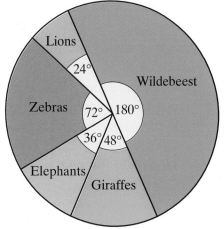

Exercise 8C

1   The pie chart shows which sport 36 pupils played yesterday.

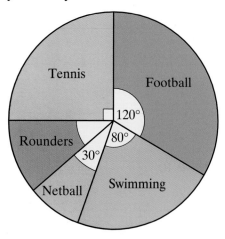

(a) What is the size of the missing angle?
(b) What angle represents one pupil?
(c) Copy and complete the table:

Sport	Angle on pie chart	Number of pupils
Football	120°	
Swimming	80°	
Netball	30°	3
Rounders		
Tennis		

2   This table shows the number of fruit trees in Hugh's garden:

(a) On a pie chart what angle would represent one tree?
(b) What angle would represent the cherry trees?
(c) Draw the pie chart.

Tree	Number
Apple	9
Pear	6
Cherry	4
Peach	3
Plum	2

3 The table shows the time, to the nearest hour, spent on homework last night for a class:

Time spent	0	1	2	3	4
No. of pupils	2	5	8	4	1

(a) How many pupils were there in the class?
(b) On a pie chart what angle would represent one pupil?
(c) Draw a pie chart to represent this data.

4 The table shows the main course chosen by pupils in Year 9:

Main course	Roast	Salad	Vegetarian	Curry	Fish	Rolls
No. of pupils	15	10	9	6	12	8

(a) Represent this data by drawing:
   (i) a pie chart   (ii) a bar chart.
(b) Comment on any advantage one chart has over the other.
(c) What proportion of the pupils chose:
   (i) curry   (ii) salad?

5 The papers bought by pupils yesterday were:

Paper	Daily Mail	The Sun	Telegraph	The Mirror	The Times
Number	6	24	18	20	4

(a) How many papers were bought?
(b) Represent this data using a pie chart.
(c) What proportion bought:
   (i) the Telegraph   (ii) the Sun?

6 Last week Riaz spent his pocket money:

School dinners	£2.50
Clothes	£6.00
Books and magazines	£3.00
Tuck shop	£2.00
Saved	£4.50

(a) Draw a pie chart to represent this data.
(b) What percentage of his pocket money did he save?

8.4 Scatter diagrams

Another useful way of comparing data is by drawing a
scatter diagram.

Example 2

The marks of ten pupils in an examination are shown in the table:

Paper 1	36	44	62	50	32	84	38	54	48	74
Paper 2	40	56	66	60	42	72	36	62	52	78

You can use the pairs of marks as
coordinate pairs on a diagram,

   e.g. $(36, 40)$
      $(44, 56)$

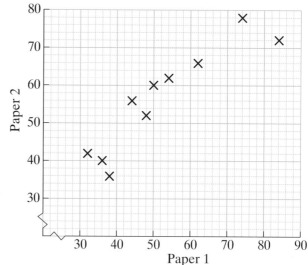

You can see that it looks like there
is a relationship between the marks.
For example, pupils who got high
marks on Paper 1 also got high
marks on Paper 2.

■ **The relationship between two sets of data is called correlation.**

These diagrams show different types of correlation:

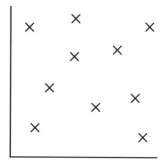

Positive correlation   **Negative correlation**   If there is **no correlation**
the points will be randomly
distributed.

Example 3

This table shows the time taken, in minutes, by groups of pupils to plant some trees:

No. in group	15	4	13	10	18	7	16	2	12	8
Time taken	12	22	13	18	9	21	7	27	11	17

(a) Draw a scatter graph.
(b) Describe the correlation.

(a)

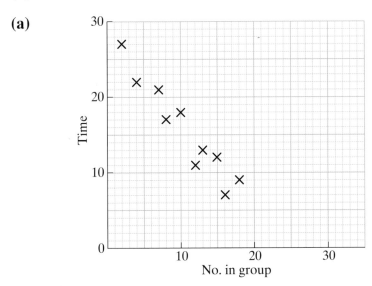

(b) There is negative correlation which means the more people in the group the less time it takes to plant the trees.

Example 4

This scatter graph shows the marks for two tests.
Describe the correlation between the two tests.

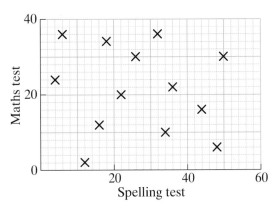

There is no obvious relationship between the tests, so there is no correlation.

Exercise 8D

1 The scatter graph shows the relationship between score and time taken on a general knowledge test.

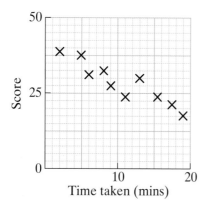

(a) What type of correlation is this?
(b) What does the correlation mean?
Give a reason for this correlation.

2 The table shows the height and diameter of a number of trees.

Height in metres	33	30	26	35	26	42	47	28	22	38
Diameter in cm	140	130	125	135	110	150	155	125	110	145

(a) Draw a scatter diagram to illustrate this data.
(b) What type of correlation is this?
(c) If a tree had a diameter of 105 cm what height would you expect it to be?

3 The table shows the scores in three rounds of a quiz:

General knowledge	30	58	29	11	47	66	31	70	55	44	20	38
People and places	33	63	40	31	56	57	51	63	49	42	38	45
Sport	21	37	20	18	40	51	38	54	36	30	28	39

(a) Draw scatter graphs to compare:
    (i) General knowledge and People and places.
    (ii) People and places and Sport.
(b) What type of correlation does each have?
(c) Comment on your findings.

4   **(a)** What type of correlation would you expect between each of the following:

  (i) Height and weight
  (ii) Distance left to travel and time taken
  (iii) Shoe size and height
  (iv) Number of library books borrowed and cars sold.

  (b) Sketch possible scatter graphs for the examples in part **(a)**.

5   This table shows marks from two Biology papers with some marks missing:

Paper 1	64	88	11		59	21	82	44	75		70	36	26
Paper 2	54	72	16	32	50	23		40	60	52	58	35	

  (a) Draw a scatter graph using the data available.
  (b) Estimate the missing marks.

8.5 Line of best fit

When there is good correlation it is often useful to draw a straight line along the slope of the points.

■   **A line which passes as closely as possible to all the plotted points on a scatter graph is called the line of best fit.**

Example 5

Here are 10 pupils' marks for two tests:

Paper 1	44	30	10	22	5	18	40	15	25	34
Paper 2	32	25	16	23	12	18	32	16	20	26

  (a) Plot the points using (Paper 1, Paper 2) as coordinates.
  (b) Draw a line of best fit.
  (c) Describe the correlation between the 2 tests.
  (d) If Georgina scored 30 on Paper 2, what would you expect her to get on Paper 1?
  (e) If Sherlena scored 8 on paper 1, what would you expect her to get on Paper 2?

(a), (b)

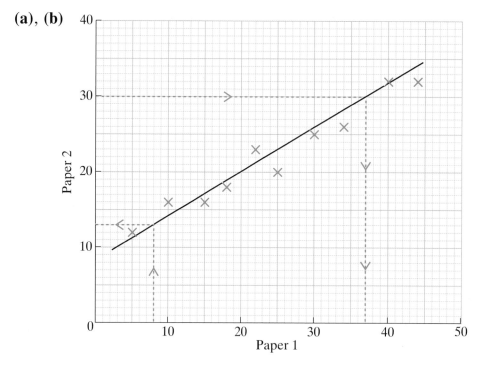

(c) There is a positive correlation between the marks for Paper 1 and Paper 2.

(d) Georgina would be expected to get about 37 on Paper 1.

(e) Sherlena would be expected to get about 13 on Paper 2.

Exercise 8E

1 Pupils are given a French written examination and an oral test. The marks were:

Written	50	41	60	74	64	49	70	81	36	54
Oral	11	9	12	16	14	13	15	18	8	12

(a) Draw a scatter diagram.

(b) Calculate the mean of the written exam and the oral test.

(c) Plot this point on your scatter diagram.

(d) Draw a line of best fit.

(e) Hannah scored 65 in her written exam. Predict her oral mark.

2 This table shows the marks obtained by twelve pupils in end of term tests:

Geography	35	16	58	32	14	21	11	31	43	36	47	10
Science	56	70	28	57	67	66	77	54	45	51	38	75
Maths	46	66	26	55	58	56	68	50	34	42	32	70
English	59	48	78	70	46	67	62	74	64	55	75	48
Art	45	59	31	52	40	60	55	42	30	44	34	36

(a) Draw scatter diagrams for each of the following. Place
the underlined subject on the x-axis in each case. Draw the lines of best fit.

   (i) <u>Geography</u> and Science

   (ii) <u>Geography</u> and English

   (iii) <u>Maths</u> and Science

   (iv) <u>English</u> and Art

   (v) <u>Science</u> and Art

(b) In each case state what kind of correlation there is, if any.

(c) Calculate the mean of each subject.

(d) Dennis scored 40 in Maths but was absent from
Science. Estimate the mark he might have got.

3 The marks for the Music and Physics practical tests are
given in the table:

Music	40	9	12	31	8	20	15	32	25	36
Physics	15	23	34	7	8	5	14	12	22	37

(a) Draw a scatter diagram to illustrate this data.

(b) Comment on the correlation.

8.6 Histograms

Bar charts are used to represent **discrete** data.

When **continuous** data is grouped into classes you can draw a histogram.

■ **Histograms display grouped continuous data.**

Histograms look like bar charts but there are no gaps between the bars. All the
bars on the histograms in this chapter have the same width.

If you do A-level maths you will come across histograms with different width
bars for different sized class intervals.

Example 6

This table shows the lengths of Mo's runner beans:

Length (cm)	0–4	5–9	10–14	15–19
Frequency	2	1	12	3

Draw a histogram to represent this data.

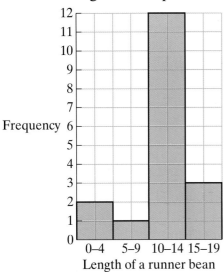

Length of a runner bean

There is one bar for each group of data. The class intervals are the same size so the bars are the same width. There are no gaps between them.

Exercise 8F

1   The length of thirty pencils to the nearest centimetre is given in the table:

Length	0–4	5–9	10–14	15–19	20–24
Number	4	8	10	7	1

(a) In which class interval would a pencil of length 14.7 cm be?

(b) Draw a histogram to represent this data.

2   The height of forty pupils, to the nearest centimetre, is given in the table.

Height	150–159	160–169	170–179	180–189	190–199	200–209
Number	3	6	9	12	8	2

(a) Janice is 169.4 cm tall. Which class interval would she be in?

(b) Draw a histogram to represent this data.

3 Soujit measured the height, in centimetres, of fifty
rockery plants. His results were:

16.4   3.6 10.6 18.4   7.8 15.9 10.6 20.1   7.2 25.4
23.5   5.4 15.0 11.6   2.4 17.7   6.7 12.8   3.9 16.4
10.2 16.1   9.7   7.3 23.4   8.3 11.5 24.8   6.2   4.7
 5.8 13.6 22.4 14.3   5.0 17.8   2.8 11.9 25.3   8.5
28.6   2.7 12.6   4.2 19.5   9.1 22.3 17.6 14.5 27.4

(a) Using 0–4, 5–9 etc. draw a frequency table.
(b) Draw a histogram to illustrate his findings.

4 The times taken by a group of pupils to complete a
spelling test are shown in the table:

Time (min)	0–4	5–9	10–14	15–19	20–24	25–29
No. of pupils	2	6	11	14	9	8

(a) How many pupils took the test?
(b) Which is the modal interval?
(c) Draw a histogram to represent this data.

5 The weight of deliveries to a butcher's shop
in a 90 day period is shown in the table:

Weight (kg)	30–34	35–39	40–44	45–49	50–54	55–59	60–64
Number	12	7	18	23	15	9	6

(a) How many goods weighed more than 49.5 kg?
(b) Draw a histogram to represent the deliveries.

6 State whether a bar chart or a histogram would
normally be drawn to illustrate each of the following:

(a) The number of houses built in each of the
first six months of the millenium in
Greenwich.
(b) How long it took to deliver papers each
day last week.
(c) The number of minutes the train stopped
at various stations.
(d) The number of chocolates in each of
twelve boxes.
(e) The lengths of a number of different
coloured rods.

8.7 Frequency polygons

■ **You can use frequency polygons to compare two sets of data.**

You draw a frequency polygon by joining the mid-points of a histogram.

These histograms show the ages of patients undergoing heart surgery at a local hospital in 1998 and 1999.

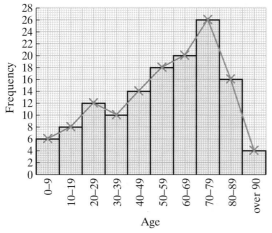
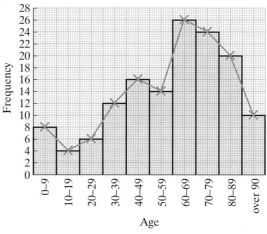

You can compare the data by drawing both frequency polygons on the same graph.

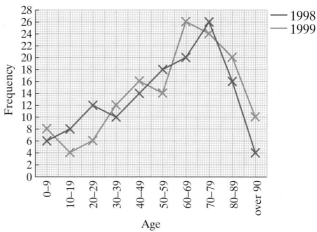

Exercise 8G

1   Two angling societies measured the length of each fish caught. The results were:

Length (cm)	0–4	5–9	10–14	15–19	20–24	25–29	30–34	35–39
Carpers	4	9	14	19	12	8	3	2
Trouters	2	5	8	15	22	14	9	4

(a) Draw a histogram to represent each society's results.
(b) Join the mid-points of each class interval to make a frequency polygon.
(c) Draw the two frequency polygons on the same graph.
(d) Comment on the differences.

2 The table shows the time, in minutes, taken by students from two schools to complete an obstacle course:

Time (min)	5–9	10–14	15–19	20–24	25–29	30–34
Redhill School	1	9	15	11	4	2
Bagshot School	2	5	10	14	8	4

(a) Draw frequency polygons to compare the data.
(b) Write three sentences to illustrate your findings.

3 Mandy measured the handspan, to the nearest centimetre, of everyone in Year 9 and recorded the results:

Handspan (cm)	15–17	18–20	21–23	24–26	27–29	30–32
Male	3	8	12	19	13	5
Female	6	11	16	9	7	1

(a) Draw frequency polygons to compare this data.
(b) Write three sentences to compare the results.

4 The table shows the number of packets of crisps the tuck shop sold at break time in June.

No. of packets	0–4	5–9	10–14	15–19	20–24	25–29	30–34	35–39
Upper school	4	7	11	10	15	12	5	2
Lower school	8	6	14	12	10	10	8	4

(a) Draw frequency polygons to illustrate this data.
(b) Write three conclusions you can make.
    Give your reasons.

5 The height, in centimetres, of eighty people from each
of two schools is given in the table:

Height (cm)	140–144	145–149	150–154	155–159	160–164	165–169	170–174	175–179
Overton	4	6	10	15	18	12	8	7
Redwall	5	9	14	20	15	11	4	2

(a) Draw histograms to illustrate this data.
(b) On the same grid draw frequency polygons.
(c) State three conclusions you can deduce from your
    results. Give your reasons.

Summary of key points

1 A pie chart uses a circle to represent data.

2 The relationship between two sets of data is called correlation.

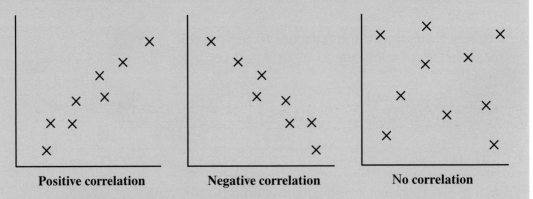

Positive correlation   Negative correlation   No correlation

3 A line which passes as closely as possible to all the plotted points on a
    scatter graph is called the line of best fit.

4 Histograms display grouped continuous data.

5 You can use frequency polygons to compare two sets of data.

9 Formulae and equations

Sir Isaac Newton used the formula
force = *mass* × *acceleration* to describe
the force needed to produce acceleration.

You need to be able to use formulae.

9.1 Substituting into formulae

■ **A formula is a general rule which allows
you to substitute numerical values to find a
solution to a particular problem.**

Example 1

Use the formula $P = 2(l + w)$ to work out the perimeter of
a rectangle with length (l) 4 cm and width (w) 2.5 cm.

$P = 2(l + w)$
$P = 2(4 + 2.5)$
$P = 2 \times 6.5$
$P = 13\,\text{cm}$

Don't forget **BIDMAS**.
Always work out the
brackets first.

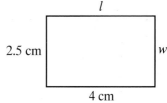

Exercise 9A

1 Use the formula $P = 2(l + w)$ to find the perimeter of
the rectangles:
(a) $l = 4, w = 3$ (b) $l = 5, w = 2$
(c) $l = 4, w = 3.5$ (d) $l = 2.5, w = 3.4$
(e) $l = 7, w = 1.6$ (f) $l = 10, w = 5.5$

2 Use the formula $A = 3r^2$ to find the approximate area
of these circles:
(a) $r = 2$ (b) $r = 5$ (c) $r = 2.5$ (d) $r = 1.6$

Don't forget $3r^2$
means $3 \times r^2$

3 The cost in pounds, C, of hiring a car is given by the
formula $C = 20 + 0.1m$ where m is the number of
miles travelled.
Work out the value of C if a car is hired and travels:
(a) 100 miles   (b) 50 miles   (c) 120 miles
(d) 70 miles   (e) 500 miles   (f) 1000 miles

4   The cost in pence, C, of making badges is given by the formula $C = 50 + 2n$ where n is the number of badges made. Work out the cost of making:
    (a) 10 badges   **(b)** 3 badges   **(c)** 100 badges
    (d) 1000 badges   **(e)** 50 badges   **(f)** 500 badges

5   Use the formula $y = 2(x^2 - 3)$ to work out the value of y when:
    (a) $x = 2$ **(b)** $x = 5$ **(c)** $x = 2.5$
    (d) $x = 3.2$ **(e)** $x = 1$ **(f)** $x = 0$

6   Use the formula $y = (x + 2)^2 - 5$ to work out the value of y when:
    (a) $x = 3$ **(b)** $x = 10$ **(c)** $x = 2$
    (d) $x = 0.5$ **(e)** $x = 8$ **(f)** $x = 0$

9.2 Using formulae with positive and negative numbers

Here are two thermometers. They are both measuring the same temperatures. One is marked in degrees Celsius (°C) and the other is marked in degrees Fahrenheit (°F).

To change from °C to °F you can use the formula:

$$F = \frac{9}{5}C + 32$$

Example 2

Use the formula to change these temperatures in °C to °F:
(a) $0\,°C$ (b) $15\,°C$ (c) $-10\,°C$

(a) $F = \dfrac{9}{5} \times 0 + 32$ (b) $F = \dfrac{9}{\overset{}{\underset{1}{5}}} \times \overset{3}{\cancel{15}} + 32$ (c) $F = \dfrac{9}{\overset{}{\underset{1}{5}}} \times \overset{-2}{-\cancel{10}} + 32$

$\quad\quad F = 0 + 32$ $F = 27 + 32$ $F = -18 + 32$

$\quad\quad F = 32\,°F$ $F = 59\,°F$ $F = 14\,°F$

Exercise 9B

1   Use the formula $F = \frac{9}{5}C + 32$ to change these
temperatures in °C to °F.
   (a) 5 °C   **(b)** 20 °C   **(c)** 25 °C   **(d)** −20 °C
   (e) −5 °C   **(f)** −40 °C   **(g)** 100 °C   **(h)** −30 °C

2   Use the formula $C = \frac{5}{9}(F - 32)$ to change these
temperatures in °F to °C.
   (a) 32 °F   **(b)** 50 °F   **(c)** 68 °F   **(d)** 212 °F
   (e) 0 °F   **(f)** −4 °F   **(g)** −22 °F   **(h)** 14 °F

Hint:
remember
BIDMAS.

3   The formula $s = ut + \frac{1}{2}at^2$ is used to work out the
distance s travelled after time t under an acceleration a
with initial velocity u. Use the formula to work out
when:
   (a) $t = 5, a = 10, u = 0$
   (b) $t = 5, a = -10, u = 0$
   (c) $t = 3, a = 4, u = 5$
   (d) $t = 10, a = -5, u = 20$
   (e) $t = 3, a = -10, u = -10$
   (f) $t = 2, a = 0, u = 3$

4   The formula $v = u + at$ is used to work out the velocity
of an object that travels for t seconds under
acceleration a. The initial velocity is u.
Work out v when:
   (a) $u = 0, a = 5, t = 2$
   (b) $u = 10, a = 5, t = 2$
   (c) $u = 5, a = -10, t = 3$
   (d) $u = -5, a = -2, t = 10$
   (e) $u = 10, a = 0, t = 3$
   (f) $u = -10, a = -10, t = 2.5$

5   The formula $F = \dfrac{mv^2}{r}$ is used to describe
motion in a circle. Work out F when:
   (a) $m = 6, v = 2, r = 8$
   (b) $m = 8, v = 1, r = 2$
   (c) $m = 2, v = -3, r = 8$
   (d) $m = 3, v = -2, r = 6$
   (e) $m = 1.5, v = -1, r = 3$
   (f) $m = 9, v = -8, r = 18$

6 Use the formula $y = (x - 3)^2$ to work out the value of y when:

    (a) $x = 5$ **(b)** $x = 10$ **(c)** $x = 2$ **(d)** $x = 1.5$

    (e) $x = -2$ **(f)** $x = -1$ **(g)** $x = -1.5$ **(h)** $x = 1.2$

9.3 Writing your own formulae

You need to be able to write your own formulae.

Example 3

A rectangle is twice as long as it is wide.
Write down a formula for the perimeter and use it to find
the perimeter when the width is 2 cm.

First draw a diagram.
Then, let the width be x
so the length will be $2 \times x$ or $2x$.

$$\text{Perimeter } P = x + 2x + x + 2x$$
$$P = 6x$$

When the width is 2 cm, $P = 6 \times 2 = 12$ cm.

Example 4

Rosa is paid each Friday. She receives
£4.50 for each hour she works. Each week
she gives £12 to her favourite charity.
Write down a formula for the amount she
has left each week.

The formula is:
Amount left $= £4.50 \times$ *Hours worked* $- £12$
$$A = 4.5H - 12$$

Exercise 9C

1 A rectangle is three times as long as it is wide. Write
down a formula for the perimeter.
Use your formula to find the perimeter when the width is:
    (a) 2 cm   **(b)** 5 cm   **(c)** 10 cm **(d)** 2.5 cm **(e)** 1.2 cm

2 The two equal sides of an isosceles triangle are twice as long as the other side. Write down a formula for the perimeter and use it to find the perimeter when the length of the shortest side is:

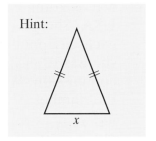

Hint:

(a) 2 cm   (b) 5 cm   (c) 10 cm
(d) 2.5 cm   (e) 2.4 cm   (f) 3.2 cm

3 A rectangle is twice as long as it is wide. Write down a formula for the *area* of the rectangle and use it to find the area when the width is:

(a) 2 cm   (b) 10 cm   (c) 4 cm
(d) 3.5 cm   (e) 1.8 cm   (f) 4.5 cm

4 Year 9 are producing a school newsletter. The cost of printing is 8p per sheet plus the setting up cost of £16.

(a) Write the setting up cost in pence.
(b) Write down a formula for the cost of printing *n* sheets.
(c) Use your formula to work out the cost (in pounds and pence) of printing:
    (i)   100 sheets
    (ii) 50 sheets
    (iii) 1000 sheets
    (iv) 30 sheets.

5 The cost of hiring a car is £30 plus 20p per mile. Write down a formula for the cost of hiring a car and travelling *m* miles. Use your formula to work out the cost (in pounds and pence) of travelling:

(a) 100 miles   (b) 200 miles   (c) 60 miles
(d) 150 miles   (e) 500 miles   (f) 20 miles

6 A rectangle is 2 cm longer than it is wide. Write a formula for the perimeter of the rectangle. Use your formula to work out the perimeter when the width is:

(a) 4 cm   (b) 1.2 cm   (c) 6 cm
(d) 22 cm   (e) 19.5 cm   (f) 3.5 cm

7   Mel is going on holiday to the USA. She gets 1.5 US dollars for each UK pound she changes, but she has to pay a 2 dollar commission. Write a formula for the number of dollars she gets, and use your formula to work out how much she gets for:

(a) 3 pounds
(b) 20 pounds
(c) 9 pounds
(d) 80 pounds
(e) 63 pounds.

9.4 Solving equations

An **equation** is a mathematical sentence.

■   **Every equation has a letter in it. Finding a number value for that letter which makes the sentence true is called *solving the equation*.**

■   **The letter in an equation represents an unknown value. It is called a variable.**

> The equation $x + 3 = 9$ is only true if $x = 6$. The **solution** to this equation is $x = 6$.

Equations with one operation

Example 5

Solve $x + 5 = 7$
(-5 from each side) $x = 7 - 5$
                         $x = 2$

> You can think of an equation as a balance:
>
> $x + 5$ 7
>   ▲
>
> -5 is the inverse of $+5$ so you take 5 from both sides. The equation still balances.
>
> x $7 - 5$
>   ▲

Example 6

Solve $\quad 3x = 12$

$(\div 3) \qquad x = 12 \div 3$

$\qquad\qquad x = 4$

$\div 3$ is the inverse of $\times 3$

■ **When you solve an equation using a balance you are using inverse operations.**

Exercise 9D

1 Find the value of the letter in each of these equations:

(a) $x + 3 = 6$ (b) $x + 5 = 8$ (c) $x + 3 = 2$

(d) $a + 5 = 2$ (e) $b - 3 = 6$ (f) $c - 3 = 2$

(g) $d - 5 = 1$ (h) $e - 6 = -2$ (i) $3f = 9$

(j) $4g = 8$ (k) $7h = 28$ (l) $3p = 2$

(m) $\dfrac{x}{5} = 2$ (n) $\dfrac{y}{3} = 2$ (o) $\dfrac{z}{4} = 8$

(p) $\dfrac{c}{3} = \dfrac{1}{2}$ (q) $a + 3 = -5$ (r) $a - 6 = -10$

(s) $4r = -12$ (t) $5p = -20$ (u) $\dfrac{x}{3} = -2$

Don't forget:
$-$ is the inverse of $+$
$+$ is the inverse of $-$
$\div$ is the inverse of $\times$
$\times$ is the inverse of $\div$
$\dfrac{x}{3}$ means $x \div 3$

Equations with two operations

When you have two operations in an equation you must eliminate numbers after the $+$ or $-$ first.

Then you can deal with the term containing the variable (letter).

$2x + 5 = 7$

Deal with the $+5$ first.

Example 7

Solve $\qquad\qquad 3x - 5 = -17$

$(+5 \text{ to each side}) \qquad 3x = -17 + 5$

$\qquad\qquad\qquad\quad 3x = -12$

$(\div 3) \qquad\qquad\qquad x = -4$

Deal with the -5 first by $+5$. Then deal with $3x$ by $\div 3$: $-12 \div 3 = -4$.

Exercise 9E

1   Solve these equations:
   (a) $2x + 1 = 7$ **(b)** $3x - 2 = 7$
   (c) $3p + 5 = 23$ **(d)** $5x - 2 = 8$
   (e) $2p + 5 = 3$ **(f)** $5p - 2 = -12$
   (g) $10p + 2 = 7$ **(h)** $7r - 3 = 4$
   (i) $5x - 1 = 4$ **(j)** $3p + 5 = -1$
   (k) $3q + 7 = 7$ **(l)** $2r - 3 = -3$
   (m) $3x - 2 = 13$ **(n)** $2t + 1 = 2$
   (o) $2t + 1 = -2$ **(p)** $5b + 2 = 4$
   (q) $3c - 2 = -5$ **(r)** $2g + 3 = -4$
   (s) $3h - 3 = 1$ **(t)** $5p - 1 = 3$
   (u) $2x + 2 = 11$

Equations with brackets

■   **When equations have brackets, always multiply out the brackets before solving the equation.**

Example 8

Solve $2(x + 3) = 7$
Multiply out the brackets first: $2x + 6 = 7$

> Don't forget: $2(x + 3)$ means multiply each term inside the bracket by 2.

Then solve the equation:
(-6) $2x = 7 - 6$
                $2x = 1$
$(\div 2)$ $x = \frac{1}{2}$ or 0.5

> Subtract 6 from each side. Divide each side by 2.

Exercise 9F

1   Solve these equations:
   (a) $2(x + 1) = 6$ **(b)** $3(x - 1) = 12$ **(c)** $5(x + 2) = 10$
   (d) $5(x - 1) = 15$ **(e)** $4(p - 2) = 8$ **(f)** $3(q + 1) = 15$
   (g) $3(c + 2) = 18$ **(h)** $5(p - 1) = 10$ **(i)** $7(r + 2) = 7$
   (j) $2(r + 7) = 14$ **(k)** $3(p - 7) = 3$ **(l)** $5(r + 1) = 10$
   (m) $10(x + 1) = 20$ **(n)** $3(p + 2) = 21$ **(o)** $5(x + 2) = 5$
   (p) $7(b - 6) = 14$ **(q)** $5(c - 2) = 15$ **(r)** $3(t + 5) = 3$
   (s) $2(r + 5) = 4$ **(t)** $3(t - 1) = -6$ **(u)** $5(g - 2) = -15$

Equations with the variable on both sides

Sometimes you will have to solve equations where the variable (letter) appears on both sides of the equals sign.

■ **To solve equations with the letter on both sides you need to keep the letter on the side of the equation that has the biggest number of letters.**

Example 9

Solve the equation $5x + 3 = 2x + 9$

You need the letter on one side of the equation. Subtract $2x$ from both sides of the equation.

$(-2x) \qquad 5x + 3 - 2x = 9$

Now solve the equation in the normal way.

$$3x + 3 = 9$$
$(-3) \qquad\qquad 3x = 6$
$(\div 3) \qquad\qquad\; x = 2$

> $2x$ is smaller than $5x$ so you keep the letter on the left-hand side of the equation.

> $5x - 2x = 3x$
> $9 - 3 = 6$
> $6 \div 3 = 2$

Example 10

Solve the equation $\qquad 2x + 2 = 5 - 3x$
$(+3x) \qquad\qquad 2x + 2 + 3x = 5$
$\qquad\qquad\qquad\quad 5x + 2 = 5$
$(-2) \qquad\qquad\qquad 5x = 3$
$(\div 5) \qquad\qquad\qquad\; x = \frac{3}{5}$ or 0.6

> $2x$ is bigger than $-3x$ so you keep the letter on the left-hand side of the equation.

Exercise 9G

1   Solve these equations:
   (a) $2x + 1 = x + 2$
   (b) $3x + 2 = 2x + 5$
   (c) $5x - 2 = 4x + 3$
   (d) $4x - 3 = 3x + 5$
   (e) $7x + 2 = 8x - 3$
   (f) $6x + 2 = 5x - 9$
   (g) $3y + 2 = 4y - 3$
   (h) $5p - 3 = 3p + 5$
   (i) $4p + 5 = 2p + 9$
   (j) $7p - 3 = 4p + 6$
   (k) $3x + 2 = 7 - 2x$
   (l) $4x + 3 = 5x - 2$
   (m) $7p - 3 = 8p + 5$
   (n) $2p + 3 = -2p + 19$
   (o) $3x + 6 = 5 - 4x$
   (p) $8x - 2 = 10x + 8$
   (q) $3p - 5 = 5 - 2p$
   (r) $7r - 3 = 5 + 3r$
   (s) $3r + 2 = 5 - 4r$
   (t) $12 - 5r = 5 - 2r$

> Hint: In (e) you should subtract $7x$ from both sides, leaving the variable on the right-hand side.

9.5 Writing and solving your own equations

You need to be able to solve problems with algebra by writing your own equations.

Example 11

Karl thinks of a number,
doubles it and adds 5.
His answer is 27.
What is the number?

Call the number Karl thinks of x
He doubles it so it becomes $2x$
He adds 5 so it becomes $2x + 5$
The answer is 27 so the equation is

$$2x + 5 = 27$$

You can then solve this equation.

$$2x + 5 = 27$$
$(-5) \qquad 2x = 27 - 5 = 22$
$(\div 2) \qquad x = 11$

Karl's number was 11.

Example 12

Rajit thinks of a number. He adds 5 and then multiplies by 2. His answer is 27. What is the number?

Let x be the number.
Add 5 to x so it becomes $x + 5$
Double it so it becomes $2(x + 5)$
The answer is 27 so $2(x + 5) = 27$

Solve the equation $\qquad 2x + 10 = 27$
$(-10) \qquad\qquad\qquad 2x = 17$
$(\div 2) \qquad\qquad\qquad x = 8\frac{1}{2}$ or 8.5

Rajit's number was $8\frac{1}{2}$.

> Don't forget:
> $2 \times (x + 5)$ must have a bracket.

Exercise 9H

Write an equation and use it to solve these problems:

1   Bob thought of a number. He added 5. His answer was 22. What was the number?

2 Zac thought of a number. He took away 7. His answer was 12. What was the number?

3 Sue thought of a number. She doubled it and added 5. Her answer was 35. What was the number?

4 Adam thought of a number. He multiplied it by 3 and took away 7. His answer was 25.
What was the number?

5 Helen thought of a number. She added 5 and then doubled it. Her answer was 24.
What was the number?

6 Robyn thought of a number. She added 10 and then multiplied by 3. Her answer was 36.
What was the number?

7 The perimeter of this isosceles triangle is 16 cm.
Work out the value of x.

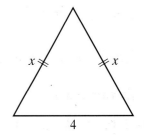

8 The length of the sides of a triangle are consecutive numbers. The perimeter is 12 cm.
What are the lengths of the sides?

Hint:

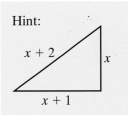

9 The difference between the length and width of a rectangle is 5 cm. The perimeter of the rectangle is 50 cm. What are the dimensions of the rectangle?

10 The difference between the length and width of another rectangle is 4 cm. The perimeter of the rectangle is 28 cm.
Work out the area of the rectangle.

9.6 Inequalities

This is Mark's stall. He has lots of apples but only a few cauliflowers. If a is the number of apples and c is the number of cauliflowers, then a **is greater than** c.

Mathematically, this is written as:

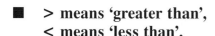

> This statement reads 'a is greater than c'. You always read inequalities from left to right, just like ordinary sentences.

- \> means 'greater than',
  \< means 'less than'.

> The thinner end points towards the smaller number. The thicker end points towards the larger number.

Example 13

Put the correct sign between these numbers:

(a) 7, 10
7 is less than 10
$7 < 10$

(b) 3, −4
3 is greater than −4
$3 > -4$

Example 14

Write down all the integers that satisfy both of these inequalities:

$$x > 3, \qquad x < 8$$

x must be greater than 3 and less than 8 so there are 4 numbers. The answer is 4, 5, 6, 7.

> Remember:
> An integer is a positive or negative whole number.

> A number **satisfies** an inequality if it makes that inequality true.
>
> $x = 3$ satisfies the inequality $x < 7$ because $3 < 7$.

Exercise 9I

1   Put the correct sign between these numbers to make a
    true statment:
    (a) 7, 4   **(b)** 3, 6   **(c)** 5, 0
    (d) 0, 7   **(e)** 3.5, 3   **(f)** −2, 0
    (g) 2, −2   **(h)** −5, −3   **(i)** −4, −8
    (j) 7, −10   **(k)** −1, −3   **(l)** −2, −4
    (m) −5, −1   **(n)** 2, −5   **(o)** 0.95, 1

2   Write down whether these statements are true or false.
    If they are false, write down the correct sign between
    the numbers.
    (a) $4 > 7$ **(b)** $7 > 4$ **(c)** $0 > -2$
    (d) $-2 < -1$ **(e)** $5 > -1$ **(f)** $-1 < 2$
    (g) $-1 < -5$ **(h)** $6 < 8$ **(i)** $4 > 9$
    (j) $3.5 < 5.3$ **(k)** $6.2 > 6.15$ **(l)** $4.9 > 5$
    (m) $-0.5 > 1$ **(n)** $-0.5 < -0.4$ **(o)** $-3 < -3.1$

3   Write down all the integers that satisfy both of these
    inequalities.
    (a) $x > 2, x < 7$ **(b)** $x > 0, x < 4$
    (c) $x > -2, x < 2$ **(d)** $x > -5, x < -1$
    (e) $x > 0, x < 7$ **(f)** $x > -2, x < 4$
    (g) $x < 4, x > 2$ **(h)** $x < 3, x > -2$
    (i) $x < 0, x > -5$ **(j)** $x < 7, x > -1$

9.7 Inequalities on a number line

A good way of showing inequalities is by shading a number
line.

Example 15

Draw a number line from 0 to 10. Shade in the inequality
    $x > 6$.

x is greater than 6 so you circle the 6 and shade the rest of
the number line up to 10:

6 is not included so
you use an open
circle, O.

Example 16

Draw a number line from −5 to +5.
Shade in the inequalities
$$x > -2 \text{ and } x < 3.$$

x is greater than −2 and less than 3 so you circle the −2 and 3 and shade between them.

> Another way of writing this is
> $-2 < x < 3$
> This means x is between −2 and 3.

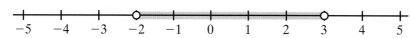

Exercise 9J

1 Draw 5 number lines from 0 to 10. Shade in these inequalities:

   (a) $x > 4$ **(b)** $x < 4$ **(c)** $x > 5$
   (d) $x < 2$ **(e)** $x > 1$

2 Draw 4 number lines from 0 to 10. Shade in these inequalities

   (a) $x > 3$ and $x < 7$
   (b) $x > 4$ and $x < 8$
   (c) $x < 7$ and $x > 2$
   (d) $x < 5$ and $x > 4$

3 Draw 6 number lines from −5 to +5. Shade in the inequalities:

   (a) $-1 < x < 2$
   (b) $-3 < x < 3$
   (c) $-2 < x < 4$
   (d) $-3 < x < -1$
   (e) $-1 < x < 1$
   (f) $1 < x < 3$

4 Write down the inequalities represented by the shading on these number lines:

   (a)
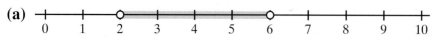

   (b)
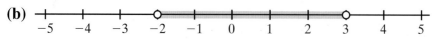

   (c)
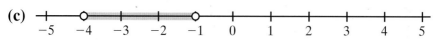

9.8 Solving inequalities

The two sides of an equation do not
always balance.
An equation that doesn't balance is called
an inequality.

■ **You can solve inequalities using
inverse operations.**

Example 17

Solve the inequality $2x + 1 > 5$

You solve an inequality in the same way as you solve an
equation.
First eliminate the $+1$ by subtracting 1 from each side:

(-1) $2x > 5 - 1$

             $2x > 4$

$(\div 2)$ $x > 4 \div 2$

             $x > 2$

The answer is $x > 2$.

> You should keep
> the letter on the
> left-hand side of the
> inequality.

Exercise 9K

1   Solve these inequalities:

   (a) $x + 4 > 6$ **(b)** $x - 3 < 2$

   (c) $x + 5 > 6$ **(d)** $x + 4 < 2$

   (e) $x - 5 > 3$ **(f)** $2x > 8$

   (g) $3x < 12$ **(h)** $\dfrac{x}{2} > 4$

   (i) $\dfrac{x}{7} < 2$ **(j)** $5x < -10$

   (k) $\dfrac{x}{3} > -2$ **(l)** $2x + 1 < 7$

   (m) $2x - 1 > 5$ **(n)** $3x + 4 < 7$

   (o) $5x - 2 > 8$ **(p)** $3p - 2 < 4$

   (q) $5r - 3 < 2$ **(r)** $7x - 2 < 12$

9.9 Solving equations by trial and improvement

Sometimes it's not possible to work out an exact solution to an equation.

You can get very close to the answer by first guessing and then improving your guess. This is called solving by **trial and improvement**.

I think the answer is 3.

I think 3.5 is closer.

Example 18

Solve $x^2 - x = 10$ by trial and improvement.
Give your answer correct to one decimal place.

You know that 3^2 is 9 so $x = 3$ might be a good first guess:
$$3^2 - 3 = 9 - 3 = 6.$$ This answer is too small.

Try $x = 4$:
$$4^2 - 4 = 16 - 4 = 12.$$ This answer is too big.

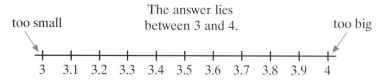

too small

The answer lies between 3 and 4.

too big

3   3.1   3.2   3.3   3.4   3.5   3.6   3.7   3.8   3.9   4

Try half way between 3 and 4, that is $x = 3.5$:
$$3.5^2 - 3.5 = 12.25 - 3.5 = 8.75$$ Too small

Use a calculator for more complicated values of x.

The answer lies between 3.5 and 4. Try $x = 3.7$:
$$3.7^2 - 3.7 = 9.99$$ Too small, but not by much.

Try 3.8:
$$3.8^2 - 3.8 = 10.64$$ Too big.

So the solution correct to one decimal place must be either $x = 3.7$ or $x = 3.8$.

To check which is the answer, you have to check half way between.

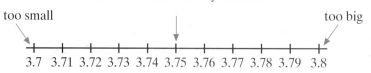

too small

too big

3.7   3.71   3.72   3.73   3.74   3.75   3.76   3.77   3.78   3.79   3.8

You should always check the half way point in the next decimal place.

$$3.75^2 - 3.75 = 10.3125$$ Too big.

So the answer must lie between 3.7 and 3.75.

The solution correct to one decimal place is $x = 3.7$.

It is helpful to set out your calculations in the form of a table.

Example 19

Solve $x^2 + x = 13$ by trial and improvement. Give your answer correct to one decimal place.

Value of x	Value of $x^2 + x$	Results compared with 13	The solution lies between
3	$3^2 + 3 = 12$	Too small	
4	$4^2 + 4 = 20$	Too big	3 and 4
3.5	$3.5^2 + 3.5 = 15.75$	Too big	3 and 3.5
3.2	$3.2^2 + 3.2 = 13.44$	Too big	3 and 3.2
3.1	$3.1^2 + 3.1 = 12.71$	Too small	3.1 and 3.2
3.15	$3.15^2 + 3.15 = 13.0725$	Too big	3.1 and 3.15

The solution correct to one decimal place is $x = 3.1$.

Exercise 9L

1   Solve these equations by trial and improvement. Give your answers correct to one decimal place.
    (a) $x^2 - x = 5$ **(b)** $x^2 + x = 7$
    (c) $x^2 + 2x = 30$ **(d)** $x^3 = 10$
    (e) $x^2 = 8$ **(f)** $x^2 - 3x = 5$

2   A square has an area of $30 \, cm^2$. What is the length of each side? Give your answer correct to one decimal place.

3   The volume of a cube is $100 \, cm^3$. What is the length of the edge of the cube? Give your answer correct to one decimal place.

4   The area of this shape is
    $1.5x^2 + 0.5x$
    Work out the value of x if
    the area of the shape is $50 \, cm^2$.
    Give your answer to one decimal place.

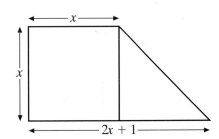

Summary of key points

1   A formula is a general rule which allows you to substitute numerical values to find a solution to a particular problem.

2   Every equation has a letter in it. Finding a number value for that letter which makes the sentence true is called solving the equation.

3   The letter in an equation represents an unknown value. It is called a variable.

4   When you solve an equation using a balance you are using inverse operations.

5   When equations have brackets, always multiply out the brackets before solving the equation.

6   To solve equations with the letter on both sides you need to keep the letter on the side of the equation that has the biggest number of letters.

7    $>$ means 'greater than'   The thinner end
     $<$ means 'less than'   points towards the
                                      smaller number.
                                      The thicker end
                                      points towards the
                                      larger number.

8   You can solve inequalities using inverse operations.

10 Fractions and ratio

People have been calculating with fractions for centuries. Ancient documents from Egypt and Babylon reveal that fractions were used for weighing and dividing four thousand years ago!

10.1 Mixed numbers and improper fractions

Fractions and mixed numbers are used in everyday life to describe all kinds of things.

Korangi Rice

Soak $2\frac{1}{4}$ cups of basmati rice for at least $\frac{1}{2}$ hour.
Fry $\frac{1}{3}$ of the onions, the zeera and a clove of garlic until soft.
Then add the drained rice, peas and $4\frac{1}{2}$ cups of water.
Mix in about $\frac{1}{4}$ teaspoon of chilli powder and $\frac{1}{2}$ tablespoon of salt

This recipe uses fractions to describe the amounts of the ingredients used.

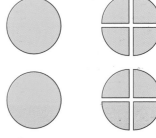

This car takes $9\frac{1}{2}$ gallons of petrol for a full tank.

You can also write mixed numbers as improper fractions.

Improper fractions are also sometimes called 'top-heavy' fractions.

For example $2\frac{1}{4} = 1 + 1 + \frac{1}{4}$

$$= \frac{4}{4} + \frac{4}{4} + \frac{1}{4}$$

$$= \frac{4 + 4 + 1}{4}$$

$$= \frac{9}{4}$$

$2\frac{1}{4} \qquad = \qquad \frac{9}{4}$

Similarly, an improper fraction can be written as a mixed number.

$$\frac{25}{9} = \frac{9+9+7}{9}$$

$$= \frac{9}{9} + \frac{9}{9} + \frac{7}{9}$$

$$= 1 + 1 + \frac{7}{9}$$

$$= 2\frac{7}{9}$$

- ■ **A mixed number has a whole number part and a fraction part. For example: $1\frac{1}{3}, 9\frac{1}{2}, 2\frac{1}{4}$.**
- ■ **An improper fraction has the numerator bigger than the denominator. For example: $\frac{5}{2}, \frac{8}{3}, \frac{19}{7}$.**

Example 1

Change $\frac{11}{5}$ to a mixed number.

$$\frac{11}{5} = \frac{5}{5} + \frac{5}{5} + \frac{1}{5}$$

$$= 1 + 1 + \frac{1}{5}$$

$$= 2\frac{1}{5}$$

$11 \div 5 = 2$ with a remainder of 1 part
$\frac{11}{5} = 2\frac{1}{5}$

Example 2

Write $3\frac{1}{4}$ as an improper fraction.

3 is $1 + 1 + 1$, so $3 = \frac{4}{4} + \frac{4}{4} + \frac{4}{4}$

$3\frac{1}{4} = \frac{4}{4} + \frac{4}{4} + \frac{4}{4} + \frac{1}{4} = \frac{13}{4}$

There are 4 quarters in 1 so there are 12 quarters in 3; plus 1 extra quarter makes thirteen quarters.

Exercise 10A

1   Change these improper fractions into mixed numbers:

(a) $\frac{12}{5}$ (b) $\frac{19}{3}$ (c) $\frac{9}{5}$ (d) $\frac{11}{7}$

2 Change these mixed numbers into improper fractions:

(a) $2\frac{1}{5}$ **(b)** $7\frac{1}{2}$ **(c)** $3\frac{7}{8}$ **(d)** $1\frac{11}{12}$

3 Put these mixed numbers and fractions in descending order:

$$1\frac{1}{2}, \ \frac{100}{99}, \ \frac{9}{4}, \ 5\frac{1}{6}, \ 2\frac{2}{3}$$

> Descending means starting at the top and going down.

4 Write these numbers in ascending order:

$$\frac{17}{8}, \ 2\frac{5}{6}, \ \frac{4}{3}, \ \frac{10}{3}, \ 2\frac{1}{2}$$

> Ascending means starting at the bottom and working up.

5

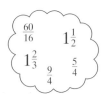
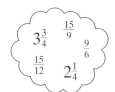

For each fraction in the first cloud, find a fraction in the second cloud with the same value.

> Remember: you can find equivalent fractions by multiplying or dividing the top and bottom of a fraction by the same number.

10.2 Simplifying fractions

$\frac{3}{4}, \frac{6}{8}, \frac{9}{12}, \ldots, \frac{45}{60}, \ldots$ are all equivalent fractions.

They all have the same value.

$\frac{3}{4}$ is the simplest form of this set of fractions.

■ **Fractions can be simplified if the numerator and the denominator have a common factor greater than 1.**

> Simplifying fractions is sometimes called cancelling.

Example 3

Write $\frac{18}{21}$ in its simplest form.

Factors of 18: 1, 2, **3**, 6, 9, 18
Factors of 21: 1, **3**, 7, 21

3 is the highest common factor of 18 and 21.

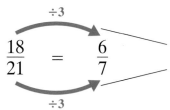

$\div 3$

$\dfrac{18}{21} = \dfrac{6}{7}$

$\div 3$

To reduce a fraction to its simplest form, you divide the numerator and the denominator by the highest common factor.

$\frac{18}{21} = \frac{6}{7}$ in its simplest form.

Exercise 10B

1 Find the highest common factor of these pairs of numbers:

Hint: Write down all the factors of each number first.

(a) 9, 36   **(b)** 5, 30   **(c)** 16, 24

(d) 51, 6   **(e)** 8, 48

2 Write each of these fractions in its simplest form:

(a) $\frac{9}{12}$ **(b)** $\frac{15}{27}$ **(c)** $\frac{16}{32}$

(d) $\frac{10}{25}$ **(e)** $\frac{6}{21}$

3 Cancel these fractions where possible:

(a) $\frac{18}{36}$ **(b)** $\frac{17}{51}$ **(c)** $\frac{11}{12}$

(d) $\frac{25}{28}$ **(e)** $\frac{22}{23}$

4 Write these improper fractions as mixed numbers in their simplest form:

(a) $\frac{24}{20}$ **(b)** $\frac{50}{8}$ **(c)** $\frac{63}{49}$

(d) $\frac{28}{14}$ **(e)** $\frac{20}{12}$

10.3 Adding and subtracting mixed numbers

Mixed numbers often occur in recipes and when describing times and distances.

"If I visit Amphill then Borford I'll have covered $1\frac{1}{2}$ miles + $2\frac{1}{5}$ miles."

"If I add another packet of flour I'll have $1\frac{1}{2}$ lb + 1 lb."

Adding mixed numbers

■ **To add mixed numbers add the whole number part
and then add the fractions.**

Example 4

Work out

$1\frac{1}{2} + 2\frac{1}{5}$

First add the whole numbers:

$1 + 2 = 3$

Then add the fractions using equivalent fractions:

$\frac{1}{2} + \frac{1}{5} = \frac{5}{10} + \frac{2}{10} = \frac{7}{10}$

2 and 5 are both
factors of 10

> Remember:
> To add or subtract
> fractions with different
> denominators find
> equivalent fractions with
> the same denominator.

$1\frac{1}{2} + 2\frac{1}{5} = 3 + \frac{7}{10} = 3\frac{7}{10}$

Example 5

Fiona and Noel bought $1\frac{3}{8}$ metres of wood for a kitchen
unit. They then decided to make another unit so had to
buy $3\frac{1}{5}$ metres of wood. How much wood did they buy
altogether?

The total amount of wood is:

$1\frac{3}{8} + 3\frac{1}{5}$

$1 + 3 = 4$

8 and 5 are both
factors of 40

$\frac{3}{8} + \frac{1}{5} = \frac{15}{40} + \frac{8}{40} = \frac{23}{40}$

$1\frac{3}{8} + 3\frac{1}{5} = 4\frac{23}{40}$

Altogether they bought $4\frac{23}{40}$ metres of wood.

Subtracting mixed numbers

■ **To subtract mixed numbers change them into improper fractions.**

Example 6

Tony wants to know the difference between the two distances $1\frac{1}{2}$ miles and $2\frac{1}{5}$ miles.

He needs to subtract $1\frac{1}{2}$ from $2\frac{1}{5}$.

Change the mixed numbers into improper fractions:

$2\frac{1}{5} = \frac{11}{5}$ and $1\frac{1}{2} = \frac{3}{2}$

$2\frac{1}{5} - 1\frac{1}{2} = \frac{11}{5} - \frac{3}{2} = \frac{22}{10} - \frac{15}{10} = \frac{7}{10}$

The difference between the two distances is $\frac{7}{10}$ mile.

Example 7

Ben and Levi ran an 800 metre race. Ben's time was $3\frac{1}{5}$ minutes and Levi's time was $1\frac{3}{4}$ minutes. How much slower was Ben than Levi? Write your answer as a mixed number.

To find the difference in their times subtract:

$3\frac{1}{5} - 1\frac{3}{4}$

$3\frac{1}{5} = \frac{15}{5} + \frac{1}{5} = \frac{16}{5}$ $1\frac{3}{4} = \frac{4}{4} + \frac{3}{4} = \frac{7}{4}$

$3\frac{1}{5} - 1\frac{3}{4} = \frac{16}{5} - \frac{7}{4} = \frac{64}{20} - \frac{35}{20} = \frac{29}{20} = 2\frac{9}{20}$

Ben was slower than Levi by $2\frac{9}{20}$ minutes.

4 and 5 are both factors of 20.

Exercise 10C

1 Work out:

(a) $1\frac{3}{4} + 2\frac{2}{3}$ (b) $3\frac{1}{5} - 1\frac{1}{2}$ (c) $2\frac{7}{8} - \frac{9}{10}$

(d) $3\frac{1}{7} + 4\frac{1}{4}$ (e) $2\frac{1}{7} + 1\frac{5}{14} - 3\frac{1}{2}$

2   Karen used $1\frac{1}{2}$ lbs of flour and $2\frac{1}{4}$ lbs of apples in her Celebration Pudding.

  (a) What did these ingredients weigh altogether?

Malcolm thought Karen used $\frac{1}{4}$ lb of flour more than necessary.

  (b) How much flour did he think she should have used?
  (c) How much would the ingredients then have weighed?

3   Match the questions to the answers in the clouds.
    Write down all of your working.

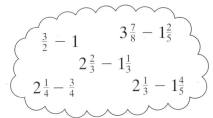
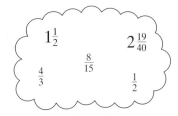

4   Andrew drives $5\frac{1}{3}$ miles to the Park and Ride.
    He then travels $8\frac{1}{4}$ miles by coach. From the
    coach he walks for half a mile to reach his office.

  (a) How far does he travel by coach and car?
  (b) How much further does he travel by coach than by car?
  (c) How far does he travel altogether?
  (d) What is the difference between the distance he walks and the distance he drives?

5   **(a)** What should be subtracted from $4\frac{4}{5}$ to give $1\frac{1}{3}$?
  (b) Which is bigger: $2\frac{4}{9}$ or $2\frac{7}{12}$?

6   Anastasia, Mairead and Helena went shopping.
    Anastasia bought $1\frac{1}{2}$ lb of carrots and $3\frac{1}{2}$ lb of potatoes.
    Mairead bought $\frac{3}{4}$ lb of cheese and $\frac{1}{2}$ lb of dates. Helena
    bought $2\frac{1}{2}$ lb of apples and $1\frac{3}{4}$ lb of pears.
    Which of these statements are true?

  (a) Anastasia's shopping weighed more than Mairead's and Helen's altogether.
  (b) Mairead's shopping weighed $2\frac{1}{4}$ lb.
  (c) Helena's shopping was heavier than Anastasia's.
  (d) The apples weighed less than the dates, cheese and carrots altogether.

10.4 Multiplying fractions

Sehan bought $\frac{3}{4}$ lb of cheese. She gave half of her cheese to her friend. To find out the weight of half of the cheese you need to find $\frac{1}{2}$ of $\frac{3}{4}$ lb.

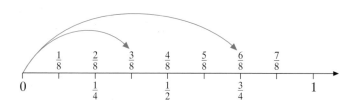

$\frac{1}{2}$ of $\frac{3}{4}$ is $\frac{3}{8}$. $\frac{1}{2}$ of $\frac{3}{4}$ means $\frac{1}{2} \times \frac{3}{4}$.

> $\frac{3}{4}$ is equivalent to $\frac{6}{8}$.
> $\frac{6}{8}$ is $\frac{3}{8} + \frac{3}{8}$ so half of $\frac{6}{8}$ is $\frac{3}{8}$.

Multiplying two fractions

Example 8

Work out $\frac{4}{5} \times \frac{2}{5}$

The shaded area represents $\frac{4}{5} \times \frac{2}{5}$

The shaded area is $\frac{8}{25}$. $\frac{4}{5} \times \frac{2}{5} = \frac{8}{25}$

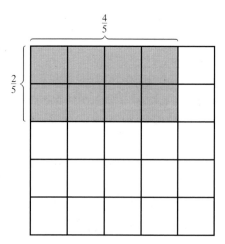

■   **To multiply two fractions, multiply the numerators and multiply the denominators.**

Example 9

Work out $\frac{1}{2}$ of $\frac{3}{5}$

$\frac{1}{2}$ of $\frac{3}{5}$ means $\frac{1}{2} \times \frac{3}{5}$

$$\frac{1}{2} \times \frac{3}{5} = \frac{1 \times 3}{2 \times 5} = \frac{3}{10}$$

Example 10

Work out $\frac{4}{5} \times \frac{5}{12}$

$$\frac{4}{5} \times \frac{5}{12} = \frac{4 \times 5}{5 \times 12} = \frac{20}{60} = \frac{1}{3}$$

$\frac{20}{60}$ simplifies to $\frac{1}{3}$. Always write your answers in simplest form.

Exercise 10D

1 Work out:

(a) $\frac{2}{3} \times \frac{1}{4}$ (b) $\frac{5}{7} \times \frac{2}{5}$ (c) $\frac{3}{8} \times \frac{5}{16}$

(d) $\frac{3}{10} \times \frac{20}{39}$ (e) $\frac{3}{4}$ of $\frac{7}{9}$ (f) $\frac{1}{8}$ of $\frac{3}{7}$

2 Three quarters of the students at Newton High School passed their mathematics exams. Two thirds of these students were girls.
   (a) What fraction of the students at the school were girls who passed?
   (b) What fraction of the students at the school were boys who passed?

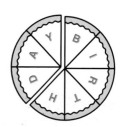

3 Twins Stella and Daniel were celebrating their birthday with friends. Stella had five eighths of the cake. Her friends ate only four fifths of her share.
   (a) What fraction of the whole cake did they eat?

   Daniel's friends ate two thirds of his share.
   (b) What fraction of the whole cake did they eat?

4 Ravi travels seven eighths of a mile to school by bike. Half way there he gets a puncture. What distance had he travelled before the puncture happened?

5 Christabel's food dish contains half of a tin of Purrfeast cat food. She eats three quarters of it.

(a) What fraction of the whole tin did she eat?

(b) What fraction of the original tin was still in her food dish?

Multiplying a fraction by a whole number

◆◆◆ ◆◆◆ ◆◆◆ ◆◆◆ ◆◆◆ $5 \times 3 = 15$

◆◆ ◆◆ ◆◆ ◆◆ ◆◆ $5 \times 2 = 10$

◆ ◆ ◆ ◆ ◆ $5 \times 1 = 5$

◁▷ ◁▷ ◁▷ ◁▷ ◁▷ $5 \times \frac{1}{2} = \frac{5}{2}$

◁◮ ◁◮ ◁◮ ◁◮ ◁◮ $5 \times \frac{1}{4} = \frac{5}{4}$

5 lots of a quarter is 5 quarters, or $\frac{5}{4}$.

You can write 5 as a fraction, $\frac{5}{1}$ and then multiply in the normal way.

$$5 \times \frac{1}{4} = \frac{5}{1} \times \frac{1}{4} = \frac{5}{4}$$

■ **To multiply a fraction by a whole number: write the whole number as a fraction over one.**
Multiply the numerators, and multiply the denominators.

For example, 5 is written as $\frac{5}{1}$.

Example 11

Multiply $\frac{3}{10}$ by 7.

7 is the same as $\frac{7}{1}$ so $\frac{3}{10} \times 7 = \frac{3}{10} \times \frac{7}{1}$

$$\frac{3}{10} \times \frac{7}{1} = \frac{3 \times 7}{10 \times 1} = \frac{21}{10} = 2\frac{1}{10}$$

$\frac{21}{10} = \frac{10}{10} + \frac{10}{10} + \frac{1}{10}$
$= 2 + \frac{1}{10} = 2\frac{1}{10}$

So $\frac{3}{10}$ multiplied by 7 is $2\frac{1}{10}$.

Exercise 10E

1   Work out, simplifying your answer where possible:

   (a) $5 \times \frac{3}{10}$ **(b)** $\frac{3}{5} \times 2$ **(c)** $6 \times \frac{2}{3}$

   (d) $8 \times \frac{3}{4}$ **(e)** $6 \times \frac{5}{11}$ **(f)** $\frac{4}{7} \times 4$

2   On a seven day holiday Jennifer spent one third of each day walking. How much time did she spend walking in total?

3   Suresh fills seven eighths of his 16 flower beds with new plants. How many flower beds are filled with plants?

4   Tabitha has 6 bars of chocolate. She gives $\frac{2}{7}$ of it to Emily. How much chocolate does Tabitha have left?

Multiplying mixed numbers

■   **To multiply mixed numbers, change them to improper fractions then multiply in the normal way.**

Example 12

Work out $2\frac{1}{4} \times 1\frac{3}{5}$.

Write the mixed numbers as improper fractions:

$2\frac{1}{4} = \frac{9}{4}$ $1\frac{3}{5} = \frac{8}{5}$

Now multiply in the normal way.

$$2\frac{1}{4} \times 1\frac{3}{5} = \frac{9}{4} \times \frac{8}{5} = \frac{9 \times 8}{4 \times 5} = \frac{72}{20} = 3\frac{3}{5}$$

Always write your answer in its simplest form.

Example 13

Carolyn soaks $2\frac{1}{4}$ kilograms of lentils to make soup. Each kilogram of lentils needs $1\frac{1}{2}$ litres of water. How much water does she require altogether?

To work out the total amount of water needed you need to multiply the fractions.

$$2\frac{1}{4} \times 1\frac{1}{2} = \frac{9}{4} \times \frac{3}{2} = \frac{9 \times 3}{4 \times 2} = \frac{27}{8} = 3\frac{3}{8}$$

Carolyn will need $3\frac{3}{8}$ litres of water.

Exercise 10F

1   Work out, giving your answers in their simplest form:

(a) $2\frac{1}{4} \times 1\frac{1}{10}$ (b) $2\frac{1}{2} \times 2\frac{1}{5}$ (c) $3\frac{1}{5} \times \frac{3}{8}$

(d) $6\frac{1}{4} \times 1\frac{1}{5}$ (e) $1\frac{1}{4} \times \frac{9}{10}$ (f) $\frac{5}{6} \times 1\frac{1}{5}$

2   The dimensions of Christian's rectangular hi-fi are $1\frac{1}{4}$ feet by $1\frac{3}{4}$ feet. He needs to work out the surface area he needs for it in his new flat. Show how he can do this and find the area of the base of the hi-fi.

3   Ami has bought a circular mirror. Its radius is $4\frac{1}{2}$ cm. Taking the value of π to be $3\frac{1}{7}$, work out the area of Ami's wall the mirror will cover.

> Remember: the area of a circle is πr^2, or $\pi \times r \times r$.

4   A parallelogram has length $6\frac{4}{5}$ cm and perpendicular height $4\frac{1}{5}$ cm.

(a) Work out the area of the parallelogram.

Half of the parallelogram is red.

(b) Work out the area of the shaded section.

> Hint:
> Area of parallelogram
> = length × perpendicular height

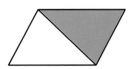

10.5 Dividing fractions

You will need to be able to solve problems by dividing fractions.

Example 14

Anna is baking muffins. She makes 4 lb of muffin mix. Each muffin uses $\frac{1}{5}$ lb of mix. How many muffins can Anna make?

Anna divides her 4 lb into $\frac{1}{5}$ portions:

$$4 \div \tfrac{1}{5}$$

There are 5 lots of $\frac{1}{5}$ in a whole so there are 4 lots of 5 fifths in 4 lb of muffin mix.

$$4 \times 5 = 20$$

Anna can make 20 muffins.

$4 \div \frac{1}{5}$ is the same as $4 \times \frac{5}{1}$ or 4×5.

- **To find the reciprocal of a fraction turn it upside down.**
- **To divide fractions replace the dividing fraction with its reciprocal and change the division sign to multiplication.**

The reciprocal of $\frac{1}{5}$ is $\frac{5}{1}$ or just 5.

Example 15

Work out $\frac{1}{4} \div 3$

$$3 = \tfrac{3}{1}$$

So the reciprocal of 3 is $\frac{1}{3}$.

$$\tfrac{1}{4} \div 3 = \tfrac{1}{4} \times \tfrac{1}{3}$$

$$= \frac{1 \times 1}{4 \times 3}$$

$$= \tfrac{1}{12}$$

Example 16

Work out $\frac{2}{5} \div \frac{3}{4}$

The reciprocal of $\frac{3}{4}$ is $\frac{4}{3}$.

$$\tfrac{2}{5} \div \tfrac{3}{4} = \tfrac{2}{5} \times \tfrac{4}{3}$$

$$= \frac{2 \times 4}{5 \times 3}$$

$$= \tfrac{8}{15}$$

Exercise 10G

1 Find the reciprocal of each fraction.

(a) $\frac{3}{5}$ (b) $\frac{7}{8}$ (c) $\frac{5}{6}$ (d) $\frac{12}{5}$ (e) $1\frac{1}{2}$

> To find the reciprocal of a mixed number first change it to an improper fraction.
> For example:
> $$1\frac{2}{3} = \frac{5}{3}$$
> The reciprocal of $\frac{5}{3}$ is $\frac{3}{5}$

2 Change the whole numbers to fractions over 1 to work out:

(a) $\frac{2}{3} \div 8$ (b) $\frac{4}{5} \div 16$ (c) $\frac{13}{15} \div 39$

(d) $\frac{7}{16} \div 14$ (e) $\frac{3}{4} \div 12$ (f) $\frac{9}{10} \div 18$

3 Work out:

(a) $\frac{2}{3} \div \frac{8}{9}$ (b) $\frac{3}{8} \div \frac{5}{7}$ (c) $\frac{7}{19} \div \frac{9}{14}$

(d) $\frac{6}{7} \div \frac{24}{35}$ (e) $\frac{3}{4} \div \frac{7}{12}$ (f) $\frac{2}{5} \div \frac{9}{17}$

4 Work out:

(a) $1\frac{1}{4} \div \frac{5}{6}$ (b) $2\frac{1}{2} \div 3\frac{1}{3}$ (c) $1\frac{1}{5} \div 2\frac{1}{10}$

(d) $3\frac{1}{5} \div 4$ (e) $6\frac{1}{4} \div 2\frac{1}{2}$ (f) $\frac{8}{9} \div 1\frac{1}{4}$

> Hint: Change the mixed numbers to improper fractions first.

5 Ed buys a watermelon weighing $\frac{3}{4}$ kg. He divides it into equal pieces each weighing $\frac{3}{16}$ kg. How many pieces of melon does he have?

6 Jason is making rock cakes for a school fete. It takes him $\frac{2}{3}$ hour to make 24 cakes.

(a) What is the time taken per cake?

Keri took $\frac{3}{4}$ hour to make 36 rock cakes.

(b) What was Keri's time taken per cake?

7 True or false:

(a) The reciprocal of $1\frac{1}{7}$ is $\frac{8}{7}$.

(b) $\frac{2}{3} \div \frac{4}{5} < \frac{2}{3} \times \frac{3}{8}$.

(c) $\frac{3}{5} \div \frac{2}{3}$ is the same as $\frac{2}{3} \div \frac{3}{5}$.

(d) The area of a rectangular flower bed is $\frac{4}{5}$ square metre. The length of one side is $\frac{2}{3}$ metre. The length of the other side is $\frac{8}{15}$ metre.

> Remember:
> < means less than.

8   Mr Keane shares $2\frac{1}{2}$ lb of chocolate between a class of 12. How much chocolate does each pupil get?

9   The base area of Desire's rectangular playpen is $3\frac{1}{2}$ m². If the width is $2\frac{1}{3}$ m, find the length of the playpen in metres.

10   Cameron works steadily on his homework and completes $\frac{7}{8}$ in $1\frac{1}{2}$ hours. How much of his homework does he complete in 1 hour?

10.6 Ratio

The garden is divided into 9 equal parts.

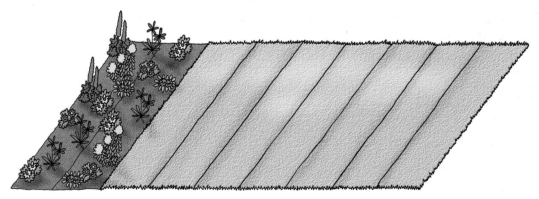

Two parts are flowers and seven parts are grass. Describing this in fractions you would say that $\frac{2}{9}$ of the garden is flowers and $\frac{7}{9}$ of the garden is grass.

However, in ratios, you compare two quantities.

So in the garden you would say there are two parts flowers to seven parts grass, or that the ratio of flowers to grass is 2 to 7.

This is written as $2 : 7$.

You could also say that there are 7 parts grass to 2 parts flowers, or that the ratio of grass to flowers is 7 to 2. This is written as $7:2$.

■   **A ratio compares two or more quantities of the same kind.**

Example 17

(a) What fraction of the octagon is red?
(b) What fraction of the octagon is blue?
(c) Write the ratio of red parts to blue parts.
(d) Write the ratio of yellow parts to blue parts.
(e) Write the ratio of blue parts to red parts to yellow parts.

(a) There are eight parts in the whole shape and one is red, so $\frac{1}{8}$ of the octagon is red.
(b) Three parts are blue, so $\frac{3}{8}$ of the octagon is blue.
(c) There is one red part to three blue, so the ratio is 1 to 3, written as $1:3$.
(d) There are four yellow parts to three blue parts so the ratio is 4 to 3, written as $4:3$.
(e) There are three blue parts to one red part to four yellow parts. The ratio is 3 to 1 to 4, written as $3:1:4$.

You can use ratios to compare three or more quantities in exactly the same way.

Example 18

Jane, Moira and Michael are comparing their weekly pocket money. Jane gets £3, Michael gets £4 and Moira gets £7. Write down the ratio of:

(a) Moira's pocket money to Michael's pocket money.
(b) Michael's pocket money to Jane's pocket money.
(c) Moira's pocket money to Michael's pocket money to Jane's pocket money.

(a) Moira gets £7. Michael gets £4. The ratio is $7:4$.
(b) Michael gets £4. Jane gets £3. The ratio is $4:3$.
(c) The ratio is $7:4:3$.

Simplifying ratios

There are six blue jerseys
and three red jerseys on
this line.
The ratio of red to blue is
$3:6$.
For each red jersey there
are two blue jerseys.
You can write the ratio of
red to blue as $1:2$.

■ **You can simplify a ratio if you can divide its numbers
   by a common factor.**
■ **If the numbers in the ratio do not have a common
   factor the ratio is in its simplest form.**

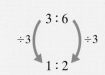

The ratio $1:2$ is
the simplest form
of the ratio $3:6$.

Example 19

Express these ratios in their simplest form:

(a) $80:50$ **(b)** $16:24$

(a) The highest common factor of 80 and 50 is 10:

$$\div 10 \left(\begin{array}{c} 80:50 \\ 8:5 \end{array}\right) \div 10$$

(b) The highest common factor of 16 and 24 is 8:

$$\div 8 \left(\begin{array}{c} 16:24 \\ 2:3 \end{array}\right) \div 8$$

Exercise 10H

1   Write these ratios in their simplest form:

   (a) $5:15$ **(b)** $30:18$ **(c)** $14:49$
   (d) $3:6:12$ **(e)** $56:24:16$ **(f)** $18:12:30$

2 Chris is sorting out his music and film collection.
He has 80 CDs, 16 DVDs, 96 VHS tapes and
120 minidiscs.

(a) Write down the ratio of CDs to DVDs.
(b) Write down the ratio of VHS tapes to minidiscs.
(c) What is the ratio of CDs to VHS tapes to DVDs?
(d) Write down the ratio of minidiscs to VHS tapes to
CDs to DVDs.

> Always write your
> answers in their
> simplest form.

3 Write these ratios in their simplest form.

(a) 350 grams to 7 kg
(b) 2 hours to 180 minutes
(c) £4.50 to 75p
(d) 1 litre of milk to $\frac{1}{2}$ litre of milk
(e) 8 years to 4 years 8 months

> Make the units the
> same before you
> write each ratio.

4 In a class there are 24 boys and 18 girls. Find the ratio of:

(a) boys to girls
(b) girls to boys
(c) boys to the total number of students
(d) girls to the total number of students.

5 Paul and Ivalor are making chocolate mousse. Paul
uses 4 ounces of cream to 6 ounces of chocolate.
Ivalor uses 6 ounces of cream to 9 ounces of
chocolate.
Which of the following statements are true?

(a) The ratio of cream to chocolate is the same in both
Paul and Ivalor's recipes.
(b) The ratio of cream to chocolate in Paul's mousse is
3 : 2
(c) $\frac{6}{15}$ of Ivalor's mixture is cream.
(d) $\frac{2}{3}$ of Paul's mixture is cream.
(e) $\frac{3}{5}$ of Ivalor's mixture is chocolate.
(f) The ratio of chocolate to cream is the same in both
recipes.

10.7 Proportion

In a football team there are eleven players including one goalkeeper. The ratio of goalkeeper to the other players is 1 : 10.

In two football teams there are 22 players including two goalkeepers. The ratio of goalkeepers to the other players is 2 : 20.

1 : 10 and 2 : 20 are equivalent ratios.

The ratio of goalkeepers to the other players will be the same for any number of football teams.

You say that the number of goalkeepers and the number of players are in **direct proportion**.

■ **Two or more quantities are in direct proportion if their ratio stays the same as the quantities increase or decrease.**

> You sometimes say the quantities are **directly proportional** to each other.

Example 20

Petrol consumption and distance travelled are in direct proportion. Karla can drive 40 miles on 3 litres of petrol. How many litres of petrol will she need to drive 120 miles?

The ratio of miles to petrol is 40 : 3. The quantities are in direct proportion so the ratio for the longer journey will be equivalent:

120 miles is three times 40 miles…   ×3 ⟨ 40 : 3 ⟩ ×3   …so three times as much petrol is needed.

120 : 9

Karla needs 9 litres of petrol.

Exercise 10I

1 Say whether you think each of these quantities will be in direct proportion or not.
   (a) Number of identical chocolate bars bought and cost.
   (b) Number of pupils in a class and their average height.
   (c) Area of a single tile and area of this whole patio.
   (d) Perimeter of a square and length of one side.

2 Derek's aquarium contains 3 frogs, 2 eels, 4 goldfish and 5 snails.

   (a) Write down the ratio of snails to goldfish to frogs to eels.

   He decides to increase the number of snails to 10. He wants to keep the numbers in the aquarium in direct proportion.

   (b) How many more frogs does he need?
   (c) How many more goldfish does he need?
   (d) How many more eels does he need?

3 Colette makes a fruit punch. The ratio of orange juice to lemonade to grapefruit juice is $4 : 7 : 3$.
   She keeps the quantities in direct proportion. How much lemonade does she need if she uses:

   (a) 400 ml of orange juice
   (b) 6 l of grapefruit juice
   (c) 120 ml of grapefruit juice?

4 A carpenter makes cabinets. The ratio of height to width to depth is $5 : 4 : 3$.

   The carpenter keeps height, width and depth in direct proportion.

   (a) How wide should a 105 cm tall cabinet be?
   (b) Find the depth of a cabinet that is 88 cm wide.
   (c) Find the width and depth of a cabinet that is 3 m tall.

5 Katherine and Ruth have rocking horses. The saddle height and the girls' heights are in direct proportion. Katherine is 60 cm tall and her horse's saddle is 48 cm high.

    (a) Write down the ratio of Katherine's height to the height of her saddle.

    (b) If Ruth is 75 cm tall, how high is her saddle?

10.8 Calculating with ratios

You will need to be able to solve more difficult ratio problems.

■ **You can solve ratio and proportion problems by reducing one side of the ratio to one.**

Example 21

Faith paints 48 m of fencing in 6 days. How much fencing did she paint in 4 days?

The ratio of number of days to length of fencing painted is:

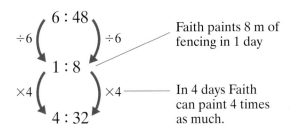

Faith paints 8 m of fencing in 1 day

In 4 days Faith can paint 4 times as much.

Faith painted 32 m of fencing in 4 days.

Example 22

A pancake recipe uses 120 grams of flour and 300 ml of milk for every 2 eggs. How much flour and milk are needed if you make pancakes with 7 eggs?

The ratio of the quantities is

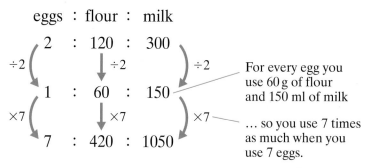

eggs : flour : milk

2 : 120 : 300

$\div 2$ $\div 2$ $\div 2$

1 : 60 : 150 — For every egg you use 60 g of flour and 150 ml of milk

$\times 7$ $\times 7$ $\times 7$

7 : 420 : 1050 — … so you use 7 times as much when you use 7 eggs.

You need 420 g of flour and 1050 ml, or 1.05 l of milk.

Exercise 10J

1   Peter walks 10 miles in 3 hours. How long would it take him to walk

    (a) 1 mile   **(b)** 12 miles?

    Hint: Write the time in minutes.

2   Aiden buys 3 CDs for £36. How much would it cost to buy

    (a) 1 CD   **(b)** 5 CDs?

3   A grasshopper can leap 169 times in 13 minutes.
    How many times can it leap in 11 minutes?

4   Pen wants her garden to contain flowers, vegetables and grass in the ratio:

    flowers : vegetables : grass
    7   :   14   :   28

    Her first plan for the garden includes 5 square metres of flowers. What area does she need for:

    (a) vegetables   **(b)** grass?

    She designs a new plan that uses 12 square metres of flowers. What area does she now need for:

    (c) vegetables   **(d)** grass?

5 Three elephants Rica, Amal and Sanjit get fed peanuts at a wildlife park. The number of peanuts they each get is directly proportional to their weight.

Rica weighs 400 kg, Amal weighs 1600 kg and Sanjit weighs 800 kg.

(a) Write down the ratio of the elephants' weights.

Rica gets 70 peanuts.

(b) How many peanuts does Amal get?
(c) How many peanuts do they get in total?

10.9 Using ratios as scales

Architects often use scale drawings when they are designing houses.

■ **A scale is a ratio used to show the relationship between the length on a diagram or model and the actual length it represents.**

For example, 1 : 100 means 1 cm on the diagram represents 100 cm or 1 m in real life.

Example 23

Jamal makes a model of a battleship with scale 1 : 75.

What do these lengths on the model represent in real life:

(a) 5 cm　　　　**(b)** 1.2 m?

(a) 1 cm represents 75 cm in real life.
　　5 cm represents $5 \times 75 = 375$ cm or 3.75 m.
(b) 1 m represents 75 m in real life.
　　1.2 m represents $1.2 \times 75 = 90$ m.

Exercise 10K

1   A mobile phone company uses a scale of $1:3$ for a
    drawing of a phone used in an advert. The height of
    the actual phone is 12 cm.

    (a) What height is the phone shown in the advert?
    (b) On the drawing, the phone is $\frac{2}{3}$ cm wide. How wide
        is the actual phone?
    (c) On the drawing the phone has a $\frac{1}{2}$ cm aerial. How
        big is the aerial on the actual phone?

2   This Ordnance Survey map uses a scale of
    $1:50\,000$. The distance between the Youth
    Hostel and the church is $4\frac{1}{2}$ km.

    (a) How many metres are there in a
        kilometre?
    (b) How many centimetres are there in a
        kilometre?
    (c) How many centimetres are there in
        $4\frac{1}{2}$ kilometres?
    (d) What length on the map represents the
        distance between the Youth Hostel and
        the church?
    (e) David walks from the church to the
        campsite, a distance of 14 cm on the map.
        What is the actual distance?

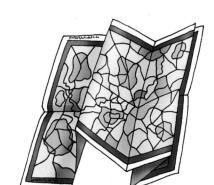

3   An architectural model of a palace uses a scale of
    $1:50$.

    (a) How tall is the actual clock tower if the clock tower
        on the model is 70 cm tall?
    (b) How wide is the main gate on the model if the
        actual main gate is 10 m wide?
    (c) If the base of the palace measures 120 m by 70 m,
        what are the dimensions of the base on the
        model?

4   An aeroplane has a wingspan of 36 m. What scale
    would a model be if the wingspan on the model was:

    (a) 1 m   (b) 36 cm
    (c) 12 cm   (d) 8 m?

Summary of key points

1 A mixed number has a whole number part and a fraction part. For example: $1\frac{1}{3}$, $9\frac{1}{2}$, $2\frac{1}{4}$.

2 An improper fraction has the numerator bigger than the denominator. For example: $\frac{5}{2}$, $\frac{8}{3}$, $\frac{19}{7}$.

3 Fractions can be simplified if the numerator and the denominator have a common factor greater than 1.

4 To add mixed numbers add the whole number part and then add the fractions.

5 To subtract mixed numbers change them into improper fractions.

6 To multiply two fractions multiply the numerators and multiply the denominators.

7 To multiply a fraction by a whole number: write the whole number as a fraction over one.
Multiply the numerators and multiply the denominators.

8 To multiply mixed numbers, change them to improper fractions then multiply in the normal way.

9 To find the reciprocal of a fraction turn it upside down.

10 To divide fractions replace the dividing fraction with its reciprocal and change the division sign to a multiplication.

11 A ratio compares two or more quantities of the same kind.

12 You can simplify a ratio if you can divide its numbers by a common factor.

13 If the numbers in the ratio do not have a common factor the ratio is in its simplest form.

14 Two or more quantities are in direct proportion if their ratio stays the same as the quantities increase or decrease.

15 You can solve ratio and proportion problems by reducing one side of the ratio to one.

16 A scale is used to show the relationship between the length on a diagram or model and the actual length it represents.

11 Probability

This television station predicts that the probability that it will rain is $\frac{2}{5}$. You can write this as 40% or 0.4.

Probability uses numbers to say how likely something is to happen.

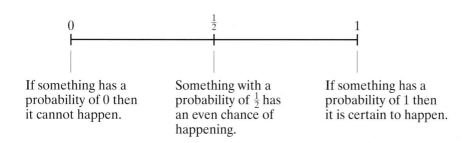

If something has a probability of 0 then it cannot happen.

Something with a probability of $\frac{1}{2}$ has an even chance of happening.

If something has a probability of 1 then it is certain to happen.

■ **All probabilities have a value from 0 to 1.**

You can write probabilities as fractions, decimals or percentages.

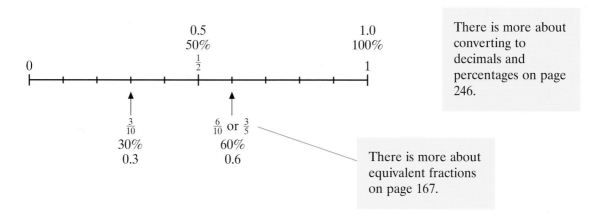

There is more about converting to decimals and percentages on page 246.

There is more about equivalent fractions on page 167.

11.1 Calculating probabilities

When you spin this wheel there are five possible outcomes.

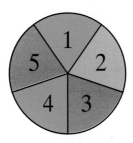

Spinning the wheel is an **event**.
The result is an **outcome**.

Two of the possible outcomes are red.

The probability of landing on red is '2 out of 5'.

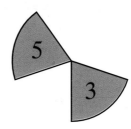

You write this

$\qquad$ Probability (red) $= \frac{2}{5}$

or $\qquad$ $P(\text{red}) = \frac{2}{5}$

Notice that

$\qquad$ $P(\text{red}) + P(\text{green}) + P(\text{blue}) = \frac{2}{5} + \frac{2}{5} + \frac{1}{5} = 1$
$\qquad$ $P(\text{not red}) = 1 - P(\text{red})$

■ **The probability that an event will happen is:**

$$P(\text{event}) = \frac{\text{number of successful outcomes}}{\text{total number of possible outcomes}}$$

■ **The probabilities of all the possible outcomes of an event add up to 1.**

■ **P(event not happening) = 1 − P(event happening)**
P(event not happening) = 100% − P(event happening)

Use this if probabilities are given as percentages.

Example 1

A card is chosen at random from an ordinary pack of playing cards.

Remember:
at random means each card is equally likely to be chosen.

Write the probability that:
(a) a red card is chosen
(b) a 3 is chosen
(c) a king is chosen.

Always write your answer in **simplest form**.

(a) $P(\text{red card}) = \frac{26}{52} = \frac{1}{2}$ **(b)** $P(3) = \frac{4}{52} = \frac{1}{13}$

(c) $P(\text{king}) = \frac{4}{52} = \frac{1}{13}$

$$\frac{4}{52} \xrightarrow[\div 4]{\div 4} = \frac{1}{13}$$

Example 2

(a) Write the probability of getting each of the colours on the spinner as a fraction, decimal and percentage.
(b) What is the probability that you will not get yellow?

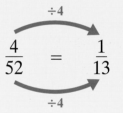

(a)

Colour	fraction	decimal	percentage
red	$\frac{1}{2}$	0.5	50%
yellow	$\frac{1}{4}$	0.25	25%
blue	$\frac{1}{4}$	0.25	25%

(b) $P(\text{yellow}) = \frac{1}{4}$
   so $P(\text{not yellow}) = 1 - P(\text{yellow})$
                  $= \frac{3}{4}$

Exercise 11A

1 Soujit chooses his breakfast cereal at random from this variety pack:

Find the probabilities of these events. Give your answers as fractions, decimals and percentages.
(a) Soujit chooses Wheaty-bits.
(b) Soujit chooses Bang, bubble and crunch.
(c) Soujit chooses Choco-charms or Multi-muesli.
(d) Soujit doesn't choose Milky-pops.

Hint:
Find the answer as a fraction first. Then convert it to a decimal and percentage.

2 For each event, choose all the correct probabilities from the cloud.
(a) Rolling a 6 on an ordinary dice.
(b) Rolling less than 3 on an ordinary dice.
(c) Rolling a 1 or a 2 on a 10-sided dice.
(d) Choosing a spade when picking one card at random from a normal pack of cards.
(e) Choosing a red card when picking one card at random from a normal pack of cards.

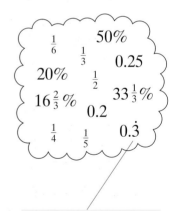

$\frac{1}{6}$ 50% $\frac{1}{3}$ 0.25   20% $\frac{1}{2}$ $33\frac{1}{3}\%$ $16\frac{2}{3}\%$ 0.2 $\frac{1}{4}$ $\frac{1}{5}$ 0.$\dot{3}$

This means 'zero point three recurring', or 0.333333...

3 A bag contains red, blue and green counters.
A counter is chosen at random from the bag.
The probability of choosing a red counter is 20%.
The probability of choosing a green counter is 30%.
(a) Write these probabilities as fractions with the same denominator.
(b) Find the probability of choosing a blue counter. Give your answer as a fraction and a percentage.

4 Some cards are missing from this pack.
   A card is chosen at random.
   The probability of choosing a spade is 22%.
   The probability of choosing a heart is 0.26.
   The probability of choosing a diamond is $\frac{13}{50}$.
   (a) Write all these probabilities as fractions
       with the same denominator.
   (b) What is the probability of choosing a club?
       Give your answer as a fraction, decimal and
       percentage.
   (c) What suit do you think the missing
       cards were?

5 A box contains red, blue, white and black balls.
   A ball is chosen at random.
       P(red) = 15%   P(blue) = 0.6
       P(white) = $\frac{1}{20}$.

   Find P(black). Give your answer as a fraction,
   decimal or percentage.

Hint:
First write all the
probabilities as
fractions with the
same denominator.

6 Lydia chooses a book to read at random.
   The probability that Lydia chooses *Alice in
   Wonderland* is $\frac{4}{5}$. What is the probability
   Lydia does not choose *Alice in Wonderland*?

7 The probability that a counter chosen at
   random from a bag will be square is $\frac{2}{11}$.
   What is the probability the counter will not
   be square?

8 Computer disks are tested as they leave
   the factory.
       P(fail) = 5%
   Find P(not fail).

9 Jeneen has 20 fruit-flavoured sweets. Six are
   strawberry, seven are lemon and the rest are
   lime. She offers one to Nikole at random.
   (a) What is the probability that strawberry
       is chosen?
   (b) What is the probability that lemon is
       chosen?
   (c) What is the probability that lime is chosen?
   (d) What is the probability that strawberry is
       not chosen?
   (e) What is the probability that lime is not chosen?

11.2 Experimental probability

Sometimes you use experiments to estimate the probability of an outcome.

For example, you can estimate the probability of getting a 3 on a dice by rolling the dice several times and keeping a record of the total number of trials and the number of times the outcome was 3.

If you rolled the dice 10 times and 3 turned up 4 times, the experimental probability of rolling a 3 would be $\frac{4}{10}$ or $P(3) = \frac{4}{10}$.

When you count the number of times a certain event happens and the total number of trials you can find the experimental probability.

■ **The estimated or experimental probability that an event will happen is:**

$$\frac{\text{number of successful trials}}{\text{total number of trials}}$$

Experimental probability is used when you do not know the total number of outcomes or whether they are equally likely. For example, with an unfair six-sided dice you can use an experiment to find the chance of each outcome happening.

↓

Experimental probability means that you **do** an experiment to get the information to work out the chance of an outcome happening.

The theoretical probability is found by saying all events are equally likely.

On a normal dice there are six possible outcomes and one of them is the number 3.

The theoretical probability of rolling a 3 would be $P(3) = \frac{1}{6}$.

■ **The theoretical probability that something will happen is:**

$$\frac{\text{number of successful outcomes}}{\text{total number of possible outcomes}}$$

■ **The experimental probability may vary from one experiment to the next.**
  The theoretical probability is always the same.

You can collect the data to estimate probability in different ways, for example, by survey, by observation, or by trials.

Theoretical probability is used when you know the total number of possible outcomes and that they are all equally likely. For example, for a fair ordinary dice there are six equally likely possible outcomes.

↓

Theoretical probability means that you **think** about the event to get the information to work out the chance of an outcome happening.

Example 3

Jemima asked her class how they each got
to school that morning. She put her
results in a frequency table.

Type of transport	Tally	Frequency
car	卌	5
walk	卌 卌	10
bus	卌 卌 ||	12
bicycle	|||	3
train		0

(a) How many people did she ask?
(b) Estimate the probability that a person in the class
    walked to school.
(c) What is the estimated probability that a person in the
    class did not walk to school?
(d) What is the estimated probability that a person in the
    class took the train to school?

(a) $5 + 10 + 12 + 3 + 0 = 30$
    She asked 30 people.
(b) 10 people walked to school so the estimated probability
    is $\frac{10}{30} = \frac{1}{3}$.
(c) $P(\text{did not walk}) = 1 - P(\text{walk}) = 1 - \frac{1}{3} = \frac{2}{3}$
(d) $P(\text{train}) = 0$

Example 4

A sweet factory produces a variety pack of boiled sweets. The flavours are lime, strawberry, lemon and orange. Mary wanted to estimate the probability of picking a particular flavour from a full pack of sweets without looking. She picked out a sweet from a pack and replaced it after noting its flavour. She repeated this 20 times. Her results are shown below.

Estimate the probability of picking a lime sweet from a full pack.

Flavour	No. of times picked
lime	4
lemon	6
strawberry	7
orange	3

There were 20 trials and there were four successful trials for lime, so the estimated probability of choosing a lime-flavoured sweet is $\frac{4}{20}$.

Exercise 11B

1   Make a six-sided dice from a piece of thick card, taping a small counter on the inside of the side labelled 6.

   (a) Is this a fair dice?

   (b) What is the theoretical probability of throwing a 6 when a fair dice is thrown?

   (c) Throw your dice 60 times and record in a table the number of times 1, 2, 3, 4, 5 and 6 occur.

   (d) Estimate the probability of getting a 6 with your dice.

You could use a net like this to make your dice.

2 Using four different colours, place 20 counters in a bag. Do not reveal how many counters of each colour there are. Ask the person sitting next to you to pick out a counter, note the colour and replace it. Repeat this 20 times.

   (a) Write the estimated probabilities of each of the colours being picked.

   (b) Empty out your bag and calculate the theoretical probabilities of choosing each colour.

   (c) Were your estimated probabilities close to the theoretical calculated probabilities?

3 Mary and Tom tossed a coin 100 times. They kept a running total of the number of heads. This table shows their results.

No. of trials	No. of heads so far	P(head) as a fraction	P(head) as a decimal
10	7	$\frac{7}{10}$	0.7
20	12		
30	15		
40	18	$\frac{9}{20}$	
50	26		
60	30		
70	35		0.5
80	44		
90	45		
100	51		

Use a calculator to work out the decimals.

   (a) Copy the table and complete it.

   (b) Draw axes on graph paper. Put 'No. of trials' on the horizontal axis, from 0 to 100. Put 'P(head)' on the vertical axis, noting a scale of 1 cm to 0.2.

     Plot the values of P(head) as a decimal.

   (c) What is the theoretical probability of getting a head with a fair coin?
Draw a line across your graph at this value.
What do you notice?

4 Carry out a small survey in your class of how people get to school. Estimate the probability that someone in your class walks to school.

11.3 Expected number of outcomes

You can sometimes use the theoretical probability to work out how many times you would expect a particular outcome to happen in an experiment. You can then compare this expected number with what actually happened.

■ **Expected number of outcomes = P(event) × Number of trials**

Example 5

(a) If you toss a coin 20 times, how many tails would you expect?

(b) Imran claimed a coin was unfair. It gave only 5 tails in 20 tosses. Was he correct?

(a) The probability of getting a tail on a coin is 0.5. So if you toss the coin 20 times you would expect $0.5 \times 20 = 10$ tails.

(b) Although 5 tails in 20 tosses is less than the expected 10, you would need to toss the coin a lot more, recording the result each time, to test whether the coin is fair or not.

Exercise 11C

1   (a) The probability of taking out a red counter from this bag is 0.3.
You take out a counter 10 times, always replacing it each time. How many red counters would you expect?

(b) P(blue) = 40%
You take out a counter, note the colour, then replace the counter. You do this 100 times. How many blue counters would you expect to get?

(c) You know P(red) = 0.3 and P(blue) = 40%.
If there are only red, green and blue counters in the bag, what is P(green)?

(d) How many of each colour would you expect to take out after 30 trials, replacing the counter each time?

2   You choose a card at random from a normal pack of playing cards.
    (a) What is the probability of choosing a red card?
    (b) You choose a card at random, replace it and repeat this 20 times. How many red cards would you expect to have chosen?
    (c) How many kings would you expect in 13 trials?

3   A 12-sided dice is thrown. It sides are numbered 1 to 12.
    (a) What is P(even)?
    (b) How many even numbers would you expect after 50 throws of the dice?
    (c) What is P(prime)?
    (d) How many primes would you expect after 48 throws of the dice?

> Remember:
> Multiplying fractions is on p. 172.

11.4 Combined events

When two events happen at the same time you can use diagrams to show all the possible outcomes.

Sample space diagrams

When two coins are tossed you can draw this sample space diagram.

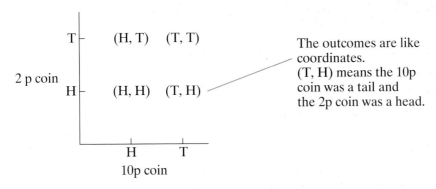

The outcomes are like coordinates.
(T, H) means the 10p coin was a tail and the 2p coin was a head.

■   **When two events happen independently you can show all the possible outcomes on a sample space diagram.**

> **Independently**
> means the outcome of one event doesn't affect the outcome of the other.

Example 6

A restaurant in Paris has a menu with two
starters, onion soup or garlic mushrooms, and
three main courses, steak, fish or chicken.

(a) Use a sample space diagram to show all
possible outcomes for choosing a starter
and a main course.
(b) A tourist does not understand the menu
and chooses a starter and main course at
random. Find the probability of the
tourist choosing soup and fish.
(c) What is the probability of choosing the
chicken with any starter?

(a)

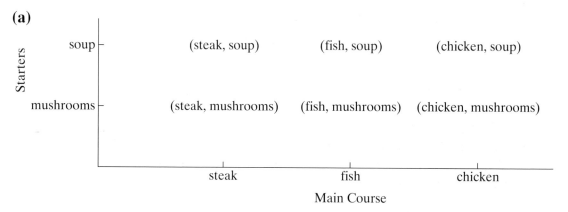

(b) There are 6 possible outcomes and only one of these is
soup and fish. The probability is $\frac{1}{6}$.
(c) There are two different starters to have with the
chicken. The probability is $\frac{2}{6} = \frac{1}{3}$.

Exercise 11D

1   Garrett is choosing his after-school activities.
He wants to choose one for Monday
and one for Wednesday.

Draw a sample space diagram to show
all the possible combinations
he could choose.

Monday	Wednesday
Football	Art
Hockey	Drama
Cricket	Music
Basketball	

2 Sarah is having a break. She can choose one drink and one snack. Use a sample space diagram to show all the possible choices she could make.

Drinks
tea
coffee
hot chocolate
cola
water

Snacks
biscuits
cake
fruit

3 Marie is going to France from England. She can choose the ferry, the Eurostar train or the plane to get to France. Then she can choose a taxi, bus or train to get to her hotel.
(a) Draw a sample space diagram to show all the possible ways she can choose to get from England to her hotel in France.

Marie chooses at random from the available options.
(b) What is P(ferry then taxi)?
(c) What is P(not ferry then taxi)?
(d) What is P(train then train)?
(e) What is the probability that she does not take a train at any point in her journey?

4 A normal dice is thrown and a fair coin is tossed.
(a) Show all the possible outcomes on a sample space diagram.
(b) What is P(1 with heads)?
(c) What is P(3 with tails)?
(d) What is P(even number with tails)?
(e) What is P(not even with not tails)?

Summary of key points

1 All probabilities have a value from 0 to 1.

2 The probability that an event will happen is:

$$P(event) = \frac{\text{number of successful outcomes}}{\text{total number of possible outcomes}}$$

3 The probabilities of all the possible outcomes of an event add up to 1.

4   P(event not happening) $= 1 -$ P(event happening)

P(event not happening) $= 100\% -$ P(event happening) —— Use this if probabilities are given as percentages.

5   The estimated or experimental probability that an event will happen is:

$$\frac{\text{number of successful trials}}{\text{total number of trials}}$$

6   The theoretical probability that something will happen is:

$$\frac{\text{number of successful outcomes}}{\text{total number of possible outcomes}}$$

7   The experimental probability may vary from one experiment to the next. The theoretical probability is always the same.

8   Expected number of outcomes $=$ P(event) $\times$ Number of trials

9   When two events happen independently you can show all the possible outcomes on a sample space diagram.

12 Number patterns

12.1 Number machines

You can use number machines to generate number sequences.

Example 1

Input the numbers 1, 2, 3, 4, 5 into this number machine.

input	output
1	9
2	18
3	27
4	36
5	45

A table is a good way to show a sequence.

Example 2

This two-step number machine performs the operations ×6 and −9.

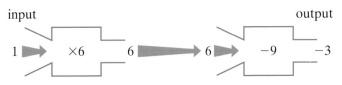

Find the output values for input values 1 to 5.

$1 \times 6 = 6 \qquad 6 - 9 = -3$

$2 \times 6 = 12 \qquad 12 - 9 = 3$

and so on.

input	output
1	−3
2	3
3	9
4	15
5	21

A two-step number machine has two operations.

The output from the first machine is the input for the second machine.

Inverse operations

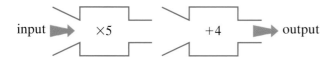

For an input value of 4
the output is

$$4 \times 5 = 20 \qquad 20 + 4 = 24$$

If you are given an *output* value, use **inverse** operations to
find the *input* value.
If 19 is the output value:

3 ◄ | ÷5 | ◄ 15 ◄ | −4 | ◄ 19

3 was the input value.

Example 3

Find the missing numbers in the table:

×3 → +2	
input	**output**
1	...
3	...
5	17
...	23
9	...

Remember:

Operation	Inverse
+	−
−	+
×	÷
÷	×

input 1 $1 \times 3 = 3 \qquad 3 + 2 = 5$

output

input 3 $3 \times 3 = 9 \qquad 9 + 2 = 11$

output 17
(use inverse)   5 ◄ | ÷3 | ◄ 15 ◄ | −2 | ◄ 17

input

output 23
(use inverse)

$7 \blacktriangleleft\!\!\!\blacktriangleleft \boxed{\div 3} \blacktriangleleft\!\!\!\blacktriangleleft 21 \blacktriangleleft\!\!\!\blacktriangleleft \boxed{-2} \blacktriangleleft\!\!\!\blacktriangleleft 23$

input

input 9 $9 \times 3 = 27$ $27 + 2 = 29$

The completed table is:

×3 ⟶ +2	
input	**output**
1	5
3	11
5	17
7	23
9	29

Exercise 12A

1 For each question:
  - Copy and complete the table to show the output numbers.
  - Describe the pattern for the output numbers.
    (The first one has been done for you.)

(a)

×9	
1	9
2	18
3	27
4	36
5	45

$\}+9$
$\}+9$

Pattern: +9

(b)

×12	
1	
2	
3	
4	
5	

(c)

−4	
1	
2	
3	
4	
5	

(d)

−5	
4	
5	
6	
7	
8	

(e)

÷5	
15	
20	
25	
30	
35	

(f)

÷2	
12	
18	
24	
30	
36	

(g)

×3	
50	
48	
46	
44	
42	

(h)

×9	
1	
3	
5	
7	
9	

(i)

+5	
−1	
0	
1	
2	
3	

(j)

−3	
−5	
−4	
−3	
−2	
−1	

(k)

×3	
21	
22	
23	
24	
25	

(l)

÷9	
9	
18	
27	
36	
45	

2 For each question:

- Copy and complete the table to show the output numbers.
- Describe the pattern for the output numbers.

(a)

×6 → −8	
1	
2	
3	
4	
5	

(b)

+10 → ×3	
1	
2	
3	
4	
5	

(c)

×10 → ÷2	
2	
4	
6	
8	
10	

(d)

÷3 → +9	
18	
24	
30	
36	
42	

(e)

−4 → ×11	
5	
6	
7	
8	
9	

(f)

×8 → ÷5	
5	
10	
15	
20	
25	

(g)

−6 → ×7	
9	
12	
15	
18	
21	

(h)

+5 → ×4	
−3	
−2	
−1	
0	
1	

(i)

×4 → −1	
0.5	
1	
1.5	
2	
2.5	

(j)

×10 → +9	
0.1	
0.2	
0.3	
0.4	
0.5	

(k)

−7 → ×8	
6	
7	
8	
9	
10	

(l)

×10 → ÷4	
10	
20	
30	
40	
50	

3 For each question copy the table and fill in the missing numbers.

(a)

×7	
2	14
…	28
…	42
8	…
10	…

(b)

×5	
…	5
3	…
5	…
…	35
9	…

(c)

+8	
21	…
…	30
…	31
24	…
…	33

(d)

+11	
1	12
11	…
…	32
…	42
41	…

(e)

÷4	
28	…
44	…
…	15
76	…
92	…

(f)

×6	
0.5	3
1	6
…	9
2	…
…	15

(g)

+9	
19	...
...	33
...	38
34	...
39	...

(h)

+19	
99	...
...	119
...	120
...	121
103	...

(i)

×8	
...	56
8	...
9	...
...	80
...	88

(j)

×8 → −5	
0	...
2	...
...	27
6	43
...	59

(k)

×2 → +11	
10	...
...	45
...	59
31	73
38	...

(l)

−4 → ×3	
4	...
...	12
...	24
16	...
20	...

(m)

+9 → −4	
1	...
...	8
5	...
7	...
...	14

(n)

÷2 → ×8	
20	80
...	160
...	240
80	...
100	...

(o)

÷4 → −4	
12	...
24	...
...	5
...	8
...	11

(p)

×6 → +9	
11	...
...	81
13	...
14	...
15	...

(q)

+12 → ×3	
...	39
3	...
5	...
...	57
9	...

(r)

−8 → ×4	
1	−28
...	−20
...	−12
7	...
...	...

12.2 Number sequences

Each number in a sequence is called a **term**.

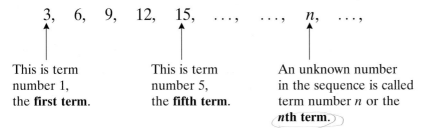

3,   6,   9,   12,   15,   ...,   ..., n,   ...,

This is term number 1, the **first term**.

This is term number 5, the **fifth term**.

An unknown number in the sequence is called term number n or the **nth term.**

■ **When investigating number sequences you can find:**

- **a rule to find the next term**
- **a general rule to find the nth term.**

> You will learn how to find the general rule for the nth term in section 12.3.

Look at this sequence:

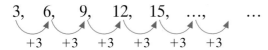

3,   6,   9,   12,   15,   ...,   ...
$+3$ $+3$ $+3$ $+3$ $+3$ $+3$

> The **difference** between each term and the next is $+3$

The next term is $15 + 3 = 18$.

The rule is **+3**.

If you know the first term and the difference you can generate a sequence of any number of terms.

Example 4

Find the next term and the rule for this sequence:

2,   6,   18,   54,   ...,   ...
$\times 3$ $\times 3$ $\times 3$ $\times 3$ $\times 3$

> You have to $\times 3$ to get the next term.

The next term is $54 \times 3 = 162$.

The rule is **×3**.

Generating a sequence

Ajay and Shareen are playing a sequence game. Ajay turns over 3 number cards and an operation card.

5	8	6	+
1st term	Difference	Number of terms	The difference must be added

Shareen uses the cards to generate a sequence.

The sequence must have 1st term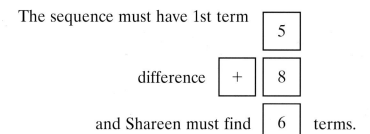

difference | + | 8

and Shareen must find | 6 | terms.

She records her sequence in a table:

Term number	Sequence
1	5
2	$5 + 8 = 13$
3	$13 + 8 = 21$
4	$21 + 8 = 29$
5	$29 + 8 = 37$
6	$37 + 8 = 45$

The sequence is:

$$5, 13, 21, 29, 37, 45$$

Exercise 12B

1   For each sequence write down:
   - the next 2 terms
   - the rule you used.

   (a) 2, 5, 8, 11, ...   **(b)** 7, 14, 21, ...
   (c) 30, 25, 20, ...   **(d)** 120, 100, 80, ...
   (e) 11, 22, 33, ...   **(f)** 4, 8, 16, ...
   (g) 64, 32, 16, ...   **(h)** 100 000, 10 000, 1000, ...
   (i) 2, 8, 32, ...   **(j)** 3, 27, 243, ...

2   Use the number and operation cards opposite to generate sequences.
   Remember:

   - The **1st card** gives the **1st term**.
   - The **2nd card** gives the **difference number**.
   - The **3rd card** tells you **how many terms** to find.
   - The **operation card** tells you **what to do with the difference number**.

   Record each sequence in a table.

(a)
| 2 | 9 | 5 | + |

(b)
| 5 | 11 | 6 | + |

(c)
| 8 | 13 | 4 | + |

(d)
| 2 | 5 | 4 | × |

(e)
| 3 | 2 | 4 | × |

(f)
| 20 | 4 | 5 | − |

(g)
| 36 | 7 | 4 | − |

(h)
| 48 | 2 | 4 | ÷ |

(i)
| 100 | 5 | 3 | ÷ |

(j)
| 19 | 12 | 6 | + |

12.3 Finding the *n*th term

You can use algebraic rules to help find any number in a
sequence. These rules are called **general rules**.
They help you find the **general** or ***n*th term**.

Example 5

Find the general rule for this sequence:

   8, 16, 24, 32, 40, …, …

Write the sequence and term numbers in a table.

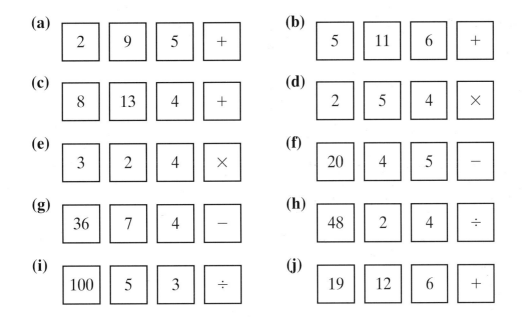

The rule for this
sequence is
'multiply the term
number by 8'.
The *n*th term is $8n$

You can use the
rule to find any term.
The 27th term
will be $8 \times 27 = 216$

Term number	Sequence
1 —×8→	8
2 —×8→	16
3 —×8→	24
4 —×8→	32
5 —×8→	40
6 —×8→	48
⋮	⋮
n —×8→	$8n$

Look for a **link**
between the term
number and the
term.

Exercise 12C

1 For each sequence find:
- the general rule
- the nth term.

(a)

Term number	Sequence
1 —×9→	9
2 —×9→	18
3 —×9→	27
4	36
⋮	⋮
n	

(b)

Term number	Sequence
1 —+5→	6
2 —+5→	7
3 —+5→	8
4	9
⋮	⋮
n	

(c)

Term number	Sequence
1	12
2	13
3	14
4	15
5	16
⋮	⋮
n	

(d)

Term number	Sequence
1	3
2	6
3	9
4	12
5	15
⋮	⋮
n	

(e)

Term number	Sequence
1	−5
2	−4
3	−3
4	−2
5	−1
⋮	⋮
n	

(f)

Term number	Sequence
1	4
2	8
3	12
4	16
5	20
⋮	⋮
n	

(g)

Term number	Sequence
1	28
2	29
3	30
4	31
5	32
⋮	⋮
n	

(h)

Term number	Sequence
1	0
2	1
3	2
4	3
5	4
⋮	⋮
n	

(i)

Term number	Sequence
1	$\frac{1}{2}$
2	1
3	$1\frac{1}{2}$
4	2
5	$2\frac{1}{2}$
⋮	⋮
n	

Hint: ÷

(j)

Term number	Sequence
1	$1\frac{1}{2}$
2	3
3	$4\frac{1}{2}$
4	6
5	$7\frac{1}{2}$
⋮	⋮
n	

Hint: ×

2   For each sequence:

- put the information into a table
- find the general rule.

(a) 8, 9, 10, 11, 12, …
(b) 5, 10, 15, 20, 25, …
(c) 6, 12, 18, 24, 30, …
(d) −2, −1, 0, 1, 2, …
(e) 22, 44, 66, 88, …
(f) 25, 50, 75, 100, …
(g) −5, −10, −15, −20, …
(h) $\frac{1}{4}$, $\frac{1}{2}$, $\frac{3}{4}$, 1, $1\frac{1}{4}$, …
(i) −4, −3, −2, −1, 0, …
(j) 1, 8, 27, 64, …

Hint: Think about powers in part **(j)**.

3   **(a)** Find the 10th term if the nth term is $5n$
      (b) Find the 8th term if the nth term is $n + 8$
      (c) Find the 5th term if the nth term is $12n$
      (d) Find the 100th term if the nth term is $n - 10$
      (e) Find the 23rd term if the nth term is $2n + 1$
      (f) Find the 16th term if the nth term is $3n - 1$
      (g) Find the 12th term if the nth term is $5n + 2$
      (h) Find the 9th term if the nth term is $n \div 3$
      (i) Find the 32nd term if the nth term is $3n \div 4$
      (j) Find the 57th term if the nth term is $7n + 5$
      (k) Find the 34th term if the nth term is $2n - 25$
      (l) Find the 84th term if the nth term is $3n + 1$

12.4 Using the difference to find the general rule

The sequence

    4, 7, 10, 13, 16, ...

can be written in a table:

Term number	Sequence
1	4
2	7
3	10
4	13
5	16
6	19
⋮	⋮
10	31
⋮	⋮
100	301
⋮	⋮
n	$3n + 1$

+3
+3
+3
+3

The difference
between terms is +3

The first part of the
general rule is $3n$

The difference between consecutive terms gives you the *first
part* of the general rule.

To find the *second part* of the general rule you need to try a few values:

Term number	3n	Sequence
1	3	4
2	6	7
3	9	10

Each time $3n$ is 1 less than the sequence.

You need to add 1 to $3n$.

The general rule is $3n + 1$.

■ **The difference between terms in a sequence gives the number to multiply n by in the general rule.**
You may need to add or subtract a number to complete the general rule.

Example 6

Find the nth term of the sequence

$3, 8, 13, 18, 23, \ldots$

Write the sequence in a table:

Term number	Sequence
1	3
2	8
3	13
4	18
5	23
⋮	⋮
n	

+5
+5
+5
+5

The rule must start with $5n$

Try a few values:

Term number	5n	Sequence
1	5	3
2	10	8
3	15	13

Each time $5n$ is 2 more than the sequence.
You need to subtract 2 from $5n$.

The general term is $5n - 2$

Example 7

Find the general term of the sequence

20, 16, 12, 8, 4, ...

Write the information in a table:

Term number	Sequence
1	20
2	16
3	12
4	8
5	4
⋮	⋮
n	

Rule starts
$-4 \times n$

Try a few values:

Term number	−4n	Sequence
1	−4	20
2	−8	16
3	−12	8

Each time $-4n$ is 24 less than the sequence. You have to add 24.

The general term is $-4n + 24$.

Exercise 12D

1   For each sequence find:
- the 10th and 100th terms
- the nth term.

(a)

Term number	Sequence
1	1
2	3
3	5
4	7
5	9
⋮	⋮
10	
⋮	⋮
100	
⋮	⋮
n	

(b)

Term number	Sequence
1	2
2	4
3	6
4	8
5	10
⋮	⋮
10	
⋮	⋮
100	
⋮	⋮
n	

(c)

Term number	Sequence
1	7
2	8
3	9
4	10
5	11
⋮	⋮
10	
⋮	⋮
100	
⋮	⋮
n	

(d)

Term number	Sequence
1	15
2	17
3	19
4	21
5	23
⋮	⋮
10	
⋮	⋮
100	
⋮	⋮
n	

(e)

Term number	Sequence
1	7
2	14
3	21
4	28
5	35
⋮	⋮
10	
⋮	⋮
100	
⋮	⋮
n	

(f)

Term number	Sequence
1	15
2	14
3	13
4	12
5	11
⋮	⋮
10	
⋮	⋮
100	
⋮	⋮
n	

(g)

Term number	Sequence
1	9
2	8
3	7
4	6
5	5
⋮	⋮
10	
⋮	⋮
100	
⋮	⋮
n	

(h)

Term number	Sequence
1	8
2	11
3	14
4	17
5	20
⋮	⋮
10	
⋮	⋮
100	
⋮	⋮
n	

(i)

Term number	Sequence
1	20
2	17
3	14
4	11
5	8
⋮	⋮
10	
⋮	⋮
100	
⋮	⋮
n	

(j)

Term number	Sequence
1	−3
2	−2
3	−1
4	0
5	1
⋮	⋮
10	
⋮	⋮
100	
⋮	⋮
n	

2 Use tables to find the general (nth) term for each sequence.

   (a) 0, 1, 2, 3, 4, …   **(b)** 11, 12, 13, 14, 15, …

   (c) 2, 6, 10, 14, 18, …   **(d)** 20, 18, 16, 14, 12, …

   (e) 5, 10, 15, 20, 25, …   **(f)** 100, 90, 80, 70, 60, …

   (g) −1, 0, 1, 2, 3, …   **(h)** 6, 11, 16, 21, 26, …

   (i) $\frac{1}{2}$, 1, $1\frac{1}{2}$, 2, $2\frac{1}{2}$, …   **(j)** 27, 24, 21, 18, 15, …

   (k) 7, 11, 15, 19, 23, …   **(l)** 3, 7, 11, 15, 19, …

   (m) 16, 21, 26, 31, 36, …   **(n)** 7, 9, 11, 13, 15, …

   (o) 10, 13, 16, 19, 22, …   **(p)** 16, 23, 30, 37, 44, …

   (q) 11, 15, 19, 23, 27, …   **(r)** −3, 1, 5, 9, 13, …

   (s) −3, −1, 1, 3, 5, …   **(t)** −1, 2, 5, 8, 11, …

   (u) −2, 3, 8, 13, 18, …   **(v)** 1, −3, −7, −11, −15, …

   (w) −2, −7, −12, −17, −22, …   **(x)** 8, 6, 4, 2, 0, …

   (y) 17, 14, 11, 8, 5, …   **(z)** 87, 75, 63, 51, 39, …

Summary of key points

1 When investigating number sequences you can find:
   - a rule to find the next term
   - a general rule to find the nth term.

2 The difference between terms in a sequence gives the number to multiply n by in the general rule. You may need to add or subtract a number to complete the general rule.

13 Decimals

13.1 Writing decimal numbers in size order

Sometimes you will need to sort measurements and decimal numbers in order of size.

Five pupils ran two 100 m races and their times were recorded. The differences between each pupil's two times (in seconds) were

2.18, 2.6, 4.3, 2.42, 3.06

Write these time differences in order of size, starting with the largest.

First look at the **whole number** part:

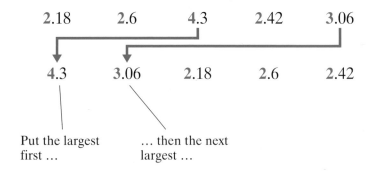

2.18, 2.6 and 2.42 all have 2 units.
Sort them using the **tenths** digit.

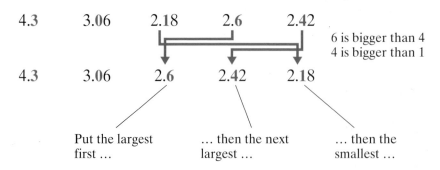

Now the time differences are in size order:
4.3, 3.06, 2.6, 2.42, 2.18.

■ **To sort decimal numbers in order of size:**
- **first compare the whole numbers**
- **next compare the tenths**
- **then compare the hundredths, and so on.**

Example 1

Sort these lengths in order, smallest first:

   0.387   0.411   0.382   0.425   0.41

There are no units, so sort by **tenths** first:

     0.387   0.411   0.382   0.425   0.41

     0.387   0.382   0.411   0.425   0.41

Next sort by **hundredths**:

     0.387   0.382   0.411   0.425   0.41

     0.387   0.382   0.411   0.41   0.425

Then by **thousandths**:

     0.387   0.382   0.411   0.41   0.425

     0.382   0.387   0.41   0.411   0.425

Hint: think of 0.41 as 0.410.

Exercise 13A

1   Rearrange these decimal numbers in order of size, starting with the largest:
- **(a)** 0.52, 0.61, 0.58, 0.66, 0.8
- **(b)** 5.4, 5.12, 5.75, 4.13, 4.09
- **(c)** 4.2, 2.6, 4.03, 4.15, 2.46
- **(d)** 0.32, 0.075, 0.307, 0.2, 0.09
- **(e)** 2, 4.53, 4.09, 2.48, 2.6
- **(f)** 0.07, 0.14, 0.009, 0.106, 0.034
- **(g)** 0.08, 0.9, 0.04, 0.2, 0.325
- **(h)** 3.09, 2.08, 3.2, 2.3, 2.16

2 Put these numbers in order of size, smallest first:
   (a) 3.74, 4.8, 4.15, 3.08, 4.22
   (b) 0.45, 0.09, 0.48, 0.032, 0.5
   (c) 6, 8.34, 6.02, 8.08, 6.009
   (d) 1.002, 0.24, 1.09, 1.15, 0.08

13.2 Adding and subtracting decimal numbers

You can add and subtract decimals in the same way as you
add and subtract sums of money.

Example 2

Alice sent a parcel containing two books. One
book weighed 1.4 kg and the other weighed
0.73 kg. The packaging weighed 75 g. Work out
the total weight, in kg, of the parcel.

First change 75 g to 0.075 kg.

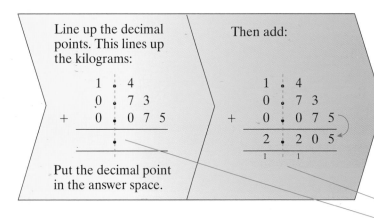

Line up the decimal
points. This lines up
the kilograms:

```
      1 . 4
      0 . 7 3
  +   0 . 0 7 5
  _____
        .
```

Put the decimal point
in the answer space.

Then add:

```
      1 . 4
      0 . 7 3
  +   0 . 0 7 5
  _____
      2 . 2 0 5
        1   1
```

Make sure you line
the decimal points
up – not the numbers.

The total weight is 2.205 kg.

■ **To add or subtract decimals:**
   ● **line up the decimal points**
   ● **put the point in the answer**
   ● **add or subtract.**

Example 3

Work out $72.64 - 35.328$. Show all your working.

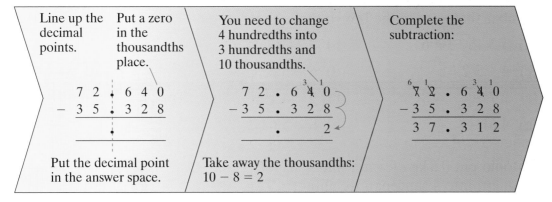

| Line up the decimal points. | Put a zero in the thousandths place. | You need to change 4 hundredths into 3 hundredths and 10 thousandths. | Complete the subtraction: |

$$\begin{array}{r} 7\ 2\ .\ 6\ 4\ 0 \\ -\ 3\ 5\ .\ 3\ 2\ 8 \\ \hline \end{array}$$

Put the decimal point in the answer space.

$$\begin{array}{r} 7\ 2\ .\ 6\ \overset{3}{\cancel{4}}\ \overset{1}{0} \\ -\ 3\ 5\ .\ 3\ 2\ 8 \\ \hline .\ \ \ \ \ 2 \end{array}$$

Take away the thousandths: $10 - 8 = 2$

$$\begin{array}{r} \overset{6}{\cancel{7}}\ \overset{1}{\cancel{2}}\ .\ 6\ \overset{3}{\cancel{4}}\ \overset{1}{0} \\ -\ 3\ 5\ .\ 3\ 2\ 8 \\ \hline 3\ 7\ .\ 3\ 1\ 2 \end{array}$$

The answer is 37.312.

Example 4

Without doing any working on paper, write down the number that should go in the box to make these true:

(a) $2.6 + \square = 3$ (b) $7 - 3.87 = \square$

(a) $2.6 + \square = 3$ The number in the box must be less than 1
You can work out mentally that $0.6 + 0.4 = 1$
so $2.6 + 0.4 = 3$

The answer is 0.4.

(b) $7 - 3.87 = \square$ $7 - 3.87$ is approximately $7 - 4 = 3$
You can work out mentally that
$0.87 + 0.13 = 1$
so $1 - 0.87 = 0.13$
$7 - 3.87 = 7 - 3 - 0.87$
$= 4 - 0.87$
$= 3 + 1 - 0.87$
$= 3 + 0.13$
$= 3.13$

The answer is 3.13.

Exercise 13B

1 Show all your working.
   (a) £53.64 + £32.57   (b) 3.95 kg + 2.67 kg
   (c) 137.5 + 0.72   (d) 3.29 + 16 + 0.538

2 **(a)** £6.84 − £2.47   **(b)** £15.20 − £9.78
    (c) 8.2 − 3.5   **(d)** 13.6 − 8.73

3 Without doing any working on paper, write down the number that goes in the box to make these true:

    (a) $5.3 + \boxed{} = 6$ **(b)** $7.24 + \boxed{} = 8$

    (c) $4 - 3.2 = \boxed{}$ **(d)** $6 - 5.6 = \boxed{}$

    (e) $2.7 + \boxed{} = 8$ **(f)** $9 - 4.1 = \boxed{}$

    (g) $4.61 + \boxed{} = 7$ **(h)** $8 - 5.63 = \boxed{}$

4 Antonio put 0.8 kg of water and 450 g of spaghetti into a saucepan weighing 1.27 kg. Work out the total weight of the saucepan and its contents.

5 Ali cut lengths of 0.76 m and 1.28 m from a five metre length of string. Work out the length of string left over.

13.3 Changing decimal numbers to fractions and fractions to decimals

■ **You can write decimal numbers as fractions using a place value diagram.**

Example 5

Change 0.15 into a fraction in its simplest form.

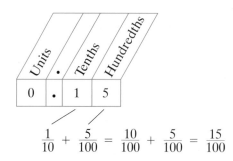

$$\frac{1}{10} + \frac{5}{100} = \frac{10}{100} + \frac{5}{100} = \frac{15}{100}$$

0.15 is the same as 15 hundredths.

Simplify:

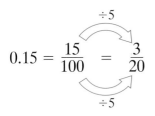

$$0.15 = \frac{15}{100} = \frac{3}{20}$$

To write the fraction in its simplest form, divide top and bottom by the common factor 5.

So 0.15 is equal to $\frac{3}{20}$.

■ **To change fractions to decimal numbers, divide the numerator (top) by the denominator (bottom).**

Example 6

Change these fractions into decimal numbers:

(a) $\frac{4}{5}$ **(b)** $\frac{5}{8}$ **(c)** $\frac{14}{25}$

(a) $\frac{4}{5}$ means $4 \div 5$, which equals 0.8.

Use these calculator keys:

| 4 | ÷ | 5 | = |

(b) $\frac{5}{8}$ means $5 \div 8$, which equals 0.625.

(c) $\frac{14}{25}$ means $14 \div 25$, which equals 0.56.

Exercise 13C

1 Change these decimals to fractions in their simplest form:

(a) 0.3 **(b)** 0.2 **(c)** 0.35 **(d)** 0.24
(e) 0.25 **(f)** 0.8 **(g)** 0.23 **(h)** 0.05
(i) 0.36 **(j)** 0.28 **(k)** 0.18 **(l)** 0.075
(m) 0.875 **(n)** 0.06 **(o)** 0.128 **(p)** 0.0625

2 Change these fractions to decimal numbers:

(a) $\frac{7}{10}$ **(b)** $\frac{19}{100}$ **(c)** $\frac{3}{100}$ **(d)** $\frac{31}{1000}$ **(e)** $\frac{3}{5}$

(f) $\frac{1}{8}$ **(g)** $\frac{7}{20}$ **(h)** $\frac{8}{25}$ **(i)** $\frac{2}{5}$ **(j)** $\frac{7}{8}$

(k) $\frac{3}{40}$ **(l)** $\frac{5}{16}$ **(m)** $\frac{3}{25}$ **(n)** $\frac{19}{20}$ **(o)** $\frac{68}{125}$

13.4 Rounding to the nearest whole number

If you do not need an accurate answer, you can give your answer to the nearest whole number.

■ **To round to the nearest whole number, look at the digit in the first decimal place:**
  - **If it is 5 or more, round the whole number up to the next whole number.**
  - **If it is less than 5, do not change the whole number.**

45.7

More than 5 so round up to 46

Example 7

Round these decimals to the nearest whole number.
(a) 36.2   **(b)** 43.5   **(c)** 0.82   **(d)** 29.64

(a) 36.2 is between 36 and 37.
  The digit in the first decimal place is 2 so round to 36.
(b) 43.5 is between 43 and 44.
  The digit in the first decimal place is 5 so round up to 44.
(c) 0.82 is between 0 and 1.
  The digit in the first decimal place is 8 so round up to 1.
(d) 29.64 is between 29 and 30.
  The digit in the first decimal place is 6 so round up to 30.

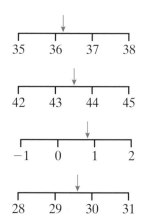

Exercise 13D

In questions **1** to **6** round the decimals to the nearest whole number.

1	**(a)** 4.8	**(b)** 3.2	**(c)** 6.5	**(d)** 4.82
2	**(a)** 16.398	**(b)** 5.701	**(c)** 10.49	**(d)** 29.6
3	**(a)** 0.7	**(b)** 11.299	**(c)** 49.35	**(d)** 200.09
4	**(a)** 19.52	**(b)** 3.99	**(c)** 237.35	**(d)** 79.08
5	**(a)** 4.189	**(b)** 299.8	**(c)** 4699.7	**(d)** 32.199
6	**(a)** 89.21	**(b)** 0.82	**(c)** 39.5	**(d)** 3999.54

13.5 Rounding to a number of decimal places

You sometimes need to use more exact figures.
If you round to whole numbers, the first finishers
in this race all have the same time:

- **To round (or correct) numbers to a given
  number of decimal places (d.p.), look at the
  digit in the next decimal place.**

Example 8

Write 5.2583 correct to 2 decimal places.

Look at the digit in the third decimal
place.

5.25**8**3

5.2583 is between 5.25 and 5.26.

Units	.	First decimal place (1 d.p.)	Second decimal place (2 d.p.)	Third decimal place (3 d.p.)	Forth decimal place (4 d.p.)
5	•	2	5	**8**	3

The digit in the third decimal place is 8, so you
round up to 5.26.

So 5.2583 = 5.26 (correct to 2 decimal places).

You can write this as 5.26 (to 2 d.p.).

Example 9

Round 6.3295   **(a)** to 1 d.p.   **(b)** to 2 d.p.   **(c)** to 3 d.p.

(a) To round to 1 d.p. look at the digit in the second
    decimal place. The digit is 2 so round down.

       6.3295 = 6.3 (to 1 d.p.)

6.3|295

(b) To round to 2 d.p. look at the digit in the third decimal
    place. The digit is 9 so round up.

       6.3295 = 6.33 (to 2 d.p.)

6.32|95

(c) To round to 3 d.p. look at the digit in the fourth
    decimal place. The digit is 5 so round up.

       6.3295 = 6.330 (to 3 d.p.)

6.329|5

You must include the final zero,
as '3 d.p.' means that three
decimal places must be shown.

In calculations you sometimes get an answer that repeats. These are called **recurring decimals**.

Recurring decimals

0.444 444 4 ... is called **0.4 recurring**. It is written **0.$\dot{4}$** (with a dot over the 4) for short.

3.247 247 247 ... is written **3.$\dot{2}4\dot{7}$** (with dots over the 2, 4 and 7).

0.444 444 ...

These dots show that the number goes on forever.

Example 10

Change these fractions to decimals, giving your answers to 3 decimal places:

(a) $\frac{1}{3}$ **(b)** $\frac{2}{3}$ **(c)** $\frac{3}{11}$

(a) $\frac{1}{3}$ means $1 \div 3$, which equals 0.333 333 ... (or 0.$\dot{3}$).

So $\frac{1}{3} = 0.333$ (to 3 d.p.)

0.333$_|$ 33 ...

(b) $\frac{2}{3}$ means $2 \div 3$, which equals 0.666 66 ... (or 0.$\dot{6}$).

So $\frac{2}{3} = 0.667$ (to 3 d.p.)

0.666$_|$ 66 ...

(c) $\frac{3}{11}$ means $3 \div 11$, which equals 0.272 727 ... (or 0.$\dot{2}\dot{7}$).

So $\frac{3}{11} = 0.273$ (to 3 d.p.)

0.272$_|$ 72 ...

Rounding money answers to the nearest penny

Rounding amounts of money is the same as rounding to 2 d.p.

Example 11

Fourteen people share equally the £72.50 bill for hiring a minibus. How much does each person pay? Give your answer to the nearest penny.

Work out £72.50 ÷ 14

Look at the digit in the third decimal place of £5.178 571 492.

£5.17**8** 571 429
The digit in the third decimal place is 8 so round up to £5.18.

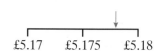
£5.17   £5.175   £5.18

■ **To round an answer in pounds to the nearest penny, look at the digit in the third decimal place:**
  ● **If it is 5 or more, round up the whole number of pence.**
  ● **If it is less than 5, do not change the whole number of pence.**

£2.37514

5 so round up to £2.38.

Example 12

The answer to a calculation is £354.283 24. Write this answer to the nearest penny.

£354.28**3** 24 is between £354.28 and £354.29.
The digit in the third decimal place is 3 so you round down.

The answer is £354.28 (to the nearest penny).

Exercise 13E

1   Round each number to 1 d.p.
    (a) 13.86   **(b)** 35.74   **(c)** 8.372   **(d)** 0.725

2   Round each number to 2 d.p.
    (a) 5.428   **(b)** 13.333   **(c)** 4.235   **(d)** 0.0535

3   Round each number to 3 d.p.
    (a) 4.8632   **(b)** 2.0008   **(c)** 5.2465   **(d)** 0.0397

4   Round each number to 4 d.p.
    (a) 2.465 28   **(b)** 0.032 73   **(c)** 0.000 45   **(d)** -2.699 97

5   Change these fractions to decimals, giving your answers correct to 3 decimal places.
    (a) $\frac{4}{9}$ **(b)** $\frac{5}{18}$ **(c)** $\frac{5}{7}$ **(d)** $\frac{7}{24}$

    (e) $\frac{1}{6}$ **(f)** $\frac{4}{15}$ **(g)** $\frac{5}{11}$ **(h)** $\frac{3}{7}$

Questions **6** to **9** are the answers to calculations. Write the answers to the nearest penny.

6   **(a)** £4.382   **(b)** £6.728   **(c)** £12.329
7   **(a)** £8.465   **(b)** £0.9254   **(c)** £21.7281
8   **(a)** £134.539 12   **(b)** £6831.8619   **(c)** £13.237 415
9   **(a)** £179.197 25   **(b)** £1639.8327   **(c)** £243.9982

In questions **10** and **11** give your answers to the nearest penny.

10 The price of a package holiday is £325. Holly pays for the holiday in six equal instalments. Work out the amount of one instalment.

11 Jasreet buys a telescope. The cash price is £316.78. Jasreet pays a deposit of one fifth of the cash price. How much is the deposit?

13.6 Rounding decimals to a number of significant figures

You will often be asked to round answers to 3 significant figures (for example). This is sometimes called 'giving the answer correct to 3 significant figures' or 'to 3 s.f.' for short. 'Significant' means 'important'.

There is more about significant figures on page 94.

The method is similar to the one used to round to a number of decimal places, but instead of counting the digits from the decimal point, you count from the first significant digit.

■ **To round (or correct) numbers to a given number of significant figures (s.f.), start counting the significant figures from the first non-zero digit on the left.**

Example 13

Round 0.023 804
(a) to 1 s.f.   **(b)** to 2 s.f.   **(c)** to 3 s.f.   **(d)** to 4 s.f.

			First significant figure	Second significant figure	Third significant figure	Fourth significant figure	Fifth significant figure					1 s.f.	2 s.f.	3 s.f.	4 s.f.	5 s.f.	
(a)	0	·	0	2	3	8	0	4	=	0	·	0	2					(to 1 s.f.)
(b)	0	·	0	2	3	8	0	4	=	0	·	0	2	4				(to 2 s.f.)
(c)	0	·	0	2	3	8	0	4	=	0	·	0	2	3	8			(to 3 s.f.)
(d)	0	·	0	2	3	8	0	4	=	0	·	0	2	3	8	0		(to 4 s.f.)

This zero shows that you have rounded to four s.f.

Exercise 13F

1 Round these numbers
- to 1 s.f.
- to 3 s.f.

(a) 0.072 86 (b) 0.2735 (c) 28.241 (d) 31.273
(e) 0.004 329 (f) 5.0632 (g) 568.73 (h) 0.018 24
(i) 0.1563 (j) 0.004 387 (k) 0.2934 (l) 0.5702
(m) 42.182 (n) 9.245 (o) 0.067 83 (p) 0.008 247
(q) 3.006 14 (r) 2.040 92 (s) 0.036 81 (t) 0.002 396

2 Write these to the number of significant figures given in the brackets.

(a) 0.078 21 (2 s.f.) (b) 3.7825 (1 s.f.)
(c) 23.965 (4 s.f.) (d) 3628.9 (1 s.f.)
(e) 2143.7 (2 s.f.) (f) 43.982 (3 s.f.)

13.7 Multiplying decimals

Multiplying by 10, 100 and 1000

You can multiply decimal numbers by 10, 100 and 1000 in the same way that you multiply whole numbers by 10, 100 and 1000.

■ **To multiply decimals:**
- **by 10, move the digits one place to the left**
- **by 100, move the digits two places to the left**
- **by 1000, move the digits three places to the left.**

$$28.63 \times 10 \quad = 286.3$$
$$52.65 \times 100 \ = 5265$$
$$0.89 \times 1000 = 890$$

Example 14

Without using a calculator, write down the answers to:
(a) 2.91×10 **(b)** 0.28×1000

(a) $2.91 \times 10 = 29.1$ Move the digits 1 place to the left.
(b) $0.28 \times 1000 = 280$ Move the digits 3 places to the left.

Multiplying by whole numbers

You need to know how to multiply decimal numbers by small whole numbers without using a calculator.

Example 15

Find the cost of 7 pairs of socks at £2.35 a pair.

$$\begin{array}{r} 235 \\ \times \quad 7 \\ \hline 1645 \\ \hline {\scriptstyle 2\,3} \end{array}$$

Multiply the numbers together, ignoring the decimal point.

The number 235 is 100 times 2.35, so 1645 is 100 times the actual answer.
To find the actual answer divide 1645 by 100.

The cost of the socks is £16.45.

Notice that the answer and the original number have the same number of digits after the decimal point:

$$235 \times 7 = 1645$$
$$2.35 \times 7 = 16.45$$

Two digits on the right of the decimal point.
The original number has two decimal places.

■ **When you multiply a decimal number by a whole number, the answer has the same number of digits after the decimal point as the original decimal number.**

Example 16

Work out 8.26×3.

$$
\begin{array}{r}
826 \\
\times \quad 3 \\
\hline
2478 \\
\hline
{\scriptstyle 1}
\end{array}
$$

Remember to show the carry numbers.

8.26

Two digits on the right of the decimal point, so the answer has two digits on the right of the decimal point.

The answer is 24.78.

To multiply decimal numbers by larger whole numbers you can use long multiplication.

Example 17

Work out 5.82×43.

5.82×3 ———————— 17.46

5.82×40 ———————— 232.8

5.82×43 ———————— 250.26

Remember to keep the decimal point in the same place.

So $5.82 \times 43 = 250.26$.

Multiplying by another decimal number

To multiply a decimal number by another decimal number without using a calculator, you could convert the decimal numbers to fractions.

For example, to work out 0.3×0.8:

$$0.3 \times 0.8 = \frac{3}{10} \times \frac{8}{10} = \frac{3 \times 8}{10 \times 10} = \frac{24}{100} = 0.24$$

There is more on multiplying fractions on page 172.

So $0.3 \times 0.8 = 0.24$.

In the same way, to work out 7.3×4.2:

$$7.3 \times 4.2 = \frac{73}{10} \times \frac{42}{10}$$

$$= \frac{73 \times 42}{10 \times 10}$$

$$= \frac{3066}{100}$$

$$= 30.66$$

Work out 73×42
by long multiplication:

$$
\begin{array}{r}
73 \\
\times \quad 42 \\
\hline
146 \\
2920 \\
\hline
3066 \\
\hline
\end{array}
$$

■ **If you multiply a number with one digit on the right of the decimal point by another number with one digit on the right of the decimal point, the answer has two digits on the right of the decimal point.**

$7.3 \times 4.2 = 30.66$

Example 18

Work out 4.6×7.4.

4.6×7.4 is approximately $5 \times 7 = 35$.

By long multiplication: $46 \times 74 = 3404$.

The answer will have two digits to the right of the decimal point.

So $4.6 \times 7.4 = 34.04$.

You can use the approximate answer to work out where the decimal point goes.

Exercise 13G

Write down the answers in questions **1** and **2** without any working:

1 (a) 4.38×100 (b) 58.4×10 (c) 0.326×10
    (d) 0.054×10 (e) 8.54×1000 (f) 0.08×100

2 (a) 7.82×100 (b) 58.34×10 (c) 2.867×1000
    (d) 2.94×10 (e) 28.7×100 (f) 0.02×1000

3 Find the cost of:
   (a) 7 books at £2.35 each
   (b) 3 kg of apples at £0.54 per kg
   (c) 8 oranges at £0.36 each
   (d) 4 CDs at £11.28 each.

Work out the answers in questions **4** and **5**, showing all your working.

4   **(a)** 6.7×2 **(b)** 3.8×3 **(c)** 9.2×5
   (d) 4.26×4 **(e)** 13.7×8 **(f)** 3.19×6

5   **(a)** 28.24×9 **(b)** 5.7×5 **(c)** 29.83×7
   (d) 7.68×5 **(e)** 8.15×4 **(f)** 12.36×8

6   Work out:
   (a) 5.23×24 **(b)** 6.41×52 **(c)** 4.53×27
   (d) 21.43×43 **(e)** 61.42×35 **(f)** 78.26×56

7   Find the answers:
   (a) 0.4×0.6 **(b)** 0.7×0.3 **(c)** 1.3×0.6
   (d) 2.4×3.1 **(e)** 4.5×2.9 **(f)** 5.7×8.6

8   Find the total cost, in pounds, of three pizzas at £2.45 each and six drinks at 52 pence each.

9   Calculate the total cost of three shirts which cost £14.65 each and five pairs of socks which cost £2.83 a pair.

10   Find the total weight of 32 pairs of shoes if each pair weighs 1.24 kg.

13.8 Dividing decimals

Dividing by 10, 100 and 1000

You can divide decimal numbers by 10, 100 and 1000 in the same way that you divide whole numbers by 10, 100 and 1000.

■   **To divide decimals:**
   ● **by 10, move the digits one place to the right**
   ● **by 100, move the digits two places to the right**
   ● **by 1000, move the digits three places to the right.**

$76.85 \div 10 \ = 7.685$
$47.6 \div 100 \ = 0.476$
$782 \div 1000 = 0.782$

Example 19

Without using a calculator, write down the answers to:
(a) $42.18 \div 100$ **(b)** $9.3 \div 1000$

(a) $42.18 \div 100 = 0.4218$ Move the digits 2 places to the right.

(b) $9.3 \div 1000 = 0.0093$ Move the digits 3 places to the right.
To do this you need to put in two zeros.

Dividing by small whole numbers

You also need to know how to divide decimal numbers by small whole numbers without using a calculator.

■ **To divide a decimal number by a whole number, line up the decimal points and divide as normal.**

Example 20

Work out:
(a) $23.8 \div 7$ **(b)** $0.36 \div 8$

(a) $23.8 \div 7$ is approximately $20 \div 7 =$ approximately 3.

$$\begin{array}{r} 3.4 \\ \hline 7\,)\,23.8 \end{array}$$

Line up the decimal point in the answer.
Divide as normal.

The answer is 3.4.

(b) $0.36 \div 8$ is approximately $0.4 \div 8 =$ approximately 0.05.

$$\begin{array}{r} 0.045 \\ \hline 8\,)\,0.360 \end{array}$$

Remember to include carry numbers.
Add a nought and carry the 4 to make 40.

The answer is 0.045.

Dividing by decimal numbers

■ **To divide by a decimal number:**
● **make it into a whole number by multiplying it by a power of 10**
● **multiply the number you are dividing into by the same power of 10.**

Example 21

Work out $76.23 \div 0.9$.

$76.23 \div 0.9$ is approximately $80 \div 0.9 = \dfrac{80}{0.9} = \dfrac{800}{9} =$ about 88.

You need to change 0.9 to a whole number by multiplying by 10.

$$76.23 \div 0.9 = \frac{76.23}{0.9} = \frac{762.3}{9}$$

$\times 10$

$\times 10$

$$\begin{array}{r} 84.7 \\ 9\overline{)762.3} \end{array}$$

So $76.23 \div 0.9 = 84.7$.

Exercise 13H

1 Work out:
  (a) $493 \div 10$ **(b)** $74.2 \div 100$ **(c)** $538.4 \div 10$
  (d) $982.4 \div 1000$ **(e)** $2.3 \div 100$ **(f)** $46.5 \div 1000$
  (g) $4.5 \div 100$ **(h)** $0.08 \div 10$ **(i)** $2.9 \div 1000$

2 Find one share if:
  (a) three people share £4.02 equally
  (b) four people share £213.60 equally
  (c) six people share £11.64 equally
  (d) seven people share £107.52 equally.

Work out the answers in questions **3** and **4**, showing all your working.

3 **(a)** $9.8 \div 2$ **(b)** $8.7 \div 3$ **(c)** $133.5 \div 5$
  (d) $29.22 \div 6$ **(e)** $0.714 \div 7$ **(f)** $0.432 \div 8$
  (g) $0.0072 \div 4$ **(h)** $9.045 \div 9$ **(i)** $2.104 \div 5$

4 **(a)** $7.62 \div 0.6$ **(b)** $26.36 \div 0.4$ **(c)** $8.88 \div 0.3$
  (d) $18.36 \div 0.9$ **(e)** $7.161 \div 0.03$ **(f)** $2.538 \div 0.04$

5 40.75 kg of peanuts is packed into 9 bags, each containing an equal weight of peanuts. Work out the weight of peanuts in each bag. Give your answer correct to 2 decimal places.

6 Kerry ran for 0.7 hours. The distance she ran was 6.72 km. Work out her average speed, in kilometres per hour.

13.9 Using mental methods with decimals

You can multiply and divide some decimal numbers by small whole numbers without using a calculator or doing any working on paper.

Example 22

Work these out mentally:
(a) 6.2×3 **(b)** $32.8 \div 8$

(a) 6.2×3 is approximately $6 \times 3 = 18$.
  6.2×3 is the same as $(6 \times 3) + (0.2 \times 3)$
$$= 18 + 0.6$$

So the answer is 18.6

(b) $32.8 \div 8$ is approximately $30 \div 8$, between 3 and 4.
  $32 \div 8$ is exactly 4 and $0.8 \div 8$ is exactly 0.1.
  So $32.8 \div 8 = 4 + 0.1 = 4.1$

You can sometimes multiply or divide a decimal by a large whole number by using factors.

Example 23

Work these out, using the factors of the whole number:
(a) 5.2×18 **(b)** $88.41 \div 21$

(a) 5.2×18 is approximately $5 \times 20 = 100$
  $5.2 \times 18 = 5.2 \times 3 \times 6$
  $5.2 \times 3 = 15.6$
  $15.6 \times 6 = 93.6$

  So $5.2 \times 18 = 93.6$

Remember: the results will have 1 decimal place.

$$\begin{array}{r} 156 \\ \times\ \ 6 \\ \hline 936 \\ \hline {\scriptstyle 3\ 3} \end{array}$$

(b) $88.41 \div 21$ is approximately $90 \div 20 = 9 \div 2 = 4.5$

21 is 3×7 so ...

... divide by 3 ... and divide the answer by 7

$$3 \overline{\smash{)}88.41}^{\,29.47}_{2\ 1\ 2} \qquad 7\overline{\smash{)}29.47}^{\,4.21}_{1}$$

$88.41 \div 21 = 4.21$

Hint: do the divisions on paper to help.

Exercise 13I

1 Work these out without writing down any working:

    (a) 4.3×3 **(b)** 6.3×2 **(c)** 21.2×4

    (d) 18.7×5 **(e)** $16.8 \div 4$ **(f)** $156.9 \div 3$

    (g) $54.9 \div 9$ **(h)** $27.2 \div 8$

2 Use the factors of the whole number to work out:

    (a) 3.2×15 **(b)** 6.1×14 **(c)** 4.3×24

    (d) $73.8 \div 18$ **(e)** $46.5 \div 15$ **(f)** $32.94 \div 27$

3 Use any of the methods shown in this section to find:

    (a) 7.1×6 **(b)** 8.2×9 **(c)** $24.6 \div 6$

    (d) 3.2×16 **(e)** $108.5 \div 35$ **(f)** $225.6 \div 24$

13.10 Estimating answers

In chapter 6 you used rounding to check whole number calculations. You can check calculations with decimals in the same way.

- **To estimate an answer to a calculation round all the numbers to one significant figure and do the calculation with the rounded numbers.**

Example 24

Estimate the answer to:

(a) £12.45 $\times$ 7.2   **(b)** £21.06 $\div$ 3.9   **(c)** $\dfrac{17.228 + 22.84}{2.1}$

(a) Rounding 12.45 and 7.2 to 1 s.f. gives 10 and 7.
So the estimate for £12.45 $\times$ 7 is £10 $\times$ 7 = £70.

Actual answer: £89.64

(b) Rounding 21.06 and 3.9 to 1s.f. gives 20 and 4.
So the estimate for £21.06 ÷ 3.9 is £20 ÷ 4 = £5.

Actual answer: £5.40

(c) An estimate is $\dfrac{20 + 20}{2} = \dfrac{40}{2} = 20.$

Actual answer: 19.08

Multiplying and dividing by numbers between 0 and 1

If you multiply 7 by 0.2 the result is 1.4, which is smaller than 7.
If you multiply 62 by 0.83 the result is 51.46, smaller than 62.

■ **If you start with any number and multiply by a decimal number between 0 and 1, the result will be smaller than the number you started with.**

If you divide 42 by 0.6 the result is 70, which is bigger than 42.
If you divide 13.26 by 0.85 the result is 15.6, bigger than 13.26.

■ **If you start with any number and divide it by a decimal number between 0 and 1, the result will be bigger than the number you started with.**

Try some other calculations like these on your calculator.

So far in this chapter you have estimated answers by rounding to whole numbers.
For numbers between 0 and 1 you should round to 1 significant figure.

Example 25

For each of **(a)** and **(b)**:
- Work out an estimate for the answer.
- Use a calculator to work out the exact value.
- State whether the estimate is a reasonable approximation for the exact value.

(a) 32.45 × 0.68   **(b)** 8.019 ÷ 0.22

(a) 0.68 is between 0 and 1 so the answer will be smaller than 32.45.
To 1 s.f., 32.45 is 30 and 0.68 is 0.7, so do:

$$\frac{30}{1} \times \frac{7}{10} = \frac{210}{10} = 21$$

Using a calculator, the actual answer is 22.066, so 21 is a good estimate.

(b) 0.22 is between 0 and 1 so the answer will be bigger than 8.019.

To 1 s.f., 8.019 is 8 and 0.22 is 0.2, so do:

$$\frac{8}{1} \div \frac{2}{10} = \frac{8}{1} \times \frac{10}{2} = \frac{80}{2} = 40$$

Using a calculator, the answer is 36.45, so 40 is a good estimate.

Exercise 13J

Do not use a calculator in questions **1**, **2** and **3**.

1 Estimate these answers by rounding to 1 significant figure:
   (a) 19.45×3.2 **(b)** $17.48 \div 3.8$
   (c) $(676.8 + 13.97) \times 4.23$

2 Without doing the calculation 49.5×0.6, write down which one of these could be the correct answer: 29.7 or 297.

3 Without doing the calculation $223.6 \div 0.43$, write down which one of these could be the correct answer: 5.2, 52 or 520.

In questions **4** to **18**:

(a) Write down a calculation that you could use to estimate the answer.
(b) Do the calculation (without a calculator).
(c) Use a calculator to work out the exact answer.

4 £18.35 × 2.8   **5** £29.40 × 4.2

6 £1853.45 × 5.4   **7** £21.09 ÷ 3.7

8 £18.88 ÷ 2.95   **9** £27.02 ÷ 2.8

10 £302.15 × 8.4   **11** 18.943 ÷ 3.8

12 3.15 × 0.82   **13** 3.038 ÷ 0.4

14 3.8 × (41.3 + 19.47)   **15** 0.42 × (9.23 + 27.9)

16 $\dfrac{61.4 - 22.64}{8.16}$ **17** $\dfrac{39.12 + 21.3}{0.53}$

18 $\dfrac{18.428 + 21.64}{0.45 \times 2.1}$

Summary of key points

1 To sort decimal numbers in order of size:
   - first compare the whole numbers
   - next compare the tenths
   - then compare the hundredths, and so on.

2 To add or subtract decimals:
   - line up the decimal points
   - put the point in the answer
   - add or subtract.

3 You can write decimal numbers as fractions using a place value diagram.

4 To change fractions to decimal numbers, divide the numerator (top) by the denominator (bottom).

5 To round to the nearest whole number, look at the digit in the first decimal place:
   - If it is 5 or more, round the whole number up.
   - If it is less than 5, do not change the whole number.

   45.7

   More than 5 so round up to 46.

6 To round (or correct) numbers to a given number of decimal places (d.p.), look at the digit in the next decimal place.

7 To round an answer in pounds to the nearest penny, look at the digit in the third decimal place:
   - If it is 5 or more, round up the whole number of pence.
   - If it is less than 5, do not change the whole number of pence.

   2.375 14

   5 so round up to £2.38.

8 To round (or correct) numbers to a given number of significant figures (s.f.), start counting the significant figures from the first non-zero digit on the left.

9 To multiply decimals:
   - by 10, move the digits one place to the left
   - by 100, move the digits two places to the left
   - by 1000, move the digits three places to the left.

   $28.63 \times 10 = 286.3$
   $52.65 \times 100 = 5265$
   $0.89 \times 1000 = 890$

10 When you multiply a decimal number by a whole number, the answer has the same number of digits after the decimal point as the original decimal number.

11 If you multiply a number with one digit on the right of the decimal point by another number with one digit on the right of the decimal point, the answer has two digits on the right of the decimal point.

$7.3 \times 4.2 = 30.66$

12 To divide decimals:
- by 10, move the digits one place to the right
- by 100, move the digits two places to the right
- by 1000, move the digits three places to the right.

$76.85 \div 10 = 7.685$

$47.6 \div 100 = 0.476$

$782 \div 1000 = 0.782$

13 To divide a decimal number by a whole number, line up the decimal points and divide as normal.

14 To divide by a decimal number:
- make it into a whole number by multiplying it by a power of 10
- multiply the number you are dividing into by the same power of 10.

15 To estimate an answer to a calculation round all the numbers to one significant figure and do the calculation with the rounded numbers.

16 If you start with any number and multiply by a decimal number between 0 and 1, the result will be smaller than the number you started with.

$15 \times 0.3 = 4.5$

17 If you start with any number and divide it by a decimal number between 0 and 1, the result will be bigger than the number you started with.

$15 \div 0.3 = 50$

14 Percentages

14.1 Percentages, fractions and decimals

Percentages, fractions and decimals can be used to write amounts which are not whole numbers.

17% means '17 out of 100'.
As a fraction this is $\frac{17}{100}$.

17% and $\frac{17}{100}$ represent the same amount.

■ **You can write any percentage as a fraction with a denominator of 100.**
   For example, $9\% = \frac{9}{100}$.

Example 1

Write 55% as a fraction in its simplest form.

$$55\% = \frac{55}{100} = \frac{11}{20}$$

$\div 5$

$\div 5$ — Divide the numerator and denominator by the common factor 5.

So $55\% = \frac{11}{20}$.

You can also write a percentage as a decimal.

6% means $\frac{6}{100}$ which means $6 \div 100 = 0.06$

■ **To change a percentage to a decimal divide by 100.**
   For example, $25\% = 25 \div 100 = 0.25$

> Remember:
> To divide by 100 move the digits two places to the right.

Example 2

Change to decimals:
(a) 7%   **(b)** 12.5%

(a) $7\% = \frac{7}{100} = 7 \div 100 = 0.07$

(b) $12.5\% = \frac{12.5}{100} = 12.5 \div 100 = 0.125$

You can write decimals and fractions as percentages.

■ **To change a decimal to a percentage multiply the decimal by 100%.**

■ **To change a fraction to a percentage, first change the fraction to a decimal then multiply by 100%.**

Example 3

Change to percentages:

(a) 0.21   (b) $\frac{3}{8}$ (c) $\frac{1}{3}$

(a) $0.21 \times 100\% = 21\%$

(b) $\frac{3}{8} = 3 \div 8 = 0.375$
$0.375 \times 100\% = 37.5\%$

(c) $\frac{1}{3} = 1 \div 3 = 0.3333\ldots$
$0.3333\ldots \times 100\% = 33.\dot{3}\% \text{ (or } 33\frac{1}{3}\%)$

> $33.333\ldots$ is a recurring decimal and is written as $33.\dot{3}$

Exercise 14A

1. Change these percentages to fractions:
   (a) 13%   (b) 73%   (c) 3%
   (d) 29%   (e) 1%   (f) 91%
   (g) 49%   (h) 19%

2. Change these percentages to fractions in their simplest form:
   (a) 90%   (b) 35%   (c) 25%
   (d) 12%   (e) 60%   (f) 15%
   (g) $66\frac{2}{3}\%$ (h) 12.5%

3. Change these percentages to decimals:
   (a) 8%   (b) 62%   (c) 39%
   (d) 85%   (e) 16%   (f) 12.5%
   (g) 2.5%   (h) 8.2%

4. Change these decimals and fractions to percentages:
   (a) 0.54   (b) 0.6   (c) 0.03
   (d) 0.724   (e) $\frac{7}{10}$ (f) $\frac{3}{5}$
   (g) $\frac{6}{25}$ (h) $\frac{7}{8}$

5 Copy and complete this table of equivalent percentages, fractions and decimals.

Percentage	Fraction	Decimal
80%	$\frac{4}{5}$	0.8
23%		
	$\frac{3}{4}$	
45%		
	$\frac{3}{10}$	
		0.625
4%		
	$\frac{2}{3}$	

> 80%, $\frac{4}{5}$ and 0.8 are equivalent. They are three different ways of writing the same number.

14.2 Finding a percentage of an amount

Here are some common percentages and their equivalent fractions and decimals. It is useful to be able to recognise them.

$$25\% = \tfrac{1}{4} = 0.25 \qquad 50\% = \tfrac{1}{2} = 0.5 \qquad 75\% = \tfrac{3}{4} = 0.75$$

$$10\% = \tfrac{1}{10} = 0.1 \qquad 20\% = \tfrac{1}{5} = 0.2 \qquad 70\% = \tfrac{7}{10} = 0.7$$

$$33\tfrac{1}{3}\% = \tfrac{1}{3} = 0.\dot{3} \qquad 66\tfrac{2}{3}\% = \tfrac{2}{3} = 0.\dot{6} \qquad 1\% = \tfrac{1}{100} = 0.01$$

Sometimes you can find a percentage of an amount without using a calculator.
This method uses fractions.

Example 4

Work out 20% of £35.

Convert 20% to a fraction:

$$20\% = \tfrac{20}{100} = \tfrac{1}{5}$$

Work out $\tfrac{1}{5}$ of £35:

$$£35 \div 5 = £7$$

So 20% of £35 = £7

20% = $\frac{1}{5}$
So divide
£35 by 5

Some percentages cannot be written as simple fractions.
You will need to use a calculator.

Example 5

Work out 11% of 75 m.

First change 11% to a decimal. $11\% = 0.11$.

11% of $75 = \frac{11}{100} \times 75 = 0.11 \times 75 = 8.25$

So 11% of 75 m is 8.25 m.

■ **To find a percentage of an amount change the percentage to a fraction or a decimal and multiply the fraction or decimal by the amount.**

You can also use the $\boxed{\%}$ key on your calculator to find percentages.

Exercise 14B

1   Of the 28 people on the bus, 25% of them are going to the terminus. How many people are going to the terminus?

2   In a sale all the marked prices were reduced by 10%.
    (a) Work out the reduction for a shirt with a marked price of £17.
    (b) What was the sale price of the shirt?

3   20% of the 150 pupils in Year 9 chose basketball as their favourite sport. How many pupils chose basketball?

4   Work out:
    (a) 10% of £8   (b) 50% of £9
    (c) 20% of £15   (d) 25% of 32 m
    (e) 75% of 36 kg   (f) 30% of 20 m
    (g) 1% of £26   (h) 15% of £50
    (i) $33\frac{1}{3}\%$ of 18 cm

5   Work out:
    (a) 23% of £250   (b) 3% of £80
    (c) 15% of £24   (d) 4% of 35 kg
    (e) 5% of 32 m   (f) 17.5% of £16

14.3 Increasing and decreasing by a percentage

You can increase or decrease an amount by a percentage.

- **To increase an amount by a percentage find the percentage of the amount and add it to the original amount.**

- **To decrease an amount by a percentage find the percentage of the amount and subtract it from the original amount.**

Example 6

A shop offered a discount of 15% off the usual prices. Work out the new price of a CD usually costing £12.

Discount = 15% of £12
$$= 0.15 \times 12 = £1.80$$

Remember:
$15\% = \frac{15}{100} = 0.15$

New price = Usual price − Discount
$$= £12 - £1.80$$
$$= £10.20$$

The new price of the CD is £10.20.

Exercise 14C

1   Without using a calculator, find the new amount when:
   (a) £70 is increased by 10%
   (b) £18 is decreased by 50%
   (c) 32 m is increased by 25%
   (d) 25 kg is decreased by 10%
   (e) 16 m is increased by 75%
   (f) £600 is decreased by 3%
   (g) £150 is increased by 6%
   (h) 18 kg is decreased by $33\frac{1}{3}\%$

Remember to include the units in your answer.

2 Amina earns £320 a week working in an office. She is given a 3% pay rise. Work out Amina's new weekly wage.

3 In September the number of pupils in Year 9 was 240. By the following February the number had increased by 5%. How many pupils were there in Year 9 in February?

4 A new car was bought for £8400. After 2 years it had lost 30% of its value. Work out the value of the car after 2 years.

5 A travel agency offers a discount of 16% off a holiday usually costing £350. What is the new cost of the holiday?

6 Alan paid £425 for his saxophone four years ago. It has increased in value by 8%. Work out the value of Alan's saxophone now.

7 In a sale all the usual prices were reduced by 15%. Find the sale price of a radio usually priced at £52.

8 Last year Rebecca's bus fare to school was £2.50. This year fares have increased by 4%. What is Rebecca's bus fare now?

9 In January an office had 150 employees. By July the number of employees had decreased by 2%. How many employees were there in July?

10 Find the new amount when:
  (a) £125 is increased by 6%
  (b) £48 is decreased by 7%
  (c) 18 litres is increased by 15%
  (d) 10.8 kg is decreased by 5%
  (e) £52 is increased by 12.5%
  (f) 37.5 kg is decreased by 8%.

14.4 Making comparisons using percentages

You can write one amount as a percentage of another amount.

Example 7

Write 660 g as a percentage of 4 kg.

To compare the amounts the units must be
the same. You have to change 4 kg to 4000 g.

Step 1: Write as a fraction: $\frac{660}{4000}$

Step 2: Change the fraction to a decimal:
$660 \div 4000 = 0.165$

Step 3: Change the decimal to a percentage: $0.165 \times 100\% = 16.5\%$

So 660 g is 16.5% of 4 kg.

- ■ **To write one amount as a percentage of another:**
  - **Write one amount as a fraction of the other.**
  - **Change the fraction to a decimal.**
  - **Multiply the decimal by 100%.**

You can also use percentages to compare results of surveys and other statistics.

Example 8

In this survey people
were asked to pick
their favourite breakfast
cereal. Compare the
results for Qwik-brek,
Muesli-luxe and
Wheat-flakes.

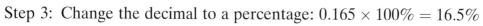

430 out of
1600 people
like
QWIK-BREK
best

2/7 of
people like
Muesli-luxe
best

31% of the
people like
Wheat-flakes
best

Change the results
to percentages:

Qwik-brek: 430 out of $1600 = \frac{430}{1600} = 0.26875$

$\qquad 0.26875 \times 100\% = 26.875\% = 26.9\%$ (to 1 d.p.)

Muesli-luxe: $\frac{2}{7} = 2 \div 7 = 0.2857\ldots = 28.57\ldots\% = 28.6\%$ (to 1 d.p.)

Wheat-flakes: 31%

The percentages show that Wheat-flakes are the most popular,
then Muesli-luxe, then Qwik-brek.

- ■ **You can use percentages to compare numerical data.**

Exercise 14D

1 900 pupils took part in a sponsored walk and 603 of them finished within 4 hours. What percentage of the pupils is this?

2 Imran sowed 70 flower seeds and 63 of them produced plants. What percentage of the seeds produced plants?

3 Katharine has 150 books and 33 of them are about History. What percentage of her books are about History?

4 Out of 125 new mugs inspected, 6 were chipped. What percentage of the mugs were chipped?

5 There are 48 cars in the staff car park and 15 of them are red. What percentage of the cars are red?

6 Write:
   (a) 27 pence as a percentage of £2.25
   (b) 900 m as a percentage of 4 km
   (c) 63 cm as a percentage of 5 m
   (d) 78 g as a percentage of 3 kg

7 Stephanie gained 43 marks out of 50 for the first Maths test and 51 marks out of 60 for the second Maths test.
   (a) Change the marks to percentages.
   (b) In which test did Stephanie do best?

8 80% of the Group 9G pupils entered the school quiz, 29 of the 32 pupils in Group 9W entered and $\frac{7}{8}$ of Group 9T entered. Use percentages to compare the entries of the three Groups.

9 In the French test Kieran gained 42 marks out of 60, in the Maths test he gained 78 out of 80 and in the Geography test he gained 41 out of 50.
   (a) Convert Kieran's test marks to percentages.
   (b) Write down his results in order, starting with the highest.

10 Of the pupils in Year 9, $\frac{3}{16}$ like Pete's band best, 22.5% like Winston's band best and $\frac{5}{24}$ like Georgia's band best. Work out the order of popularity of the three bands, starting with the most popular.

14.5 Profit and loss

If you buy an article the price you pay is called the **cost price**. If you later sell the article, the amount of money you are paid is called the **selling price**.

If you sell an item for a higher price than you paid for it you make a **profit**. If you sell it for a lower price you make a **loss**.

■ **A profit or a loss is the difference between the cost price and the selling price.**
- **If a profit is made: selling price = cost price + profit**
- **If a loss is made: selling price = cost price − loss**

Example 9

Sabia paid £7500 for a car two years ago. She recently sold the car at a loss of 28%. What price did she sell the car for?

Loss = 28% of £7500
$\qquad = \frac{28}{100} \times £7500 = 0.28 \times £7500 = £2100$

Selling price = cost price − loss
$\qquad\qquad = £7500 − £2100$
$\qquad\qquad = £5400$

Sabia sold the car for £5400.

You can write the profit or loss as a percentage of the cost price.

■ **Percentage profit $= \dfrac{\textbf{profit}}{\textbf{cost price}} \times \textbf{100\%}$**

■ **Percentage loss $= \dfrac{\textbf{loss}}{\textbf{cost price}} \times \textbf{100\%}$**

Example 10

William bought a television from a wholesaler for £336 and sold it in his shop for £399. Calculate his percentage profit.

Profit = £399 − £336 = £63

Percentage profit $= \dfrac{\text{profit}}{\text{cost price}} \times 100\%$
$\qquad\qquad\qquad = \frac{£63}{£336} \times 100\%$
$\qquad\qquad\qquad = 0.1875 \times 100\% = 18.75\%$

Percentage profit = 18.75%

Exercise 14E

1. For each of these calculate the selling price:
   (a) cost price = £80 profit = 5%
   (b) cost price = £260 profit = 12.5%
   (c) cost price = £85 loss = 14%
   (d) cost price = £170 loss = 7.5%

2. Ben bought some shirts from a wholesaler for £10.50 each. He sold them in his shop and made a 32% profit. What is the selling price of each shirt?

3. Helen bought a Hi-fi for £87.50 and later sold it at a loss of 8.4%. How much did Helen sell the Hi-fi for?

4. For each of these calculate the percentage profit:
   (a) cost price = £60 selling price = £63
   (b) cost price = £52 selling price = £65
   (c) cost price = £90 selling price = £108

5. For each of these calculate the percentage loss:
   (a) cost price = £48 selling price = £42
   (b) cost price = £125 selling price = £90
   (c) cost price = £40 selling price = £37.50

6. John bought a car for £6400 and sold it for £4832. Calculate his percentage loss.

7. A shop bought a fridge for £210 and sold it to a customer for £280. Find the percentage profit made by the shop. Give your answer to 1 decimal place.

8. Bronwen bought a bicycle for £279. She later sold it for £190. Calculate her percentage loss, correct to 1 decimal place.

14.6 Taxation

VAT

Value Added Tax (VAT) is the amount that is added to bills for services and purchases. The rate for VAT in the UK for most goods and services is $17\frac{1}{2}\%$.

Example 11

VAT at $17\frac{1}{2}\%$ is added to a telephone bill of £76.84. Work out the total amount to be paid.

VAT = 17.5% of £76.84 = $0.175 \times$ £76.84 = £13.447
$\qquad$ = £13.45 (to the nearest penny)

Total cost = £76.84 + £13.45 = £90.29 (to the nearest penny)

Here is a useful non-calculator method to work out VAT at $17\frac{1}{2}\%$:

Example 12

Without using a calculator, work out the VAT at $17\frac{1}{2}\%$ on an electrician's bill of £42.

$17\frac{1}{2}\% = 17.5\% = 10\% + 5\% + 2.5\%$

10% of £42 = $\frac{1}{10} \times$ £42 = £42 ÷ 10 = £4.20

5% is half of 10%, so 5% of £42 $\quad$ = £2.10 $\quad$ (halving)

2.5% is half of 5%, so 2.5% of £42 = £1.05 $\quad$ (halving)

Adding the three values:
$$17.5\% \text{ of } £42 = \underline{£7.35}$$

So the VAT is £7.35

Income tax

When you earn more than a certain amount of money you have to pay income tax to the government.
Some of your income is tax free (no income tax is paid on it). The rest of it (your **taxable income**) is taxed.

■ **Taxable income = total earnings − tax-free income**

For the tax year 2001–2002 (6 April 2001–5 April 2002), income tax was paid on taxable income at these rates:

Taxable income	Rate of income tax
Up to £1880	10%
£1881–£29 400	22%
Over £29 400	40%

Example 13

Mr Green's taxable income for the year 2001–2002 is
£30 120.

Calculate the amount of income tax Mr Green pays.

	£
At 10%:	1880
At 22%:	27 520 +
TOTAL	29 400
At 40%:	Any extra taxable income above £29 400

Step 1:
Tax on the first £1880 of taxable income at 10%:
10% of £1880 = 0.10 × 1880   = £188

Step 2:
The amount of taxable income to be taxed at 22% is
£29 400 − £1880 = £27 520

Tax on the next £27 520 of taxable income at 22%:
22% of £27 520 = 0.22 × £27 520   = £6054.40

Step 3:
The amount of taxable income to be taxed at 40% is
£30 120 − £29 400 = £1720

Tax on the remaining £720 of taxable income at 40%:
40% of £720 = 0.40 × 720   = £288

Total tax paid = £188 + £6054.40 + £288
              = £6530.40

Exercise 14F

In this exercise take the VAT rate to be $17\frac{1}{2}\%$.

1 Without using a calculator, work out the VAT on these
prices:
- **(a)** £40
- **(b)** £60
- **(c)** £240
- **(d)** £28
- **(e)** £720
- **(f)** £34
- **(g)** £26
- **(h)** £62.40

2 Work out the VAT on these prices:
- **(a)** £38
- **(b)** £250
- **(c)** £56.40
- **(d)** £900
- **(e)** £562
- **(f)** £27.20

3 Add VAT (to the nearest penny) to these prices:
- **(a)** £14.84
- **(b)** £63.28
- **(c)** £124.99

4   Calculate the VAT on a £24.80 bill
for a meal for three.

5   A builder charges £520 plus VAT for
repairing a roof. Work out the total bill.

6   The price of a computer is £579 plus VAT at 17.5%.
Find the full cost, inclusive of VAT, correct to the
nearest penny.

7   Two stores advertised the
same fridge.
  (a) Which is the cheaper price,
     including VAT?
  (b) What is the difference in
     the prices, including VAT?

8   Gemma's taxable income for
2001–2002 is £16 500. Using the rates for income tax
given on page 256 work out how much income tax
Gemma pays.

9   Calculate the amount of income tax payable for the
year 2001–2002 on these taxable incomes:
  (a) £5500
  (b) £17 800
  (c) £35 800

14.7 Buying on credit

If you want to buy items without paying the full cost
immediately you can buy them **on credit**. You pay a deposit
and then make a number of regular payments.

Example 14

The cash price of a cooker is £460. Leanne buys
the cooker on credit. She has to pay a deposit
of 15% of the cash price and then 24 monthly
payments of £19.50. Calculate:
(a) the total cost of buying the cooker on credit
(b) the amount Leanne would save if she paid cash.

(a) Deposit = 15% of £460 = 0.15 × £460 = £69
Total monthly payments = 24 × £19.50 = £468
Total credit cost = £69 + £468 = £537

(b) Difference in cost = £537 − £460 = £77
Leanne would save £77 if she paid cash.

Exercise 14G

For each question work out:
(a) the total cost of buying on credit
(b) the difference between the cash price and the cost of
buying on credit.

1 The cash price of a television is £585. It can
be bought with a deposit of 20% and
12 monthly payments of £46.30.

2 A car costs £8400. The credit terms are a
deposit of 15%, followed by 24 monthly
payments of £346.25.

3 A CD player costs £135. The credit agreement requires
a deposit of 12% and 12 monthly payments of £11.75.

4 The cash price for double glazing is £4520. The credit
terms are a deposit of 25% plus 36 monthly payments
of £112.60.

5 A bicycle costs £240. It can be bought on credit with a
deposit of 18% followed by 24 monthly payments of
£9.65.

6 A computer costs £749. The credit terms are a deposit
of 15% and 18 monthly payments of £41.50.

14.8 Simple interest

If you invest money in a bank savings account the bank pays you **interest**.

If you borrow money from a bank you have to pay interest to the bank. The interest is a percentage of the amount you invest or borrow.

■ **Simple interest over several years is calculated assuming that the sum of money invested or borrowed remains the same over those years and that the percentage rate of interest remains the same over those years.**

Example 15

Mark invests £250 for 3 years at an interest rate of 3.5% per annum. Calculate the simple interest he earns.

> **Per annum** (or **p.a.**) means each year.

Interest for 1 year is 3.5% of £250: $0.035 \times £250 = £8.75$

Simple interest for 3 years: $£8.75 \times 3 = £26.25$

> Remember:
> $3.5\% = \dfrac{3.5}{100} = 0.035$

Exercise 14H

1 Find the simple interest when:
 (a) £500 is invested for 2 years at 4% p.a.
 (b) £724 is invested for 5 years at 3% p.a.
 (c) £250 is invested for 3 years at 3.4% p.a.
 (d) £612 is invested for 4 years at 4.5% p.a.
 (e) £280 is invested for 3 years at $3\frac{1}{2}\%$ p.a.

2 Javed invests £185 for 5 years at 4.2% per annum.
 Work out the simple interest he earns.

3   Amy borrows £450 from a bank for 3 years at 5.4%
per annum. Calculate:
(a) the simple interest she must pay
(b) the total amount she owes after 3 years.

4   Paul wants to borrow £3500 for 3 years. He can borrow
from a bank at a simple interest rate of 6.2% per
annum or from a credit company at a simple interest
rate of 8.6% per annum. Work out the difference
between the amounts of interest he would have to pay
the bank and the credit company.

Summary of key points

1   You can write any percentage as a fraction with
denominator of 100. For example, $9\% = \frac{9}{100}$.

2   To change a percentage to a decimal divide by 100.
For example, $25\% = 25 \div 100 = 0.25$

3   To change a decimal to a percentage multiply the
decimal by 100%.

4   To change a fraction to a percentage, first change
the fraction to a decimal then multiply the decimal
by 100%.

5   To find a percentage of an amount change the
percentage to a fraction or a decimal and multiply
the fraction or decimal by the amount.

6   To increase an amount by a percentage find the
percentage of the amount and add it to the original
amount.

7   To decrease an amount by a percentage find the
percentage of the amount and subtract it from the
original amount.

8   To write one amount as a percentage of another:
● Write one amount as a fraction of the other.
● Change the fraction to a decimal.
● Multiply the decimal by 100%.

9 You can use percentages to compare numerical data.

10 A profit or a loss is the difference between the cost price and the selling price.
   - If a profit is made:
     selling price = cost price + profit
   - If a loss is made:
     selling price = cost price − loss

11 Percentage profit $= \dfrac{\text{profit}}{\text{cost price}} \times 100\%$

12 Percentage loss $= \dfrac{\text{loss}}{\text{cost price}} \times 100\%$

13 Taxable income = total earnings − tax-free income

14 Simple interest over several years is calculated assuming that the sum of money invested or borrowed remains the same over those years and that the percentage rate of interest remains the same over those years.

15 Perimeter, area and volume

15.1 Perimeter and area

Lake Garda is the largest lake in Italy and is one of the country's best known holiday resorts.

The perimeter of the lake is 158.40 kilometres (km)

The area of the lake is 369.98 square kilometres (km^2)

■ **Remember that:**

- **The distance around a two-dimensional (or flat) shape is called the perimeter of the shape.**
- **The amount of space covered by a two-dimensional shape is called the area of the shape.**

Example 1

This shape has been made from centimetre squares.

(a) Work out the perimeter of the shape.
(b) Work out the area of the shape.

The centimetre squares are rearranged to make a square.

(c) Work out the perimeter and area of the square.

(a) There are 34 centimetre edges so the perimeter of the shape is 34 cm.
(b) There are 36 centimetre squares, so the area of the shape is 36 cm^2.
(c) The centimetre squares can be rearranged to make a 6 × 6 square:

The square has four sides, each of 6 cm length.

So the perimeter of the square is 4 × 6 = 24 cm.

The square is still made from 36 centimetre squares, so the area is still 36 cm^2.

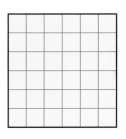

Exercise 15A

1 This shape is made of centimetre squares.

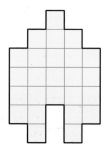

(a) Find the perimeter and area of the shape.

The squares are rearranged to form a square.

(b) Find the perimeter and area of the square.

2 24 square tiles are laid out as a 2 by 12 rectangle.

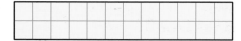

The perimeter of this rectangle is 28 units.
The area of this rectangle is 24 square units.
Use **all** of these twenty-four square tiles to make other rectangles of various sizes.
Which rectangle will have the smallest perimeter?

3 This rectangle has a perimeter of 24 cm.
Draw other rectangles with perimeters of 24 units.
Which rectangle has the largest area?

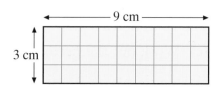

4 This irregular shape has been drawn on centimetre squared paper.

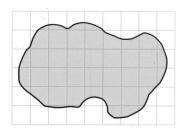

Work out an estimate of the area of the shape.

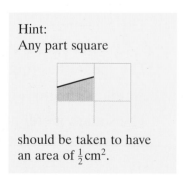

Hint:
Any part square

should be taken to have an area of $\frac{1}{2}$ cm^2.

5 Here are the first four stages in a pattern made from centimetre squares.

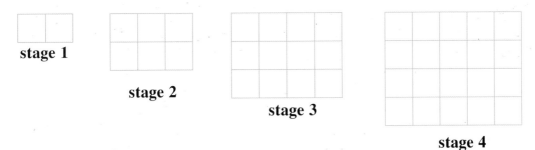

stage 1

stage 2

stage 3

stage 4

The length of each rectangle is 1 cm more than the width.
(a) Work out the perimeter and area of each rectangle.
(b) Work out the perimeter and area of the rectangle in the 10th stage. Explain how you worked out your answer.

15.2 Perimeter and area of a rectangle

The perimeter of any shape can be worked out by adding together the lengths of the sides of the shape.

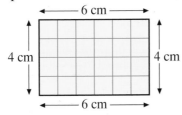

The perimeter of this rectangle is:

$$6 + 4 + 6 + 4 = 20\,\text{cm}$$

This is the same as:

$$2 \times 6 + 2 \times 4 = 12 + 8 = 20\,\text{cm}$$

You can write a **formula** in words for the perimeter:

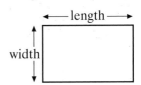

$$\text{Perimeter} = 2 \times \text{length} + 2 \times \text{width}$$
$$= 2 \times (\text{length} + \text{width})$$
$$= 2(\text{length} + \text{width})$$

Using brackets means that the '×' sign can be missed out.

You can write this using symbols:

$$Perimeter = 2(length + width)$$
$$P = 2(l + w)$$

> Remember:
> Work the brackets
> out first.

So for any rectangle:

- **Perimeter of a rectangle = 2 (length + width)**
  $$= 2(l + w)$$

You can count squares to find the area of a rectangle ...
... but there is a much easier way.

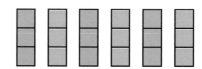

This rectangle
has area 18 cm³

Imaging splitting this
rectangle ...

... into six lots of
three squares.

You can then find the area by multiplying:

6 lots of 3 squares
$= 6 \times 3 = 18 \text{ cm}^3$

For any rectangle:

- **Area of a rectangle = length × width**
  $$= lw$$

Example 2

This diagram represents a sports field.

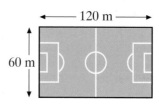

Calculate:
(a) the perimeter of the field   (b) the area of the field.

(a) The perimeter is worked out
    by the formula
$$P = 2(l + w)$$
$$= 2 \times (120 + 60)$$
$$= 2 \times 180$$
$$P = 360 \text{ metres}$$

(b) The area is worked out
    by the formula
$$A = l \times w$$
$$= 120 \times 60$$
$$A = 7200 \text{ square metres}$$

Exercise 15B

1 Calculate the perimeter and area of each of these shapes.

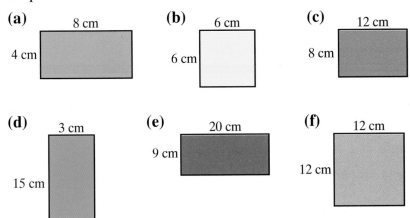

(a) 8 cm, 4 cm

(b) 6 cm, 6 cm

(c) 12 cm, 8 cm

(d) 3 cm, 15 cm

(e) 20 cm, 9 cm

(f) 12 cm, 12 cm

2 Work out the perimeter and area of a rectangle measuring:
(a) 5 cm by 3 cm
(b) 8 cm by 10 cm
(c) 12 cm by 3 cm
(d) 6 m by 14 m

3 The perimeter of a rectangle is 28 cm.
The width of the rectangle is 4 cm.
Work out:
(a) the length of the rectangle
(b) the area of the rectangle.

4 A rectangle measures 12 cm by 3 cm.
A square has the same area as the above rectangle.
Work out the length of a side of the square.

5 The diagram represents an L-shaped floor space.
Work out the area of the floor space.

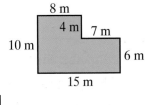

8 m
4 m 7 m
10 m
6 m
15 m

6 Work out the shaded area.

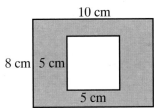

10 cm
8 cm 5 cm
5 cm

15.3 Area of a triangle, parallelogram and trapezium

Triangle

The area of a triangle is **half** the area of the surrounding rectangle.

The area of the surrounding rectangle is base × height

■ **For any triangle:**
   Area of a triangle = $\frac{1}{2}$ × base × height
   or $A = \frac{1}{2}bh$

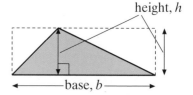

Parallelogram

A parallelogram is made from two equal triangles:
The area of the parallelogram is

   2 × area of one triangle

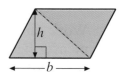

■ **For any parallelogram:**
   Area of parallelogram = $2 \times \frac{1}{2}$ × base × vertical height
   = base × vertical height
   or $A = bh$

Trapezium

This shape is a trapezium.
It has two parallel sides, the **top** and the **base**.

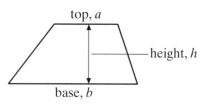

Imagine rearranging
the trapezium …

… to make a rectangle
with the same area

You can see that
   length of rectangle $= \dfrac{\text{top} + \text{base}}{2}$

■ **So for any trapezium:**
   Area of a trapezium $= \dfrac{\text{top} + \text{base}}{2}$ × height

   or $A = \frac{1}{2}(a+b)h$

Example 3

(a) Work out the area of the trapezium.
(b) A triangle has an area equal to the area of the trapezium. The length of the base of the triangle is 32 cm.
    Work out the height of the triangle.

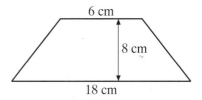

(a) The area of the trapezium $= \dfrac{\text{top} + \text{base}}{2} \times \text{height}$

$$= \dfrac{18 + 6}{2} \times 8$$

$$= 12 \times 8 = 96 \,\text{cm}^2$$

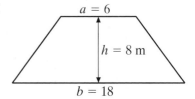

(b) The area of the triangle $= 96 \,\text{cm}^2$
    Using:

$$\text{Area of triangle} = \tfrac{1}{2} \times \text{base} \times \text{height}$$

$$96 = \tfrac{1}{2} \times 32 \times \text{height}$$

$$96 = 16 \times \text{height}$$

so height of triangle $= \dfrac{96}{16} = 6 \,\text{cm}$

Exercise 15C

1 Work out the area of each of these shapes.

(a)

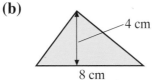

(b)

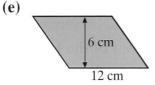

(c)

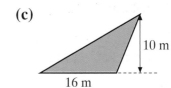

(d)

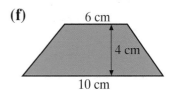

(e)

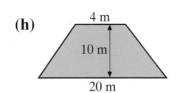

(f)

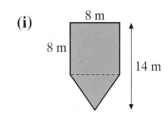

(g)

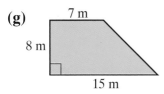

(h)

(i)

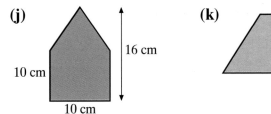

(j) 16 cm 10 cm 10 cm

(k) 9 cm 8 cm 16 cm

(l) 12 cm 3 cm 10 cm

2 Work out the area of the shaded region in each of these cases.

(a)

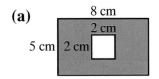

8 cm
2 cm
5 cm 2 cm

(b)

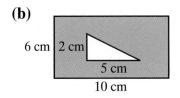

6 cm 2 cm
5 cm
10 cm

(c)

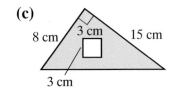

8 cm 3 cm 15 cm
3 cm

3 The diagram represents the blueprint of a swimming pool.
The pool is in the shape of a rectangle with a triangular end piece.
The overall length of the pool is 40 metres.
The width of the pool is 25 metres.
Work out the area of the surface of the pool.

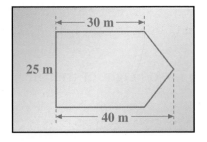

30 m
25 m
40 m

4 The diagram represents an architect's plan of the front of a house.

3 m
14 m
9 m
16 m

Work out the area of the front of the house.

5 Work out the shaded area.

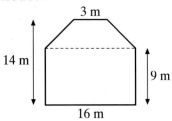

9 cm
3 cm
5 cm
15 cm

6   The diagram represents the cross-section of a tunnel.

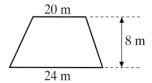

Work out the area of the cross-section.

15.4 Circumference and area of a circle

The perimeter of a circle is called the **circumference**.

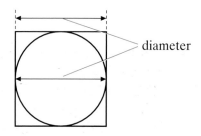

The smallest square around any circle
has sides equal to the diameter:

The circumference of the circle is:

less than 4 diameters: greater than 2 diameters:

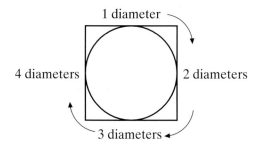
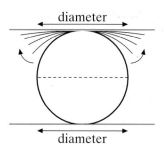

So the circumference is between 2 and 4 times its diameter.
A good estimate is about 3 times the diameter.

■   **The actual formula is:**
   Circumference of a circle = $\pi \times$ diameter

π is the number you get when you divide a circle's
circumference by its diameter.

π is a Greek letter.
It is pronounced
'pie'.

π is the same for all circles and its value is 3.14 correct to
two decimal places. π is also approximately $\frac{22}{7}$.

The area of a circle

You also use π to calculate the area of a circle.
If you draw a circle surrounded by a square the area is ...

... less than the area
of the square

... greater than half the
area of the square

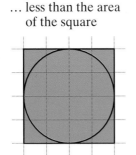

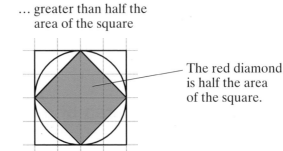

The red diamond
is half the area
of the square.

So a good estimate for the area of the circle is
approximately $\frac{3}{4}$ of the area of the square.

Since the length of a side of the square is the diameter
of the circle:

Area of circle is approximately $= \frac{3}{4} \times (\text{diameter})^2$

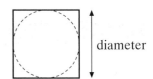

diameter

The area of the square is:
diameter $\times$ diameter $= (\text{diameter})^2$

The actual formula is:

$$\text{Area of a circle} = \frac{\pi}{4} \times (\text{diameter})^2$$

$$= \frac{\pi}{4} \times (2 \times \text{radius})^2$$

$$= \frac{\pi}{4} \times 4 \times (\text{radius})^2$$

$$= \pi \times (\text{radius})^2$$

■ **So the formula is:**
Area of a circle $= \pi \times (\text{radius})^2$

Using symbols:

■ **The formula for the circumference of a circle is:**

$$C = \pi d \quad \text{or} \quad C = 2\pi r$$

■ **The formula for the area of a circle is:**

$$A = \frac{\pi d^2}{4} \quad \text{or} \quad A = \pi r^2$$

Key:
C = circumference
A = area
r = radius

Example 4

Work out the circumference and area of this circle.

(i)   in terms of π (ii)   using $\pi = 3.14$ (iii)   using $\pi = \dfrac{22}{7}$

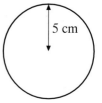

5 cm

Using $C = 2\pi r$, the circumference is $C = 2 \times \pi \times 5 = 10 \times \pi$

So   (i) $C = 10\pi$ cm

     (ii) $C = 10 \times 3.14 = 31.4$ cm

     (iii) $C = 10 \times \dfrac{22}{7} = \dfrac{220}{7}$ cm

Using $A = \pi r^2$, the area is $A = \pi \times 5^2 = \pi \times 25$

So   (i) $A = 25\pi$ cm^2

     (ii) $A = 25 \times 3.14 = 78.5$ cm^2

     (iii) $A = 25 \times \dfrac{22}{7} = \dfrac{25 \times 22}{7} = \dfrac{550}{7}$ cm^2

Exercise 15D

1   Work out the circumference and area of each of these circles. In each case **(i)** leave your answer in terms of π, and **(ii)** give your answer correct to 1 d.p.

(a)

20 cm

(b)

9 cm

(c)

6 cm

(d)

30 cm

(e)

25 cm

(f)

19 cm

2   The diagram shows a semicircle of radius 5 cm.

5 cm

Work out:

(a) the area of this semicircle

(b) the perimeter of the semicircle.

Hint:
Remember to include the base in the perimeter.

Using **(i)** $\pi = 3.14$ **(ii)** $\pi = \dfrac{22}{7}$

3   The circumference of a circle is 628 cm.
Work out:

(a) the radius of the circle

(b) the area of the circle.

4 Work out the area of the shaded region:
   (a) in cm²
   (b) in mm²

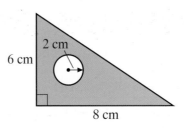

5 Work out:
   (a) the perimeter and area of the square
   (b) the circumference and area of the circle
   (c) the area of the shaded region.

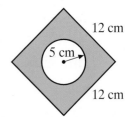

6 The circumference of a circle is 314 cm.
   Work out the area of the circle.

Example 5

This mirror is a rectangle with a semicircle at one end.

Work out:
(a) the perimeter
(b) the area.

(Take π to be 3.14)

The top of the mirror is half of a circle with radius 20 cm.
The circle would have:

$$\text{circumference} = 2 \times 3.14 \times 20$$
$$= 125.6 \text{ cm}$$

$$\text{area} = 3.14 \times 20^2$$
$$= 1256 \text{ cm}^2$$

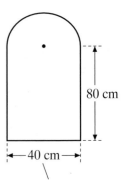

The radius of the
semicircle will
be 20 cm

(a) The perimeter of the mirror is:
   $80 + 40 + 80 + (\frac{1}{2}$ perimeter of full circle)

   $$= \quad 200 \quad + \quad 62.8$$
   $$= 262.8 \text{ cm}$$

> Remember to
> include the units in
> your answer.

(b) The area of the mirror is:
   (area of rectangle) $+ (\frac{1}{2}$ area of circle)

   $$= \quad 3200 \quad + \quad 628$$
   $$= 3828 \text{ cm}^2$$

Exercise 15E

(Assume $\pi = 3.14$)

1 The diagram represents a running track.
The shape of the field is rectangular with two
semicircular ends.
Work out:
(a) the perimeter of the track
(b) the area of the track.

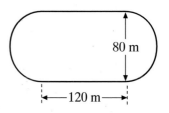

2 The diagram represents a church door.
The door is a rectangle with a semicircular top.
Work out:
(a) the perimeter of the door
(b) the area of one of the faces of the door.

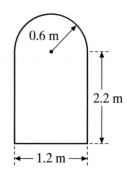

3 The diagram shows a table mat:

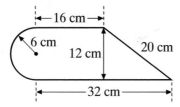

The mat is made from a rectangle with a triangle at
one end and a semicircle at the other end.
Work out:
(a) the perimeter of the table mat
(b) the area of the table mat.

4 Wendi cuts a sheet of tin into a rectangle with a
semicircle cut away from one of the ends.
Work out the perimeter and area of the
sheet of tin:
(a) in metres and metres^2
(b) in centimetres and centimetres^2.

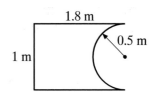

5 The diagram represents the cross-section of a
door stopper.
The cross-section is a right-angled triangle
joined to a semicircle.
Work out the area of the cross-section.

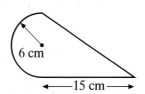

15.5 Volume

Solid shapes and hollow shapes take up space in three dimensions.

They are called 3-dimensional (or 3-D) shapes.

■ **The amount of space taken up by a three-dimensional shape is called the volume of the shape.**

Volume of a cuboid

This cuboid is made from centimetre cubes.

Each cube has a volume of $1\,cm^3$ or 1 cubic centimetre.

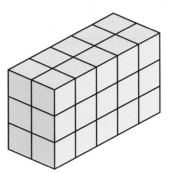

There are $2 \times 5 = 10$ cubes in each layer.

There are 3 layers, so the total number of cubes is:

$$2 \times 5 \times 3 = 10 \times 3 = 30 \text{ cubes}$$

and the volume of the cuboid is $30\,cm^3$.

The volume of this cuboid $= 2 \times 5 \times 3$
$= \text{length} \times \text{width} \times \text{height}$

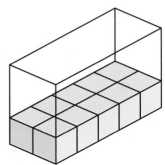

■ **For any cuboid:**
The volume of a cuboid = length × width × height

Example 6

Work out the volume of this cuboid.
Using the formula:

$$\text{volume} = 10 \times 8 \times 3 = 80 \times 3 = 240\,cm^3$$

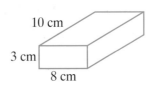

Exercise 15F

1   Work out the volume of each of these cuboids.

(a)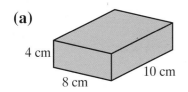

(b)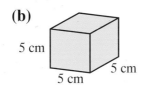

(c)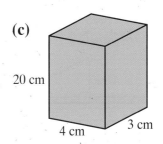

2   Work out the volume of a cuboid which measures 8 cm by 12 cm by 10 cm.

Volume of a prism

A prism is a 3-dimensional shape with a constant cross-section.
These shapes are all prisms.

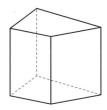 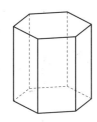 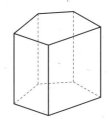

The formula for the volume of a cuboid is
> volume = length × width × height

> = area of base × height

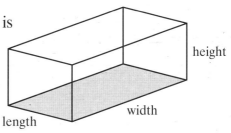

The volume of a cuboid could also be worked out by
> volume = height × width × length

> = area of cross-section × length

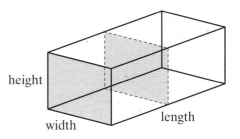

This formula will also be true for any prism.

■   **For any prism:**
   The volume of a prism is:

   volume = area of base × height

   or

   volume = area of cross-section × length.

Example 7

Work out the volume of this prism.

The cross-section of the prism is a right-angled triangle.

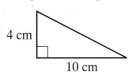

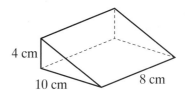

The area of the cross-section is
$$\tfrac{1}{2} \times 4 \times 10 = 2 \times 10$$
$$= 20\,\text{cm}^2$$

Remember to include the units in your answer.

Use the formula:

volume of prism = area of cross-section × length
$$= 20 \times 8 = 160\,\text{cm}^3$$

Exercise 15G

1 Work out the volume of each of these prisms.

(a)

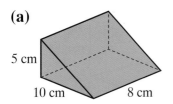

(b)

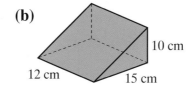

(c)

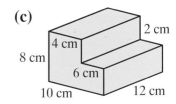

(d)

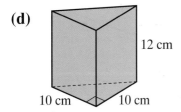

(e)

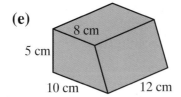

(f)

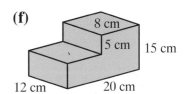

(g)

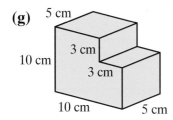

(h)

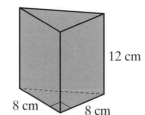

(i)

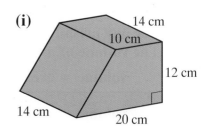

2   The diagram represents the face of a church door.

The door is 4 cm thick.

Work out the volume
of the door:
(a) in centimetres
(b) in metres.

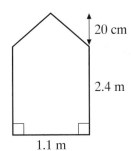

20 cm

2.4 m

1.1 m

Hint:
Make sure all
measurements are in
the same units
before you start.

3   Work out the volume of each of these prisms.

(a)

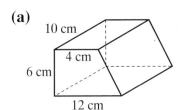

10 cm

4 cm

6 cm

12 cm

(b)

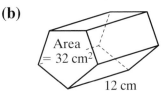

Area
= 32 cm²

12 cm

(c)

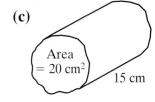

Area
= 20 cm²

15 cm

4   The diagram shows the cross-section of a prism.

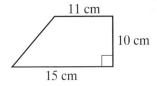

11 cm

10 cm

15 cm

The length of the prism is 8 cm.
Work out the volume of the prism.

5   The diagram shows the base of a prism.
The volume of the prism is 210 cm³.
Work out the height of the prism.

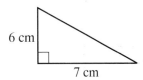

6 cm

7 cm

6   Which of these two shapes has the greater volume and
by how much?

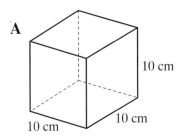

A

10 cm

10 cm

10 cm

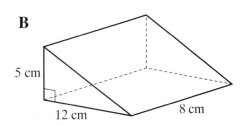

B

5 cm

12 cm

8 cm

7 The diagrams show a prism and its cross-section.

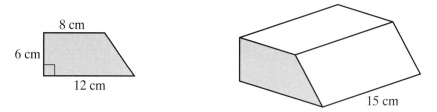

Work out the volume of this prism.

Capacity

In real life there are many three-dimensional, hollow shapes:

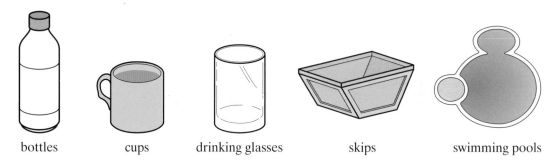

bottles   cups   drinking glasses   skips   swimming pools

■ **The volume of the inside of a hollow shape is called the capacity of the shape.**

You can measure capacity in:

Metric system   1 litre (large wine bottle) $= 1000 \, \text{cm}^3$
Imperial system   1 pint (milk bottle); 1 gallon $= 8$ pints

Example 8

The diagram shows the net of a shoe box.

Work out the capacity of the shoe box in litres.

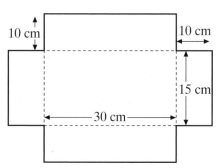

When the net is folded, it will make this shoe box:

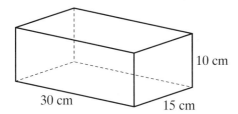

Use the formula:

   volume of cuboid = length × width × height

The volume (or capacity) of the shoe box will be

   $30 \times 15 \times 10 = 450 \times 10 = 4500 \, \text{cm}^3$

1 litre is $1000 \, \text{cm}^3$ so the capacity is $4500 \div 1000$
   $= 4.5 \text{ litres}$

Exercise 15H

1   The diagram represents the net of a box.

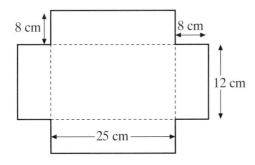

   Work out the capacity of the box.
   Give your answer in:
   (a) cubic centimetres
   (b) litres.

2   A wine box is in the shape of a cuboid.

   The capacity of the wine box is 3 litres,
   and its base is a square of side 10 cm.
   Work out the height of the wine box.

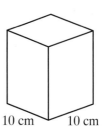

3 The diagram shows the cross-section of a swimming pool.

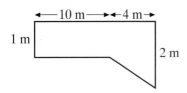

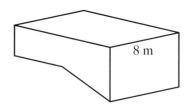

The distance across the pool is 8 metres.

Calculate the capacity of water in the pool when it is full.

4 The capacity of this juice carton is 1 litre.

The length is 9 cm and the height is 16 cm.

Work out the width of the packet.

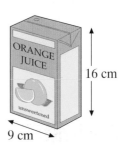

Volume of a cylinder

A cylinder is a *special type* of prism with a constant circular cross-section.

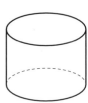

A cylinder is a prism so:

   volume of cylinder = area of base × height

Because it is a circle, the area of the base is πr^2.

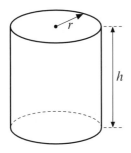

So for any cylinder:

■ **volume of cylinder $= \pi \times \text{radius}^2 \times \text{height}$**
$$= \pi r^2 h$$

Example 9

A can of drink is in the shape of a cylinder.

The base is a circle of radius 3 cm and the
height of the can is 11 cm.

Work out the capacity of the can.
(Use both $\pi = 3.14$ and $\pi = \frac{22}{7}$)

Using volume $= \pi \times r^2 \times h$, and remembering that
volume is also capacity

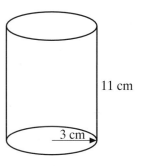

11 cm

3 cm

Capacity $= \pi \times 3^2 \times 11$

$\qquad = \pi \times 9 \times 11$ $\qquad$ or using $\pi = \frac{22}{7}$

$\qquad = 3.14 \times 9 \times 11$ $\qquad$ capacity $= \frac{22}{7} \times 9 \times 11$

$\qquad = 28.26 \times 11$ $\qquad\qquad\qquad = \frac{22}{7} \times 99$

$\qquad = 310.86 \text{ cm}^3$ $\qquad\qquad\qquad = \frac{2178}{7} \text{ cm}^3$

Exercise 15I

1 Work out the volume of each of these cylinders.
(Assume $\pi = 3.14$)

(a)

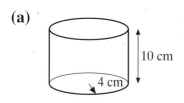

10 cm

4 cm

(b)

2 cm

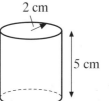

5 cm

(c)

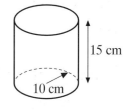

15 cm

10 cm

(d)

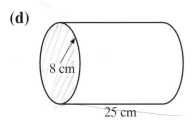

8 cm

25 cm

(e)

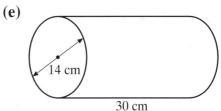

14 cm

30 cm

2 A metal rod is in the shape
of a cylinder.

The radius of the cross-section
of the rod cylinder is 4 cm and
the length is 70 cm.

Using $\pi = \frac{22}{7}$, calculate the volume of the rod.

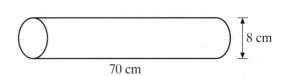

8 cm

70 cm

3 The diagram shows a swimming pool in the shape of a rectangle with a semicircular end.

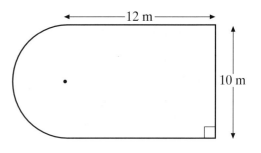

(a) Work out the area of the surface of the pool.

The depth of the pool is a constant 1.6 metres.

(b) Work out the capacity of water in the pool when it is full.

4 The cross-section of a trough is a semicircle of radius 20 cm.

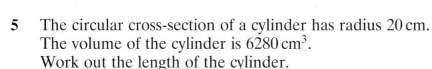

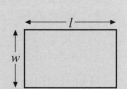

The length of the trough is 150 cm.

Work out the capacity of the trough:
(a) in cm³   **(b)** in litres.

5 The circular cross-section of a cylinder has radius 20 cm.
The volume of the cylinder is 6280 cm³.
Work out the length of the cylinder.

Summary of key points

1 The distance around a two-dimensional (or flat) shape is called the perimeter of the shape.

2 The amount of space covered by a two-dimensional shape is called the area of the shape.

3 In words, the formula for the perimeter of a rectangle is:

Perimeter = 2(length + width)

- In symbols, the formula for the perimeter, P, of a rectangle of length l and width w, is:

$$P = 2(l + w)$$

4 In words, the formula for the area of a rectangle is:

Area = length × width

- In symbols, the formula for the area, A, of a rectangle of length l and width w is:

$$A = l \times w \quad \text{or} \quad A = lw$$

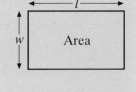

5 The formula for the area of a triangle is:

Area = $\frac{1}{2}$ × base × height or $A = \frac{1}{2}bh$

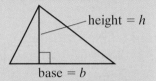

6 The formula for the area of a parallelogram is:

Area = base × vertical height or $A = bh$

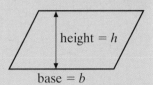

7 The formula for the area of a trapezium is:

$$\text{Area} = \frac{\text{top} + \text{base}}{2} \times \text{height}$$

or $A = \frac{1}{2}(a + b)h$

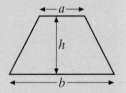

8 The formula for the circumference of a circle is:

$$C = \pi d \quad \text{or} \quad C = 2\pi r$$

9 The formula for the area of a circle is:

$$A = \frac{\pi d^2}{4} \quad \text{or} \quad A = \pi r^2$$

10 The amount of space taken up by a three-dimensional shape is called the volume of the shape.

11 The volume of a cuboid is:

volume = length × width × height

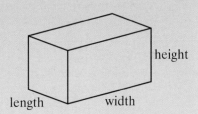

12 The volume of a prism is:

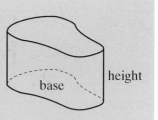

volume = area of base × height

or

volume = area of cross-section × length

13 The volume of the inside of a hollow shape is called the capacity of the shape.

14 The formula for the volume, V, of a cylinder of base radius r and height h is:

$$V = \pi \times r^2 \times h \quad \text{or} \quad V = \pi r^2 h$$

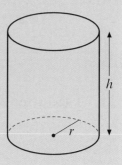

16 Using and applying mathematics

Introduction

This chapter is about the **problem-solving process**. In the chapter you will learn more about how to use and apply mathematics to **investigate** a problem solving situation.

16.1 The problem

This problem is about making kerbs of various lengths from kerbstones of different length.
At the start we just have two different kerbstones:

white kerbstones

which are of length 1 unit

red kerbstones

which are of length 2 units.

Suppose that we wanted to make a kerb of length 10 units using these white and red kerbstones. Some of the different ways of doing this are:

There are a lot of different ways and we would probably get mixed up if we tried to list them all.

Solving the problem means that if you need a kerb of a particular length, you can state how many different ways there are of making that length of kerb. You should also be able to explain why your answer is true.

Understand the problem

The first thing you need to do is make sure that you understand the problem.

In this problem you have a selection of:

white kerbstones ☐ of length 1 unit

and red kerbstones ▰ of length 2 units

You are going to investigate the **number of different ways** of making a kerb of any length.

For instance, if the kerb is of length 5 units then some of the different ways of making it are:

Have you seen the problem or something like it before?

Before starting to tackle any problem you should always ask yourself if you have seen the problem or something like it before. If you have then you may be able to benefit from that experience.

This chapter will assume that the kerbstone problem is new to you.

Exercise 16A

Here are four different ways of making a kerb of length five units using the white and red kerbstones:

Find at least **two other ways** of making a kerb of length five units.

16.2 Simplify the problem

The first stage of the problem-solving process is to make the problem as simple as you can.

Start by looking at some kerbs of very short lengths, such as 1, 2 and 3 units.

The simplest case is when the kerb is of length 1 unit.

A very simple case is called a **trivial** case.

It can be made in only **one way**. by using a single white kerbstone:

When the length of the kerb is two units it can be made in two ways:

and

When the length of the kerb is three units it can be made as:

So when the length of the kerb is three units, it can be made in three ways.

Now you have three simple results:

Length of kerb	Number of ways
1	1
2	2
3	3

At this stage you might start to think that the number of different ways of making a kerb is always equal to the length of the kerb – but you would be wrong, as the next exercise shows.

Exercise 16B

Show that there are five different ways of making a kerb of length four units.

16.3 Developing strategies

One of the most important parts of the problem solving and investigation process is developing a strategy.

For the kerbs problem it might look nice to have lots of pictures of white and red kerbstones but it is much more efficient to use letters:

w to represent white ☐   *r* to represent red ▮

You can now represent your kerbs using the letters *r* and *w* in different orders. The five different kerbs of length 4 units look like this:

> *r r* 2 red and 0 white
>
> *r w w*
> *w r w* 1 red and 2 white (in any order)
> *w w r*
>
> *w w w w* 0 red and 4 white

> You only use three different combinations of blocks to make the five different kerbs.

There are three different kerbs that use one red block and two white blocks.

There is a pattern where it seems as if the red (or *r*) *slides* down a diagonal

> *r w w*
> *w r w*
> *w w r*

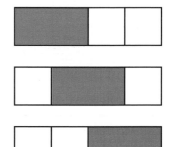

You now have three strategies that are helpful in solving the problem:

1   using letters to represent the kerbstones

2   separating the different combinations of blocks such as 1 red and 2 white, etc.

3   the *sliding* of a single letter down a diagonal.

> Strategy 3 is an example of writing your results in a **systematic** way.
> If you had written:
>
> *w w r*
> *r w w*
> *w r w*
>
> you might not have spotted a pattern.

Example 1

Use the strategies to find all eight ways of making a kerb of length five units.

A kerb of length 5 units can be made as:

2 red and 1 white	*r r w* *r w r* *w r r*	3 ways
1 red and 3 white	*r w w w* *w r w w* *w w r w* *w w w r*	4 ways
0 red and 5 white	*w w w w w*	1 way

This gives a total of $3 + 4 + 1 = 8$ ways.

Recording results and making observations

You now have five results. It is a good idea to record your results in a table:

Length of kerb	Number of different ways of making the kerb
1	1
2	2
3	3
4	5
5	8

You need to be able to make observations based on your results.

For instance, quite simply you might see that:

As the length of the kerb increases then the number of ways of making it also increases.

At a slightly higher level of difficulty and awareness you might notice that:

The pattern for the number of ways of making a kerb goes

odd	even	odd	odd	even
1	2	3	5	8

Then at an even higher level you might notice that:

The pattern for the number of ways of making a kerb, that is, the numbers:

1,   2,   3,   5,   8

is generated by the following rule.

The next number is the sum of the previous two numbers

$$3 + 5 = 8$$

1,   2,   3,   5,   8

$$2 + 3 = 5$$

Making and testing a prediction

You now have a possible rule for finding the next number in the sequence. This is called a **conjecture**. It is a statement about **what you think is happening**. The conjecture is:

The next number is the sum of the previous two numbers.

You can use your conjecture to make a **prediction**. You can add your prediction to your table of results:

Length of kerb	Number of different ways of making the kerb
1	1
2	2
3	$2 + 1 = 3$
4	$3 + 2 = 5$
5	$5 + 3 = 8$
6	$8 + 5 = 13$

Using your conjecture, you can predict that there are 13 different ways of making a kerb of length 6 units.

You now need to **test your predictions**. You can use your strategies to find the number of different kerbs of length 6 units:

| 3 red and 0 white | *r r r* | 1 way |

| 2 red and 2 white | *r r w w*
r w r w
r w w r
w r r w
w r w r
w w r r | 6 ways |

| 1 red and 4 white | *r w w w w*
w r w w w
w w r w w
w w w r w
w w w w r | 5 ways |

| 0 red and 6 white | *w w w w w w* | 1 way |

There are $1 + 6 + 5 + 1 = 13$ ways to make a kerb of length 6.

You now have 6 definite results:

Length of kerb	Number of different ways of making the kerb
1	1
2	2
3	3
4	5 ⟩ +
5	8
6	13 =

You have made a prediction, tested it and found it to be true. You can be **very confident** that the general rule is true.

However, there is far more to establishing truth in mathematics than the confidence that comes from predicting and testing. Later on in this chapter you will explain **why the rule works**.

Exercise 16C

Using the general rule:

1 **(a)** make a prediction for the number of different ways of making a kerb of length 7 units.
 (b) test that prediction.

2 make predictions for the number of different ways of making a kerb of length:
 (a) 8 units **(b)** 9 units **(c)** 10 units

16.4 Using symbols

In section 16.3 you used letters to represent the kerbstones. It will be useful to be able to write the general rule using letters and symbols.

The general rule for the kerbstones problem is:

> The next number in the sequence is the sum of the previous two numbers.

One way to write this in symbols would be to call the next number the nth number. Then you could write the rule as:

$$n\text{th} = (n-1)\text{th} + (n-2)\text{th}$$

This is a better way of writing the rule, but it is still not very elegant. You could use the symbol U_n to mean the nth term of the sequence.

You couldn't just write

$$n = (n-1) + (n-2)$$

This is an equation which can be solved to give $n = 3$.

Example 2

Write down U_5 for the sequence given by the kerbstones problem.

The sequence is:

1, 2, 3, 5, 8, 13, ...

↑
The 5th term is 8

$U_5 = 8$

Example 3

Write down the general rule for the kerbstone problem using U_n to represent the nth term of the sequence.

The rule is:

$$n\text{th} = (n-1)\text{th} + (n-2)\text{th}$$

You can write this:

$$U_n = U_{n-1} + U_{n-2}$$

Exercise 16D

1 For the kerbstone sequence:

$$1, \quad 2, \quad 3, \quad 5, \quad 8, \quad 13, \quad \ldots$$

write down the values of:
(a) U_1 **(b)** U_4 **(c)** U_7 **(d)** $U_8 + U_9$

2 Write these rules using U_n to represent the nth term of the sequence.
(a) The next number in the sequence is twice the previous number.
(b) The next number in the sequence is the previous number plus three.
(c) The next number in the sequence is the product of the previous two numbers.

> Remember:
> the product of a and b is $a \times b$ or ab.

16.5 Have you seen it before?

At any stage in the problem solving or investigative process you should ask yourself, *'Have I seen this or something like this before?'*

You might have seen the sequence

$$1, \quad 2, \quad 3, \quad 5, \quad 8, \quad 13, \quad \ldots$$

before.

The sequence is known as the **Fibonacci sequence**. It was first developed by an Italian mathematician called Leonardo of Pisa in the thirteenth century.

Example 4

For the Fibonacci sequence:

   1,   2,   3,   5,   8,   13,   21,   …

Work out the value of $\dfrac{U_5}{U_4}$

$U_5 = 8, U_4 = 5$

So $\dfrac{U_5}{U_4} = \dfrac{8}{5} = 1.6$

Exercise 16E

For the Fibonacci sequence, work out these values:

1 $\dfrac{U_6}{U_5}$

2 $\dfrac{U_{n+1}}{U_n}$ for values of n from 1 to 9

3   Draw axes on graph paper. Put n along the horizontal axis from 0 to 9. Put $\dfrac{U_{n+1}}{U_n}$ on the vertical axis from 0 to 3, using a scale of 1 cm to 0.25.
Plot your values from question **2**. What do you notice?

4   Without working out any values, write down what you think $\dfrac{U_{100}}{U_{99}}$ might be to one decimal place.

16.6 Why does it work?

You should now be confident that the solutions to the kerbstone problem are like this:

Length of kerb	1	2	3	4	5	6	7	8	9	10
Number of ways	1	2	3	5	8	13	21	34	55	89

You also know that the rule for the number sequence is:

> *The next number is the sum of the previous two numbers*

and that this rule can be written in symbols as:

$$U_n = U_{n-1} + U_{n-2}$$

The next stage of the process is to **justify** this rule. You need to say **why it works**.

A self-justifying system

Go back and look at the original problem.

The ways of making a kerb of length 3 are:

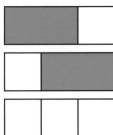

The ways of making a kerb of length 4 are:

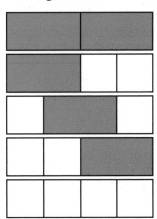

There are two ways of making a kerb of length five:

Take a kerb of length four and add a single white block to the end:

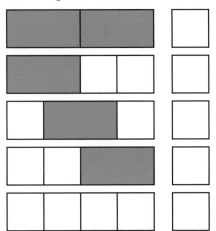

Take a kerb of length three and add a single red block to the end:

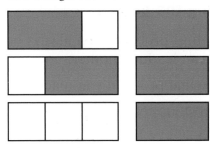

These are all eight ways of making a kerb of length five.

You now have a very powerful system for making a kerb of a particular length from your knowledge of the kerbs of the two previous lengths.

You can use the same argument to show why the general rule must be true.

There are two ways to make a kerb of length n units:

Take a kerb of length $n - 1$ units and add a single white block to the end:

Take a kerb of length $n - 2$ units and add a single red block to the end:

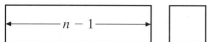 

There are U_{n-1} kerbs of length $n - 1$ units, so you make U_{n-1} kerbs in the first way.

There are U_{n-2} kerbs of length $n - 2$ units, so you make U_{n-2} kerbs in the second way.

This is all the kerbs of length n:

$$U_n = U_{n-1} + U_{n-2}$$

This way of constructing kerbs is called a **self-justifying system**. It not only tells you how to make all the kerbs of a certain length, but it also shows you **why the rule is true**.

You have now correctly established a general rule, expressed it in symbols and said why it works.

You have successfully **solved the original problem**.

Extending the problem

Mathematical problems can always be extended – one problem can lead to another.

In the original problem you made kerbs from:

white kerbstones of length 1 unit:

red kerbstones of length 2 units:

The general rule for a kerb of length n units is:

$$U_n = U_{n-1} + U_{n-2}$$

where U_n is the number of ways of making a kerb of length n units.

Changing variables

Having solved the problem with the white and red kerbstones a good mathematical question to ask is:

> *What will happen if we change the problem to making kerbs when we use*:

white kerbstones of length 1 unit:

green kerbstones of length 3 units:

You could start again with some simple lengths of kerbs and list the ways a certain length can be made.

For example, using white and green and writing:

w for ☐ and *g* for ▭

a kerb of length 6 units can be made as:

g g

g w w w
w g w w
w w g w
w w w g

w w w w w w

So using white (of length 1 unit) and green (of length 3 units), a kerb of length 6 units can be made in 6 ways.

But if you repeat the process of listing all the possibilities, as you did before, then you **have not learnt from** or **have not progressed from** or **have not reflected on** your previous experience.

The key to solving the original problem was making kerbs of a particular length from your knowledge of kerbs of previous lengths.

Using white and green blocks, you can make a kerb of length *n* units in two ways:

Take a kerb of length *n* − 1 units and add a single white block to the end:

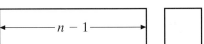

Take a kerb of length *n* − 3 units and add a single green block to the end:

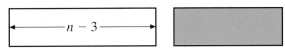

The general rule for the number of kerbs of length n units, or U_n, with green and white blocks is:

$$U_n = U_{n-1} + U_{n-3}$$

You can test this rule by checking some cases.

Example 5

(a) Show that by using white (of length 1) and green (of length 3) kerbstones, a kerb of length 6 units can be made in $U_6 = 6$ different ways.

(b) Confirm that $U_6 = U_5 + U_3$

(a) 6 units: *g g*
                  g w w w
                  w g w w
                  w w g w
                  w w w g
                  w w w w w w   so $U_6 = 6$

(b) 5 units: *g w w*
                  w g w
                  w w g
                  w w w w w   so $U_5 = 4$

     3 units: *g*
                  w w w   so $U_3 = 2$

$U_5 + U_3 = 4 + 2 = 6 = U_6$

Exercise 16F

You are making kerbs using white and green kerbstones.

1   Work out the values of:
    (a) U_7
    (b) U_8

2   Confirm that:
    (i) $U_7 = U_6 + U_4$
    (ii) $U_8 = U_7 + U_5$

16.7 Further extensions

The problem using white and green kerbstones is now solved, but that does not stop you going further.

Suppose you want to make kerbs of various length using:

white kerbstones of length 1 unit:

purple kerbstones of length 4 units:

You can use your previous experience to make a **conjecture** straight away.

This is the third problem you've looked at. It is useful to be able to label the problems in an easy way.

The first problem used white and red kerbstones, of lengths 1 and 2. You can call this the $(1, 2)$ problem.

The second problem used white and green kerbstones of lengths 1 and 3. This was the $(1, 3)$ problem.

The general rules are:

$(1, 2)$ problem: $U_n = U_{n-1} + U_{n-2}$
$(1, 3)$ problem: $U_n = U_{n-1} + U_{n-3}$

The new problem uses white and purple blocks of lengths 1 and 4. Your conjecture is:

$(1, 4)$ problem: $U_n = U_{n-1} + U_{n-4}$

> This is still only a conjecture.
> You haven't shown why it is true yet.

Exercise 16G

1   Copy and complete this table for making kerbs using white (of length 1) and purple (of length 4) kerbstones.

Length of kerb	1	2	3	4	5	6	7	8	9	10
Number of ways	1									

2   Confirm that in all cases

$$U_n = U_{n-1} + U_{n-4}$$

3 Explain why

$$U_n = U_{n-1} + U_{n-4}$$

Summary of key points

In any problem solving or investigative situation you should

1 Make sure that you understand the problem.

2 Ask yourself if you have seen the problem or something like it before. You may be able to benefit from that experience.

3 Simplify the problem.

4 Develop strategies to deal with the problem.

5 Record results and make observations.

6 Make and test predictions.

7 Make a generalisation.

8 Use symbols wherever appropriate.

9 Justify the results – explain why they work.

10 Extend the problem or investigation by changing some variables.

11 Reflect on what you have done to solve the extended problem.

12 Justify or prove any results to your extended problems.

17 Calculators and computers

This unit shows you ways of using scientific calculators, graphical calculators and computer software to help build on and extend the work you have been studying in the other units of this book.

The examples will work on Casio calculators. The spreadsheet examples are based on Microsoft *Excel* and the examples for drawing bearings are based on *WinLogo*.

17.1 Bearings and loci

You can draw bearings, constructions and loci on a computer using *WinLogo*.

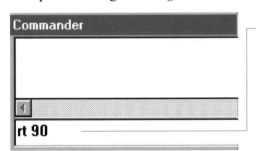

Type your instructions here and then press the Enter key before typing your next set of instructions.

Example 1

Draw on screen:

(a) a bearing of 070°

Type:
fd 100 label "N bk 100
rt 70 fd 100

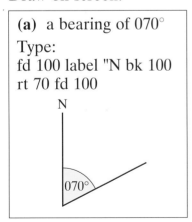

(b) a bearing of 330°

Type:
cs fd 100 label
"N bk 100
rt 330 fd 100

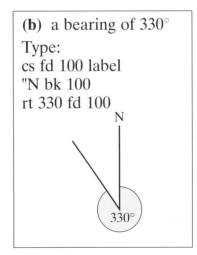

In *WinLogo* you must provide instructions to move the 'turtle' around the screen.

The turtle begins this way round:

rt 90

will turn it 90° clockwise.

fd 100

will move it forward '100' places and draw a line '100' units long.

You will find the following instructions useful in this section:

bk 100
will move it back '100' places and draw a line '100' units long.

lt 90
will turn it 90° anticlockwise.

pu
will pick the pen up and you will not be able to draw again until you enter:

pd
which puts the pen down again.

cs
clears the screen and places the turtle back at the origin [0 0].

Label "Sue
to put the word 'Sue' on screen

Exercise 17A WinLogo

1   Use *WinLogo* to draw:

   (a) a bearing of 060°   **(b)** a bearing of 120°

   (c) a bearing of 210°   **(d)** a bearing of 290°

> In parts (a) to (d) make the 'arms' of your bearing 100 units long.

   (e) a journey of 200 kilometres on a bearing of 230°, using a scale of 20 logo units to represent 50 km.

   (f) the following journey

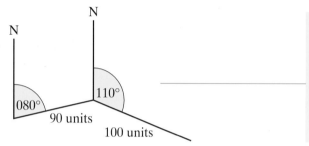

> Hint:
> After moving forward 90 units on the first leg of your journey, you will need to turn left through 80° before heading North again.

2   Use *WinLogo* to construct:

   (a) angle BAC and its bisector, where angle BAC is 50°

> Make each line 100 units long.

   (b) the line EF and its perpendicular bisector, GH

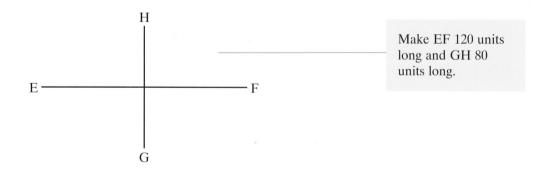

> Make EF 120 units long and GH 80 units long.

3 Use *Winlogo* to construct the following set of nested regular polygons:

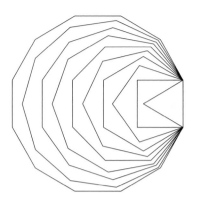

Each polygon has a side of size 40 units.

The code for the octagon is:
repeat 8 [fd 80 lt 45]

$$\frac{360°}{n}$$

the number of sides, n

For the heptagon, a polygon with 7 sides, and the 11-gon, you may use the decimal point in *WinLogo* for the left turn.

4 Use *WinLogo* to draw:

Hint:
Think of a circle as a polygon with a lot of sides, say 360.

(a) the locus of a point which is always the same distance from a given point

(b) the locus of a point which is always the same distance from AB as it is from AC in the diagram below

There is more about the locus of a point on page 25.

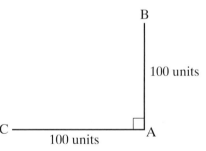

B

100 units

C

100 units

A

(c) the locus of a point which is always the same distance from the line EF below

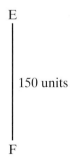

E

150 units

F

17.2 Cumulative frequencies

You can use a spreadsheet to create curves from the cumulative frequencies you met in section 4.2 and use it to estimate the median for a set of data.

Exercise 17B Spreadsheet

1   The pulse rate of 35 athletes was taken when they were resting. The results are shown in the table below

Pulse rate	Frequency	Cumulative frequency
55	1	1
56	3	4
57	4	8
58	6	14
59	5	29
60	8	27
61	4	31
62	2	33
63	2	35

In a spreadsheet:

- Enter 55 in cell A2.
- Enter the formula =A2+1 in cell A3 and copy it down to cell A10.
- Enter the frequencies from the table into cells B2 to B10.
- Enter the number 1 in cell C2.
- Enter the formula =B3+C2 in cell C3 and copy it down to cell C10.
- Highlight the cells A1 to A10 and *while holding down the Ctrl key on your keyboard*, highlight cells C1 to C10.

	A	B	C
1	Pulse	Frequency	Cumulative frequency
2	55	1	1
3	56	3	=B3+C2
4	57	4	
5	58	6	

Drag this square down to cell C10 to copy the formula down.

● Use the chart wizard to draw a cumulative frequency curve, similar to the one below:

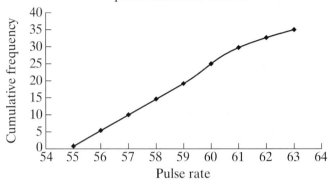

A cumulative frequency curve from the pulse rates of 35 athletes

Use a printout of your curve to *estimate*:

(a) the median pulse rate for the athletes

(b) the number of athletes with a pulse rate less than 60.5

There are 35 athletes.

$$\frac{35+1}{2} = \frac{36}{2} = 18$$

On your graph find the 18th athlete on the vertical axis and draw a horizontal line until you meet the curve. Draw a vertical line down from this point to the horizontal axis to find your estimate for the median.

2   The height of 57 mature rose bushes was measured to the nearest centimetre and the results are shown in the frequency table below:

Height in centimetres	75	76	77	78	79	80
Number of roses	3	7	12	14	13	8

(a) Enter all the data into cells A1 to G1 and A2 to G2 of a spreadsheet.

(b) Enter:
  ● "Cumulative frequency" in cell C1
  ● the number 3 in cell B3
  ● the formula =C2+B3 in cell C3 and copy it across to cell G3

(c) Highlight, with the aid of the Ctrl key on your keyboard, cells A1 to G1 and cells A3 to G3 and create a cumulative frequency curve.

At the final stage of the chart wizard choose the option to place the chart as a new sheet.

(d) Print out a copy of your cumulative frequency
curve and use it to find an estimate for the median
height of the roses.

(e) The nursery which grew the roses
wanted to restrict the height of the
roses to 785 millimetres. Use your
curve to estimate the number of roses
above this height.

For more accurate
readings from your
curve:

• double click each
axis in turn and
reduce the major
unit on the scale.

17.3 Equations of curves

You can draw curves on a graphical calculator. After you
have switched on the calculator select the **GRAPH** icon
using the arrow keys and then press the EXE key to display
a window similar to this:

```
G-Func :Y=
Y1:
Y2:
Y3:
Y4:
SEL DEL    DRAW
```

Press SHIFT F3 to bring up the V-Window

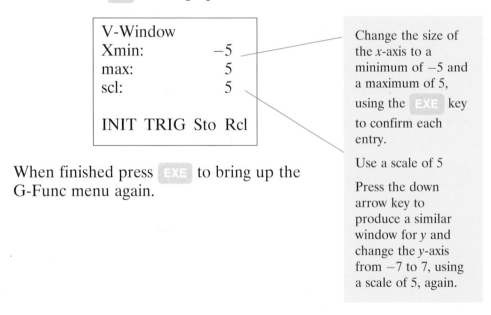

```
V-Window
Xmin:         −5
max:           5
scl:           5

INIT  TRIG  Sto  Rcl
```

Change the size of
the x-axis to a
minimum of −5 and
a maximum of 5,
using the EXE key
to confirm each
entry.

Use a scale of 5

Press the down
arrow key to
produce a similar
window for y and
change the y-axis
from −7 to 7, using
a scale of 5, again.

When finished press EXE to bring up the
G-Func menu again.

Exercise 17C Graphical calculator

1 Draw the four curves $y = x^2$, $y = x^2 + 1$, $y = x^2 - 1$ and $y = x^2 + 3$. Describe the translation from the curve $y = x^2$ to obtain each of the other 3 curves.

2 Draw the four curves $y = x^2$, $y = 2x^2$, $y = 3x^2$ and $y = 0.5x^2$. List the 4 curves in order of their width, starting with the widest.

3 Describe the shape of the curve $y = x^3 - 4x$ and write down the number of times it crosses the x-axis.

Press X,T ∧ 3 for x^3.

4 What is the connection between the curves $y = x^2$ and $y = -x^2$?

5 How many times does the line $y = 2x - 1$ meet the curve $y = x^3 - x^2 - 4x + 4$?

An alternative way to do this exercise is to use a computer software package like *Omnigraph*.

You can also use a spreadsheet to draw graphs. The graph in question 8 on page 73 could be produced as follows:

To begin question 1, press

X,T x^2 EXE

to store the equation Y1=X^2. Then press

X,T x^2 +

1 EXE

to store the equation Y2=X^2+1

Now type similar equations for Y3 and Y4.

Finally press F4

to produce your four curves.

When you have finished each question, press

SHIFT F3 EXE

to return to the GRAPH mode. Delete your equations one by one by using the arrow keys to select the equations and pressing the F2 key followed by the F1 key.

	A	B
1	x	y
2	-4	= 2*A2*A2-3
3	-3	
4	-2	
5	-1	
6	0	
7	1	
8	2	
9	3	
10	4	

Drag this square down to copy the formula down to cell B10

- -4 was entered in cell A2
- =A2+1 was entered in cell A3 and copied down to cell A10
- =2*A2*A2-3 was entered in cell B2 and copied down to cell B10

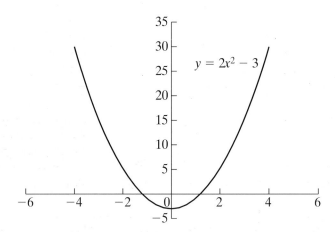

17.4 Handling data

You can use a spreadsheet to create bar charts, pie charts, scatter graphs and lines of best fit.

Exercise 17D Spreadsheet

1   The average number of words per minute typed by a group of eleven Year 8 students is shown in the frequency table below:

Student	Ali	Emma	Jill	Serge	Mario	Shaheen
Words per minute	23	35	16	32	36	11

Student	Errol	Bob	Sara	Andre	Aurore
Words per minute	19	15	22	13	27

- Enter all the data into rows 1 and 2 of a spreadsheet.

	A	B	C	D
1	Student	Ali	Emma	Jill
2	Words per minute	23	35	16

- Highlight all the data and use the chart wizard to create a bar chart. Make sure you add appropriate labels to your chart at stage 3 of the wizard.

In *Excel* a bar chart is called a column chart!

At the last stage of the wizard choose the option to place the chart as a new sheet

2 The number of ice creams sold by Henry in his shop during one week in July are shown in the following frequency table:

Day of the week	Monday	Tuesday	Wednesday	Thursday
Number of ice creams sold	62	65	78	36

Day of the week	Friday	Saturday	Sunday
Number of ice creams sold	58	91	70

- Enter the data into cells A4 to H4 and A5 to H5 of your spreadsheet.
- Use the chart wizard to create a pie chart of your data and place the chart as a new sheet at the last stage of the wizard.
- Give two reasons why you think the sales were so low on the Thursday
- Enter the formula =AVERAGE(B5:H5) in cell 15 to calculate the mean number of sales.
- Enter the formula =MEDIAN(B5:H5) in cell J5 to calculate the median number of sales.

There is more on averages in Chapter 4

3 The data in the table on the next page shows the number of goals scored, goals conceded and point totals for the 24 football clubs in the Nationwide Division One 1999/2000 season.

(a) Enter the frequency table headings and all the data into columns A, B and C of a new spreadsheet numbering the rows 1 to 25.

(b) Enter the heading "Goal difference" in cell D1.

(c) Enter the formula =A2-B2 in cell D2 and copy it down to cell D25.

(d) Use the chart wizard to create the following 3 scatter graphs – remember to place each graph as a new sheet at the final stage of the wizard:

    goals scored against points total

    goals conceded against points total

    goal difference against points total

(e) For each scatter graph describe the type of correlation.

(f) On each graph click <u>C</u>hart on the menu bar and Add T<u>r</u>endline ... (In *Excel* a line of best fit is called a trendline)

(g) Enter the formula =AVERAGE(A2:A25) in cell A26 and copy it *across* to cell C26 to calculate the mean for columns A, B and C.

(h) Enter the formula =MEDIAN(A2:A25) in cell A27 and copy it *across* to cell C27 to calculate the median for columns A, B and C.

(i) Enter the formula =MODE(A2:A25) in cell A28 and copy it across to cell C28 to calculate the mode for columns A, B and C.

	A	B	C
1	Goals scored	Goals conceded	Points total
2	79	45	91
3	78	40	89
4	71	42	87
5	88	67	82
6	65	44	77
7	69	50	76
8	64	48	74
9	62	49	74
10	49	41	67
11	62	53	66
12	55	51	62
13	45	50	57
14	57	68	57
15	53	55	56
16	57	67	54
17	59	71	54
18	55	67	54
19	55	66	51
20	46	67	51
21	41	67	51
22	43	60	49
23	52	77	46
24	48	69	36
25	38	77	36

Hold down the Ctrl key on your keyboard to highlight any columns not next to each other.

17.5 Investigating sequences

Exercise 17E Scientific calculator

1   Use a calculator to investigate the following sequence:

   • Choose any number *greater* than 4
   • If it is even: halve it
   • If it is odd: multiply it by 3 and add 1
   • If your next number is even: halve it. If it is odd: multiply by 3 and add 1
   • Continue until you reach a loop
   • Choose another number greater than 4 (but not one from the example or from your own sequence!) and start again
   • Choose a third number which has not occurred before
   • Write down your findings
   • Use your findings to help continue this 'Hailstone tree'

> **Example**
> Start with 23:
> $23 \rightarrow 70 \rightarrow 35 \rightarrow 106 \rightarrow 53 \rightarrow 160 \rightarrow 80 \rightarrow 40 \rightarrow 20 \rightarrow 10 \rightarrow 5 \rightarrow 16 \rightarrow 8 \rightarrow 4 \rightarrow 2 \rightarrow 1 \rightarrow 4 \rightarrow 2 \rightarrow 1$. Stop because the sequence reaches a loop.

> The numbers in your sequences are called 'Hailstone numbers'.
> Why do you think that they are given this name?

   • Investigate the sequences if the rule 'multiply by 3 and add 1' is changed to 'multiply by 3 and subtract 1'

17.6 Powers, factors, primes and perfect numbers

Exercise 17F Scientific calculator and the Internet

Investigation

Finding perfect numbers:

A number is said to be 'perfect' if all its factors, apart from the number itself, add up to the number:

$1 + 2 + 3 = 6$

There is more on factors, powers and primes in Chapter 6.

The factors of 6 are

- Find the next perfect number after 6
- Complete the following table to help you find the next *four* perfect numbers.

Hint:
The next perfect number is between 20 and 30.

n	$2^n - 1$	Is $2^n - 1$ a prime number?	2^{n-1}	$(2^n - 1) \times 2^{n-1}$	Is $(2^n - 1) \times 2^{n-1}$ a perfect number?
2	3	Yes	2	6	Yes
3	7	Yes	4	28	
4	15	No	8	120	
5					
6					
7					
8					
9					
10					

If $n = 4$, press:

[2] [x^y] [4] [−] [1] [=]

to give 15

If $n = 4$, press:

[2] [x^y] [3] [=]

to give 8

$n - 1$

- Use the Internet site:
  http://www.geocities.com/ResearchTriangle/Thinktank/2434/prime/primenumbers.html to check for prime numbers.

- Use the Internet site:
  http://www.hjnpwatson.demon.co.uk/javaperf.htm to check for perfect numbers.

  > Enter your number and press the Tab key on your keyboard.

- When is $(2^n - 1) \times 2^{n-1}$ a perfect number?
- List the perfect numbers you have found as the sum of their factors apart from the number itself.

Index